Dispossession and Resistance in India

Dispossession and Resistance in India

The River and the Rage

Alf Gunvald Nilsen

DISPOSSESSION AND RESISTANCE IN INDIA: The River and The Rage
Alf Gunvald Nilsen

© 2013 Alf Gunvald Nilsen

Paperback Edition Published in India 2013
Edition History: Hardback, Routledge, 2010

ISBN 978-93-5002-249-8

This edition is licensed for sale in the Indian subcontinent only.

All rights reserved. No part of this book may be reproduced or transmitted, in any form or by any means, without prior permission of the Publisher.

Published by
AAKAR BOOKS
28 E Pocket IV, Mayur Vihar Phase I, Delhi 110 091
Phone : 011 2279 5505 Telefax : 011 2279 5641
info@aakarbooks.com; www.aakarbooks.com

Printed at
Mudrak, 30 A, Patparganj, Delhi 110 091

To my mother, Ellen Nilsen, and in loving memory of my father, Alf Inge Nilsen (1940–2008)

Contents

Acknowledgements

This book originates in a simple question that I asked myself many years ago when I was an undergraduate student: what is it that happens when social movements protest officially sanctioned practices and meanings of development? The question stemmed from my encounter with an academic culture in which – not unlike James Ferguson's 'anti-politics machine' – development was overwhelmingly conceived of in technical and managerial terms, far removed from the vast diversity of popular struggles that had caught my interest and led me to the study of development in the first place. Friends put me on to the movement against dam-building in the Narmada Valley, and ten years later I emerge with this book – which I hope provides some answers to the initial question from which it emanates – and debts of gratitude that it is a pleasure to acknowledge. The usual disclaimers apply.

I would first of all like to thank the activists of the Narmada Bachao Andolan, who welcomed me to the Narmada Valley, facilitated my fieldwork, housed me and fed me, and, most importantly, shared their experiences and knowledge of popular struggle with me. I am particularly grateful to Asit Das for travelling with me and translating for me. I would also like to thank Shashank Kela for many enlightening and inspiring discussions both during and after my fieldwork. I do not expect the activists who helped me in my work to agree with everything in this book; I hope, however, that it provides arguments and analyses that are of some interest and use, perhaps most of all in terms of contributing to a debate on social movement strategy at a time when subaltern livelihoods and lifeworlds are confronted with an increasingly authoritarian and aggressive and neoliberal project.

One of the great pleasures of carrying out the work that eventually led to this book was my encounter with the good people of Sandarbh Kendra in Indore, especially Jaya Mehta and Vineet Tiwari. Since our first meeting in 2003, they have become comrades and family; the warmth of their friendship, the generosity of their help and the inspiration of sharing in their work are very precious to me.

My research on the Narmada Bachao Andolan has had several academic homes. At what was then the School of Development Studies at the University of East Anglia, John Cameron supervised my undergraduate dissertation with an appropriate blend of criticism and encouragement. The ideas that constitute the basis of this book germinated in the haven for critical thought provided by Ken Cole. Ken later co-supervised my PhD thesis when I relocated to the University of Bergen; I thank him for inspirational and instructive discussions, as well as great musical experiences over the years. At DEV, I was fortunate enough to meet and get to know Chris Burman. Over the past ten years we have been engaged in a constant discussion of each other's work, sometimes face-to-face over pints of fine real ale in equally fine Midland pubs, sometimes via sms between Norway and South Africa. I have enjoyed and benefited from every bit of it.

At the Department of Sociology, University of Bergen, Ole Johnny Olsen seized hold of my project, and for four years he supervised and made space for my work and me. Ole Johnny patiently made his way through my massive manuscripts, always made time for important discussions, put up with my stubborn refusals to see his points, and eventually taught me a lot of what I know about sociological thinking and scholarly exposition. The combination of his intellectual engagement, consistent support and, equally important, generous and caring friendship played a very large part in making this project possible; for that I am deeply grateful. My collaboration with Asun St. Clair and Mette Andersson did a lot to clarify and inspire ideas, and so did my teaching on several undergraduate and graduate courses in the department. Olav Korsnes was an excellent Head of Department during the year which I finished writing up the thesis. I am also grateful to him for chairing the commission which assessed my doctoral thesis, and the subtle hints he dropped along the way that my 700 pages of musings on dispossession and resistance did in fact make some sense.

I adapted the thesis into a book during the time I was an RCUK Fellow at the Centre for the Study of Social and Global Justice at the School of Politics and International Relations, University of Nottingham. I would like to thank Sara Motta, Adam Morton, Andreas Bieler, Tony Burns, Vanessa Pupavac, Jennifer Martinez, Sara De Jong, Bettina Renz, Rod Thornton and Matthew Rendall for their collaboration, in various ways, in making space for critical thought and engagement about questions of justice, both far from and close to home. Musab Younis, Rizwaan Sabir, Hicham Yezza and other members of the student community also inspired me during my time in Nottingham. I would like to thank Swapna and Tituk for providing a home away from home in Vashi when I first started work on the book.

I have benefited a great deal from discussions in various academic forums. The Alternative Futures and Popular Protest conference in Manchester deserves special mention, and I would like to thank Neera Chandhoke and staff and students at the Developing Countries Research Centre at Delhi University for a particularly spirited discussion of two of my papers. I also want to thank the external examiners of my thesis, David Harvey and John Harriss, for exciting discussions during my doctoral defence. Beyond demonstrating what academic engagements with a purpose should be like and how enjoyable they can be – even when the prospective doctor suffers from chicken pox – they also made me see that there was in fact a book in the thesis. I was fortunate to meet Laurence Cox at an early stage in my work on this project, and our joint exploration of what a Marxist theory of social movements might look like, coupled with Laurence's friendship and his example as an organic intellectual, have been resources of hope every step of the way.

My most heartfelt thanks go to those nearest to me. My parents-in-law, Krishna and Bhaskar Barua have welcomed me into their family with warmth and affection. My wonderful wife, Padmaja Barua, is my happiness in life, and it is her love and companionship that sustains me, every day, in so many ways. My parents, Ellen and Alf Inge Nilsen, and their unconditional love, friendship and support have always been my bedrock and my guiding light. From an early age, they instilled in me the knowledge interest that guides my work, and it was they who were the first people to teach me left from right. For all this, gratitude somehow seems like too small a word. I wish Dad was still with us, not just so he could see this book and the imprint of his belief in social justice on it, but more importantly so that he could still bless us with his warm and caring presence. It is to his memory, and to my kind and courageous Mum, that this book is dedicated.

Lillesand, July 2009

1 The river and the rage

Introducing the Narmada Valley conflict

On 31 December 2006, the concrete work on the Sardar Sarovar Project, a multi-purpose dam built on the Narmada River in Narmada district in central Gujarat, was brought to completion, with the dam standing at 120 metres (Bavadam 2007). Across the border, in western Madhya Pradesh, 127,000 people faced imminent submergence by the dam reservoir without prospects for adequate resettlement and rehabilitation. The following day activists of the Narmada Bachao Andolan (Save the Narmada Movement) – the popular movement that has been fighting against the project since the late 1980s – decried the event as 'a total betrayal and a clear message for all adivasis, farmers, fishworkers, labourers and urban poor to traders: all who are being promised rehabilitation only to be ousted, forcibly evicted in the name of development' (NBA 2007). In blatant defiance of the protests of the Narmada Bachao Andolan (NBA), the dam builders staged a ceremony in Gujarat on 19 January 2007 at which the Sardar Sarovar Project was dedicated to the Indian nation (Bavadam 2007). Following in the wake of the completion of the upstream Indira Sagar dam in Madhya Pradesh two years earlier and coinciding with the resumption of construction on the Maheshwar Hydroelectric Project and Omkareshwar Project, the events that unfolded around the completion of the Sardar Sarovar Project in late December 2006 and January 2007 constituted the endgame of a process of dispossession and resistance that has played itself out over two decades in the Narmada Valley in western and central India.

The Narmada Valley ranges across the three states of Madhya Pradesh, Maharashtra and Gujarat, with the Narmada River winding its way from the Maikal ranges in Amarkantak in Shadhol district of northern Madhya Pradesh to the Arabian Sea at Bharuch, Gujarat. Dispossession flows from the fact that the waters of the Narmada are to be tamed and harnessed by the largest multi-purpose river valley development project to date in India: the Narmada Valley Development Project (NVDP), which envisions the construction of more than 3,000 dams of varying sizes on the river, with the Sardar Sarovar Project (SSP) as its linchpin. Like all such projects, the dams of the NVDP will engender large-scale submergence of land and thus lead to the displacement of those communities for whom this land provides habitat, lifeworld and livelihood – and this will happen without adequate resettlement and rehabilitation. The lack of a satisfactory plan for resettlement and rehabilitation of dam oustees in the case of the SSP was raised as an issue by the Narmada Bachao Andolan as well as independent researchers in the mid- and late 1980s, then confirmed by the World Bank's Independent Review of the project in the early 1990s, and reconfirmed again by more recent research into the impact of the increasing height of the dam on communities living in the submergence zone of the SSP in Maharashtra and Madhya Pradesh.[1] Displacement without resettlement and rehabilitation entails that most of the oustees 'find themselves left with the option of starving to death or walking several kilometres to the nearest town, sitting in the marketplace . . . offering themselves as wage labour, like goods on sale' (Roy 2002: 103).

Resistance has flowed from the communities of adivasi subsistence peasants and caste Hindu farmers across the three riparian states that stand to lose their land and with it their habitats, livelihoods and lifeworlds to the reservoirs and canal networks of the Narmada dams. From the mid-1980s onwards, social action groups

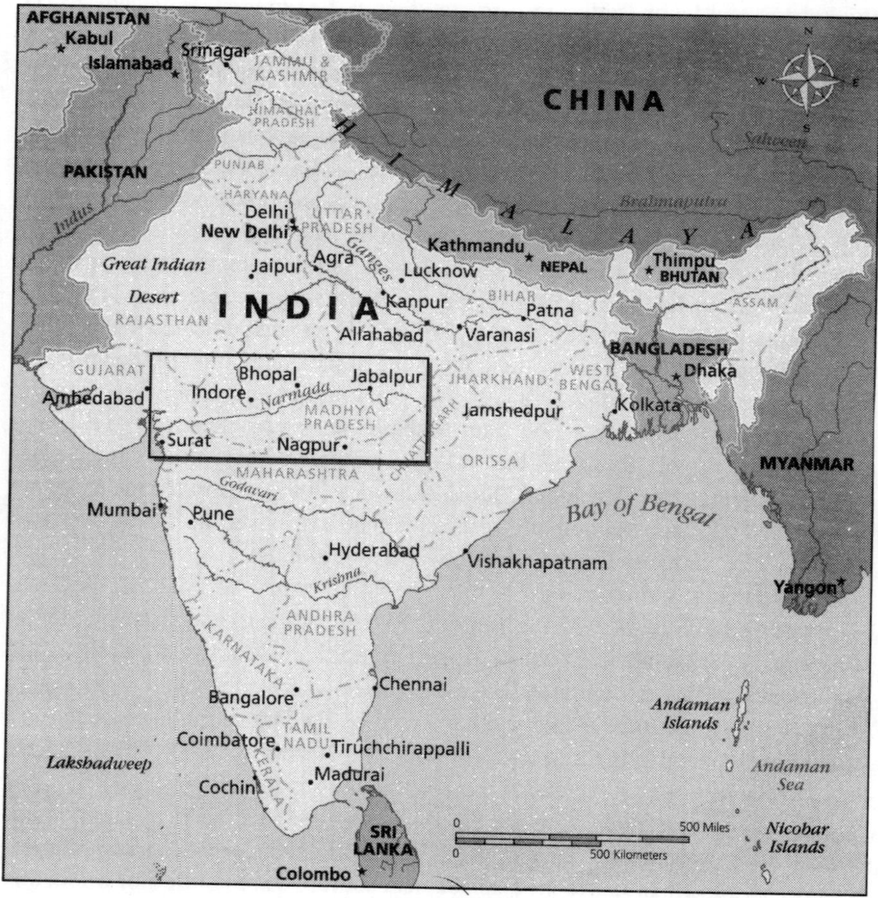

Map 1 India – the Narmada Valley is roughly indicated by the box

Source: Map provided by Eureka Cartography

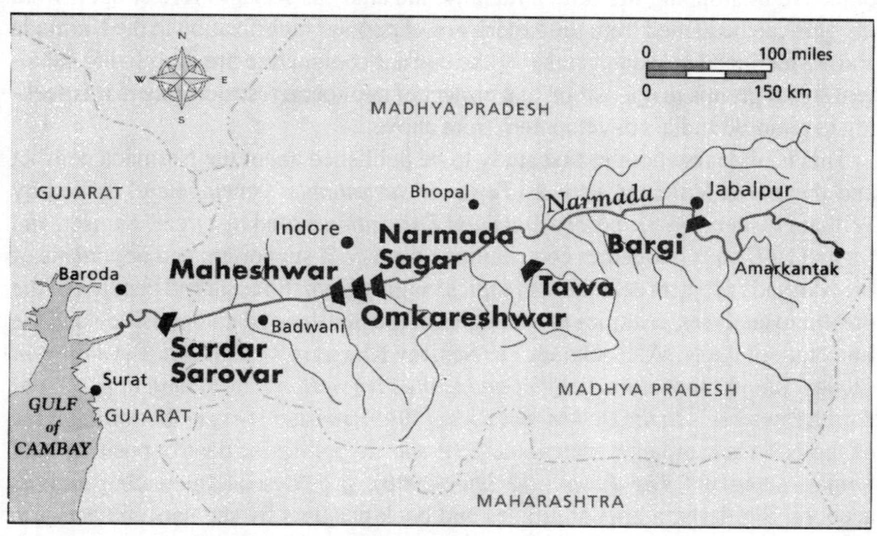

Map 2 Large dams on the Narmada River

Source: Map provided by Eureka Cartography

working with adivasi[2] communities and gradually also in caste Hindu farming communities in Maharashtra, Gujarat and Madhya Pradesh affected by the SSP started an intense questioning of the responsible authorities as to the prospects for fair and adequate resettlement and rehabilitation. By the late 1980s, several of these groups had merged into the pan-state organization Narmada Bachao Andolan (NBA). Convinced that resettlement and rehabilitation of the affected communities would not be possible, the NBA adopted a stance of total opposition to the SSP. The campaign was pursued vigorously through the 1990s, with one of its crowning achievements being the withdrawal of World Bank funding from the SSP in 1993. The NBA also extended its campaign to other dams in the Narmada Valley, such as among the communities that were affected by the completion of the Bargi dam on the upper reaches of the Narmada in the early 1990s, and in particular amongst the communities affected by the Maheshwar Hydroelectric Project from the late 1990s onwards. Finally, the campaign against dam building on the Narmada River has been embedded in a trenchant critique of India's postcolonial development project – a critique which the NBA has attempted to carry forward through a number of alliances that have unified the energies of social movements across India in opposition to social injustice, political exclusion and environmental degradation.

In this book, I present an analysis of this process of dispossession and resistance which seeks to elucidate the underlying political economy of the distributional biases of the Narmada dams, to explicate the nature of the expansive dynamic of resistance to the projects and the collective processes of learning which animated it, and to decipher the main reasons why the NBA ultimately failed to achieve its objective of stopping the SSP. Crucially, the analysis seeks to reflect upon what insights can be gained from the experience of popular mobilization in the Narmada Valley for social movements that at the current conjuncture are mobilizing subaltern social groups in opposition to a project of neoliberal restructuring that is seeking to remould India's development from above.

This is of course not the first study to be published about the Narmada conflict and the NBA. Volumes such as *Towards Sustainable Development?* edited by William Fisher (1995) and *The Dam and The Nation* edited by Drèze, Samson and Singh (1997) bring together contributions from both supporters and opponents of the Narmada projects dealing with topics ranging from the costs and benefits of the project to analyses, critiques and eulogies of the politics of dam opposition and the trajectory of the NBA. Books such as Sanjeev Khagram's *Dams and Development* (2004), Ranjit Dwivedi's *Conflict and Collective Action* (2006), and in particular Amita Baviskar's *In the Belly of the River* (1995), present fairly elaborate analyses of the NBA's campaign against the SSP and its politics of dam opposition, and Sanjay Sangvai's *The River and Life* (2000), provides an interesting activist account. Similarly, a host of articles and book chapters by scholars and activists have produced important insights about the dynamics of the Andolan and its politics (see e.g. Baviskar 1997a/b/c; Routledge 2003; Kala 2001; Udall 1995; Dwivedi 1997, 1999; Jayal 2000: Chapter 4; Patkar 1995; Patel 1995). However, in this study, I seek to bring out new insights about dispossession and resistance in the Narmada Valley through the application of a particular perspective on social movements and the struggles in which they are embroiled.

Laurence Cox (1999a: 1) has argued that mainstream sociological perspectives on social movements tend to operate with an inadequately narrow conception of the 'object' that is being studied in that they 'reify "movements" as unusual activity against essentially static backgrounds'. In its place he advocates 'a concept of social movement as the more or less developed articulation of situated rationalities, from the faltering attempt to express new needs to the development of full-blown challenges for societal hegemony' (ibid.: 1). Extant analyses of the NBA have tended to be characterized by precisely the kind of narrowness that Cox criticizes: the movement tends to be posited as a fixed institutional entity which is then studied in terms of the character of the demands it has levied on the project authorities and the state, or the ways in which it has used global norms pertaining to human rights and environmentalism to advance its opposition to the Narmada projects both nationally and internationally (see, e.g., Dwivedi 1997; Jayal 2000: Chapter 4; Khagram 2004). Relatively little attention is paid to the processes of learning internal to the movement that initially enabled the mobilization of politically marginalized groups, and then fuelled the gradual radicalization of claims and demands. Furthermore, the unfolding of the anti-dam campaign and its various strategic shifts has not been studied thoroughly in terms of how it has been rooted in cycles of learning intrinsic to the Andolan's struggle itself.

In this study, the social action groups that emerged in the Narmada Valley in the early and mid-1980s constitute the starting point of an analysis of resistance to dispossession as a process in which the scope of collective action was continually widened and deepened. Throughout the analysis my focus is on the development of activist skills, practices, forms of consciousness and knowledge, how this development has underpinned the changing nature of political demands, claims and strategies, and how this process has been animated by the conflictual dynamic of collective learning that defines the praxis of activism. The analysis engages thoroughly with those aspects of the Andolan's politics which go beyond the anti-dam struggle to articulate a critique of the postcolonial development project in India, and also seeks to relate the trajectory of the movement process in the Narmada Valley to the wider political economy of postcolonial capitalist development in India. This entails an engagement with how the process of mobilization in the Narmada Valley has articulated with the institutional manifestations and modalities of postcolonial capitalism in India – in particular the institutions, practices and discourses of the state. In the remainder of this chapter, I provide a more detailed account of the Narmada dam projects and the trajectory of the Narmada Bachao Andolan, as well as the theoretical framework which informs this study.

Dispossession and resistance in the Narmada Valley

India's modern temples and the Narmada dam projects

At the coming of Independence in 1947, India faced a colonial economic heritage of 'limited structural transformation': agriculture was the dominant sector in the economy, characterized by low productivity, low cultivation intensity, and persistent landlordism preventing accumulation and growth,[3] whereas large-scale industry was slow in the coming, contributing only 6.5 per cent of GNP and employing less than 10 per cent of the country's workforce (Corbridge and Harriss 2000). In this context, development, understood as economic modernization, came to be 'the *raison d'être* of the modern state and the source of its legitimacy' (ibid.: xvii; see also Chatterjee 1993). And within the parameters of the postcolonial development project, the construction of large dams came to occupy a central place – it was the method of choice for 'industrializing river control' and thereby securing irrigation, electricity and water supplies to underpin the effort to modernize agriculture and expand industrial production (D'Souza 2003: 4; see also Singh 1997 and Klingensmith 2007). Indeed, in 1955, when he was inaugurating the Nagarjunasagar dam – a key element of the Upper Krishna Project in Andhra Pradesh[4] – Prime Minister Jawaharlal Nehru famously stated that the project would serve as 'a stepping stone for India's prosperity and a symbol of the series of modern temples taken up' to advance development (cited in Rao 2005).

However, the roots of dam building as a development strategy can be traced back in time to the last decades of the Raj and outwards in scale to the global shift towards state-led accumulation strategies in world capitalism that occurred from the 1930s to the post-war era. Pioneered in the USA through the construction of a series of dams under the auspices of the Tennessee Valley Authority in the early 1930s, multi-purpose river valley development (MPRVD) was seized upon with great enthusiasm by 'ruling elites in different countries from across the ideological spectrum' (D'Souza 2003: 83). In India, MPRVD emerged on the agenda of the colonial state following the flooding of the Damodar River in 1943 (D'Souza 2006: 187–94), resulting in the sanctioning of large dam projects for the Mahanadi Valley and the Damodar Valley in eastern India. Importantly, the turn towards large dams reflected a reorientation in colonial development policies (D'Souza 2003, 2006). Faced with a radicalized freedom movement, a restive working class, and discontent among the Indian business class, colonial authorities came to favour a developmental ideology centred on social and economic reform. The implementation of public works and employment-generating schemes that could stem potential discontent and unrest – such as MPRVD – was promoted[5] (D'Souza 2006: 197).

Independence and its aftermath witnessed the entrenchment of MPRVD as one of many strategies by which to advance the modernization of the newly sovereign state (D'Souza 2006: 202). Dams came to be posited as the only viable option for providing irrigation and water storage facilities on the scale necessary for increasing agricultural productivity and industrial production: 'Just a year after Independence and before the beginning of planned development in India, about 160 large-scale dams were being considered, investigated or executed' (Singh 1997: 66). Since Independence in 1947, India has witnessed the construction of more than 1300 dams, and the lion's share of these came up in the heydays of the Green Revolution between 1965 and 1979 (ibid.: 82; see also Klingensmith 2007: chapters 5 and 6).

The potential for dam-building on the Narmada was first seriously investigated in the 1940s. In the mid-1960s a master plan of 13 major projects was drawn up, with one project – the future Sardar Sarovar Project – located in what was then Bombay State, and the remaining 12 located in the erstwhile Central Provinces.[6] By 1979, the design had been expanded to encompass more than 3000 dams of varying sizes, and had been named the Narmada Valley Development Project.

The Sardar Sarovar Project (SSP)

The Sardar Sarovar Project (SSP) is a multipurpose dam being constructed on the Narmada River in the district of Narmada in central Gujarat. The rationale of the dam is defined as the provision of irrigation, drinking water, electricity and flood protection. A 1,200 metres long concrete mastodon, the proposed final height of the dam is some 138 metres, with an attached canal network of 75,000 kilometres. Submerging 37,000 hectares of land, the 200 kilometres long reservoir will affect 245 villages across three states: 193 villages in Madhya Pradesh, 33 villages in Maharashtra, and 19 villages in Gujarat. Spanning such a large area, the reservoir will of course affect a diverse range of communities: 56 per cent of those who stand to be displaced belong to adivasi communities in the three states, whereas the remaining 44 per cent belong to caste Hindu farming communities in western Madhya Pradesh (Roy 2002: chapter 2).

The cost of the project – estimated as 14,000 crore[7] rupees in the Ninth Five-Year Plan (1997–2002) – is financed through the budget of Gujarat state, with contributions from the other involved state governments, funds from the central government and funds raised from financial markets by the Sardar Sarovar Narmada Nigam Limited (SSNNL), the body responsible for the construction of the project, through the public issue of bonds and placement of bonds with financial institutions.[8] The World Bank also funded the project from the late 1970s until its withdrawal in 1993.

The management of the SSP is carried out through a fairly complex institutional structure involving both central and state governments. The Ministries of Finance (MoF), Environment and Forests (MoEF), and Water Resources (MoWR) administer the central government's interests in the project. The Narmada Water Disputes Tribunal established the Narmada Control Authority (NCA) in Indore in Madhya Pradesh to watch over and coordinate state-level actions in relation to the project. Each of the riparian states has its own institutional apparatus to deal with the project. The SSNNL administers the project in Gujarat, and is thus in charge of building the actual dam. The Narmada Valley Development Authority (NVDA) is the equivalent to the SSNNL in Madhya Pradesh, catering to the development of the project on the stretches of the river that belongs to the state. Maharashtra deals with the project through extant institutions and with the assistance of the Additional Collector for Resettlement and Rehabilitation (Fisher 1995: 19).

The site of the SSP was located to Navagam in what was then Bombay State in the late 1950s. When Bombay State was divided into the states of Gujarat and Maharashtra in 1960, the Broach project as it was then called became the responsibility of Gujarat. The project has since its very beginning occupied a central place in the designs for Gujarati state-building (Sen 2000a: 1). Throughout its trajectory, the project has been virulently supported by the lobby groups of the rich farmers of South and Central Gujarat as well as by the state's emergent industrial bourgeoisie (Dwivedi 2006: 74–5). It has also featured centrally in the discourses of the political representatives of these groups from Sardar Vallabhbhai Patel in the 1960s to the present Chief Minister Narendra Modi (see Chapter 2). The project also has support from all other political parties in the state, as well as a host of right wing Hindutva organizations.

The Planning Commission sanctioned the project in 1960 and Jawaharlal Nehru laid the foundation stone on April 5, 1961 (D'Souza 2002: 4–5; Khagram 2004: 69–70). The approach roads and bridges to the dam site were built, project and staff headquarters were set up, and land was acquired for the project colony at Kevadia, displacing 4000 people in the process – most of whom have yet to be resettled (Dwivedi 2006: 63). However, the implementation of the project was to be held up by deep-running interstate rivalries between Gujarat and Madhya Pradesh for two decades (D'Souza 2002: 5–6).[9]

It was not until 1979, when the Narmada Water Disputes Tribunal (NWDT) – a body set up to resolve the conflict between the two states – delivered an award that was acceptable to all parties that the project got under way. By 1987–88, funding had been secured from the World Bank, and the necessary central ministries had given clearance to the project. However, the trajectory of the SSP now came to be shaped by popular resistance from the affected communities rather than inter-state rivalries as the grass-roots groups that would eventually come to form the NBA begun to question and challenge the project. Thus, the construction of the SSP proceeded in fits and starts until 1994 when India's Supreme Court imposed a stay on the project while it dealt with a case of public interest litigation filed by the NBA in order to stop the dam. However, in October 2000 the Supreme Court ordered that the SSP should be brought to completion, and the dam today stands at 120 metres.

The Maheshwar Hydroelectric Project (MHP)

Located in Khargone district of Madhya Pradesh, the Maheshwar Hydroelectric Project is as its name suggests being built for the purpose of electricity generation. At a height of 35 metres and with a 40 kilometres long reservoir, it is claimed that the project will produce 400 MW of electricity when it is brought to full completion. The reservoir will submerge some 5,000 hectares of agricultural land, affecting 61 villages in the region of West Nimad/Khargone in Madhya Pradesh. The cost of the project is set to 530,000,000 US dollars (Dharmidhikary n.d.; Ghose n.d; Bissell, Singh and Warth 2000; NBA 1999; Schücking 1999).

The project was conceived in 1978 under the auspices of the NVDA as part of the emerging master plan for the harnessing of the Narmada River. In 1989, it was passed on to the Madhya Pradesh Electricity Board, and then in 1993, as the first hydroelectric project in Indian history, it was privatized. The concession was awarded to the Shree Maheshwar Hydel Power Corporation Limited (SMHPCL), a company which was set up by the S. Kumars group and whose economic mainstay until then had been textiles. The project was given conditional clearing from the MoEF in 1994, and construction work began in 1997 (Ghosh 2003, 2006b). Whereas 51 per cent of its equity is controlled by S. Kumars, the SMHPCL has since the very beginning sought foreign equity for the project. The first takers were the US companies Pacgen and Bechtel, but these withdrew in 1997 and 1998 as a consequence of NBA protests. Then the German corporations Bayernwerk, Vereinigte Elektrizitätswerke Westfalen (VEW), and Siemens entered into the project. Almost half the costs were to be provided by the German Bayerische Vereinsbank as an export loan. Moreover, to protect long-term investments, both corporations also applied to the German government for an investment guarantee, and Siemens applied to the German government for an export guarantee. The export guarantee in turn was to be given by Hermes – the official export credit agency of the German government – and was to pay Siemens a token amount if the company had any losses in its dealing with the project. Thus, the mainstay of the balance would be underwritten by the German government (Bissell, Singh and Warth 2000; Schücking 1999).

Whereas Bayernwerk and VEW withdrew as a consequence of NBA protests in 1999, Siemens remained a part of the project until the summer of 2000. Following pressure from the NBA, the German government commissioned an investigation into the MHP to determine the charges that the project was in blatant violation of the human rights of the communities of the area. The report was unequivocally damning of the project,[10] especially its resettlement and rehabilitation policy, and consequently Siemens was compelled to withdraw its application for an export guarantee, and a proposed loan from the HypoVereinsbank to the MHP was cancelled. However, the vacuum left by Bayernwerk and VEW was filled by Ogden, a US company, which signed a contract for 49 per cent of the equity in March 2000. However, following massive international lobbying and NBA protest, Ogden withdrew from the project in December 2000 (Schücking 1999). This was followed by the Portuguese government turning down an application from ABB to supply a guarantee for their delivery of equipment to the project.

Ogden's withdrawal from the MHP in 2000 brought the MHP to a temporary standstill. The response of the SMHPCL was to turn to Indian financial institutions such as the Industrial Development Bank of India (IDBI), the Industrial Finance Corporation of India (IFCI), the Unit Trust of India (UTI), the State Bank of India (SBI), the Life Insurance Corporation of India (LIC), and the General Insurance Corporation (GIC). Moreover, the dam builders also resorted to funds from commercial banks and other financial institutions. The public financial institutions have been approached for financing as much as 90 per cent of the total project costs. IDBI has admitted to disbursing Rs. 30 crores – 30 per cent of a loan of Rs. 100 crores – and Rs. 50 crores as equity for the project. Despite its reassurances to NBA activists that no additional funds would be channelled to the project before certain conditions were met, the IDBI proceeded to give an additional Rs. 30 crores to the SMHPCL (Bavadam 2001). In the early days of 2004, the newly elected BJP government of Madhya Pradesh decided to support the project with a guarantee of Rs. 400 crores; construction on the project was resumed and so were the protests of the NBA (Bavadam 2004b).[11] The conflict is still ongoing, and its outcome is still uncertain.

India's new social movements and the Narmada Bachao Andolan

India's postcolonial development project was underpinned by a truce line which ran between a 'developmental state which promised to end poverty and backwardness' (Chatterjee 2004: 37) on the one hand and popular classes that had been demobilised after the attainment of independence. Following the end of the Telangana uprising in 1951, subaltern social movements by and large remained quiescent and ceded their autonomy to 'the strong hand of the Nehruvian state' (Katzenstein and Ray 2005: 14). However, India became deeply embroiled in the transnational conjuncture of resistance of 1968, the 'southern moment' of which gave rise to a critique of 'the nationalism and institutionalized elite politics . . . of the first generation of independent third world states' (Watts 2001: 172). It was the eruption of the Naxalite revolt in West Bengal in 1967 – a guerrilla insurgency headed by the Communist Party of India – Marxist-Leninist (see Bannerjee 1984) – that sounded the death knell of subaltern acquiescence and marked the onset of a decade in which India witnessed the emergence of new social movements (NSMs) that subjected the exclusionary and exploitative dimensions of state-led capitalist development to substantial critique (Vanaik 1990; Omvedt 1993; Kamat 2002; Ray and Katzenstein 2005).

During the early 1970s in India, there occurred 'a substantial radicalization of youth . . . outside the circles of the traditional left' (Vanaik 1990: 195), which in turn resulted in the organization of groups and mobilization around issues that had been neglected by the parliamentary left parties. Significant NSMs of the 1970s were the Chipko movement which championed the livelihoods of forest-dwelling communities in Uttarkhand (Guha 1989; Basu 1987; Rangan 2000), the Kerala Fishworkers' Forum which organized poor fisherfolk in Kerala against the depredations wrought on their livelihoods by mechanized trawling (Basu 1987; Shah 1988), and the Shramik Sangathana which organized Bhil adivasis in Maharashtra around issues of agricultural wages, land control and forest rights (Basu 1987; Shah 1988; Upadhyaya 1980). In 1974–75, a wave of popular uprisings shook Indira Gandhi's government to the core. Assuming the form of a protest against corruption and manipulative politics and maintaining a studied distance from established political parties, the Nav Nirman movement, as it came to be known, swept through the state of Gujarat in January 1974 and culminated in the dissolution of the legislative assembly (see Jones and Jones 1976; Wood 1975; Shah 1977). The uprising transmuted into a challenge to the national regime when it was taken up by Jayaprakash (JP) Narayan, a socialist and leading figure in the Sarvodaya movement in Bihar.[12] In Bihar, the JP movement was met with fierce repression, the consequence of which was that it was converted 'from a state agitation to a movement of all-India scope' (Frankel 2005: 534). By March 1975, JP was able to stage a massive protest in Delhi, demanding Indira Gandhi's resignation. Many commentators have pointed to this as a factor that was crucial in prompting the Prime Minister's decision to impose a national state of emergency in June of the same year (Shah 1977; Hardiman 2003; Frankel 2005). Moreover, the 1970s witnessed the mushrooming of various social action groups – a phenomenon that Kamat (2002: 10) refers to as 'the new grassroots movement' – which came to identify the dominant conception or ideology of development as the root cause of persistent poverty and increasing inequalities in Indian society. These groups particularly flourished in the wake of the Emergency, when the Janata government encouraged 'voluntary work and the formation of voluntary organizations in the countryside' (ibid.: 12).[13]

From the middle of the 1980s, India's NSMs increasingly came to be involved in a search for perspectives and agendas that could serve as a unifying platform for the diverse struggles that had emerged during the previous one-and-a-half-decades. For some movements – like the Kerala Fishworkers' Forum and the Shetkari Sangathana – this revolved around addressing gender relations and feminist politics; for others – like the Chattisgarh Mukti Morcha – it revolved around developing a red-green politics, i.e. a worker-peasant alliance around the politics of social justice and environmental sustainability (Omvedt 1993: 230–6). As Omvedt points out, the attempts to forge a common platform reached a high point with the National Rally Against Destructive Development in Harsud, Madhya Pradesh in September 1989, where between 25,000 and 50,000 activists from different social movements gathered to discuss an agenda which could unite different struggles against destructive development projects (ibid.: 269–70).[14]

Another crucial process, unfolding towards the end of the 1980s, was the increasing integration of the politics of the NSMs in a national field of force characterized by the onset of neoliberal restructuring and Hindu communalism. An important event in this process was the 'mandate of 89'. The 1989 elections sent a new opposition force, the National Front coalition, which borrowed key themes from social movements, to power (Omvedt 1993: 273). The National Front government was thus a government 'elected on a mandate of change and with social movement backing' but it was also 'a fragile coalition government marked by factionalism' which lacked a capacity for concerted political action (ibid.: 274). This became obvious when Prime Minister V. P. Singh decided to implement the recommendations of the Mandal Commission on positive discrimination for lower caste groups in 1990; as Omvedt points out, this was 'the one social movement issue that did not require a major political reformulation of the process of development' (ibid.: 280). It did, nevertheless, turn out to be an explosive move: it triggered political protest by Hindu communalist forces across the country and eventually led to the downfall of the Singh government (see Frankel 2005: 688–9). Simultaneously, the Indian economy plunged into a crippling fiscal crisis. Thus, when Narasimha Rao's Congress government assumed power in 1991, the floodgates of neoliberal restructuring were opened once and for all – despite massive protestations by NSMs, trade unions and the parliamentary left (ibid.: 590; see also Walton and Udayagiri 2002).

For some commentators, for example Basu (1987), Vanaik (1990) and Omvedt (1993), the failure of India's NSMs to decisively advance their agenda in the late 1980s and early 1990s puts the stamp of defeat upon these movements. Yet movement struggles are still vigorous in India; as Corbridge and Harriss (2000: xix) note, the attempts to reinvent India according to neoliberal and Hindu communalist elite designs are being virulently resisted 'by a diversity of social and political movements which are part of [a] long history . . . of resistance to the established order by those who have been the objects of oppression'. Indeed, this resistance is escalating in tandem with the intensification of neoliberal restructuring. In this context, it is imperative that the specific experiences of mobilization and struggle in the Narmada Valley be made relevant as 'useable knowledge for those seeking social change' (Flacks cited in Bevington and Dixon 2005: 189).

Now, the social action groups that worked among the dam-affected adivasi communities in the Narmada Valley in the early and mid-1980s – the Khedut Mazdoor Chetna Sangath in Madhya Pradesh, the Narmada Dharangrasta Samiti in Maharashtra, and the ARCH Vahini in Gujarat – all emerged as urban, educated activists that were embedded in or inspired by one or many of the new strands of oppositional grassroots politics set out to mobilize marginalized groups in the countryside. These social action groups in turn became the hub of contention over the Narmada projects as they started to question the authorities on the impact of the Sardar Sarovar Project on the affected communities and the extent to which adequate policies and plans for resettlement and rehabilitation had been put in place. The organizations soon started co-operating among themselves, as well as with NGOs and activist networks at national and transnational scales, in order to more effectively make their claims for information on the state as well as on the World Bank as a central funding agency (see Baviskar 1995; Dwivedi 2006; Jayal 2000; Khagram 2004).

The initial demands for information and resettlement and rehabilitation soon came to be radicalized as the activists pressed their claims and demands on state authorities that were unwilling to respond and as they amassed information about the SSP on their own that suggested, among other things, that the scale of displacement was far more extensive than official estimates claimed and, moreover, that the prospects for adequate resettlement and rehabilitation were slight. This process culminated in mid-1988 when the decision was made to oppose the dam *tout court* and to form a pan-state organization under the moniker Narmada Bachao Andolan. Only the ARCH Vahini – the organization that represented the dam-affected communities in Gujarat – decided not to join in this demand; they chose instead to co-operate with the state government in the implementation of resettlement and rehabilitation (see Patkar 1995; Patel 1995; Sangvai 2000a).

The demand that the SSP should be cancelled was brought to bear on state and central governments from 1990 onwards, in a campaign that united non-violent direct action with a strategic claim that the dam should be subjected to a state-led review in terms of its social and environmental impacts and economic and technical feasibility. The first year of the struggle witnessed the NBA staging several dramatic actions to get the governments of the riparian states and the federal government to commit to a review, but ultimately these efforts failed in the face of staunch opposition from the Government of Gujarat (GoG) and its Chief Minister, Chimanbhai Patel. This led the NBA to a strategic reorientation: the movement now came to focus on protest activities in the dam-affected adivasi villages, crucially centred on non-cooperation with state and project authorities, and engaged with the independent review team (the Morse Commission as it came to be known) that had been dispatched to the Narmada Valley by the World Bank as a result of intense mobilization by the transnational advocacy network that had emerged around the NBA in the late 1980s. Whilst the Andolan staged high-profile protests and resisted fierce repression on the ground in the Narmada Valley, the investigations of the Morse Commission yielded a damning report which in turn resulted in one of the movement's major victories, namely the withdrawal of World Bank funding from the SSP in 1993 (see Jayal 2000; Udall 1995; Khagram 2004; Dwivedi 2006).

Following the withdrawal of the World Bank, the Andolan again focused its energies on trying to force the state to implement a review of the SSP. Following a series of dramatic protest actions, the central government announced that a review would be carried out by a Five-Member Group (FMG). However, the work of the FMG, albeit supportive of the NBA's stance, eventually failed to have any practical ramifications. When the sluice gates of the SSP were closed during the monsoon of 1994, causing submergence and displacement in Maharashtra and Madhya Pradesh, the NBA turned to India's Supreme Court in order to stop the project. The Supreme Court in turn imposed a stay on the construction of the SSP in 1995 that remained in place for the next five years. During the Supreme Court's deliberations, the Andolan devoted its energies to constructive activities in the dam-affected adivasi communities in Maharashtra and Madhya Pradesh, and also extended its mobilizational activities to the communities that stood to be affected by the Maheshwar Hydroelectric Project (MHP) with a great deal of success (Jayal 2000; Khagram 2004; Dwivedi 2006).

However, the success in the struggle against the MHP quickly came to be overshadowed by the trajectory of the struggle against the SSP: in October 2000, the Supreme Court delivered its verdict on the case that the NBA had filed against the Indian government, stating that every endeavour should be made to bring the construction of the SSP to its completion. With this turn of events, the struggle was shifted onto its current defensive terrain, where the NBA focuses on securing resettlement, rehabilitation and compensation for the communities affected not only by the SSP, but also the Indira Sagar Project and the Maheshwar and Omkareshwar dams (see Jayal 2000; Dwivedi 2006; Khagram 2004).

Understanding movement processes

This study is informed by a theoretical framework which seeks to overcome the narrow view of social movements as organizations engaging in extra-parliamentary collective action 'within a more stable or institutionalized political order' centred on 'particular status claims made against the taken-for granted background of the economic order' (Cox 1999a: 85). Taking a broader view, I conceive of social movements as the fundamental animating forces in the making and unmaking of social structures of human needs and capacities, and as forces that emanate both from dominant and subaltern groups within a social formation – it is a perspective, then, which speaks of social movements from above as well as social movements from below (see Cox, 1999a; Cox and Nilsen 2005; Nilsen 2009).

This perspective is moored in a conception of historical materialism where praxis stands as the foundational ontological category as well as the substance of historical change and development – and praxis is in turn understood as the satisfaction of human needs through the conscious deployment of practical and corporeal capacities in historically evolving social formations.[15] Praxis is of course inherently developmental: 'the satisfaction of the first need', wrote Marx and Engels (1999: 49), 'leads to new needs; and this production of new needs is the first historical act'. And this spiral of developing needs and capacities is in turn intrinsically social and historical.

The sociality of praxis flows from the fact that human beings go about the business of satisfying their needs in a cooperative manner and this cooperation generates social formations that constitute a condition for the deployment of capacities for the satisfaction of needs. However, these lattice-works of social relations do not only function as enabling conduits, but also as structural constraints by exerting pressures and setting limits on praxis. The outcome of the exertion of pressures and the setting of limits is the formation of a dominant structure of entrenched needs and capacities that is reproduced over extended periods time in accordance with extant relations of power between dominant and subaltern groups within a social formation. However, such structures – and the social formations in which they inhere – are not static; rather they are internally contradictory totalities that constantly undergo change as a result of contention between dominant and subaltern social groups over the structuration of needs and capacities (Nilsen 2007a).

Such changes can take the form of modifications of a dominant structure of entrenched needs and capacities which leaves the overarching societal framework intact, or in the form of systemic convulsions in which such structures and the social formation that has crystallized around them are fundamentally ruptured and replaced by something new and altogether different – this is the defining feature of the historicity of praxis. The former occurs when subaltern social groups mobilize collectively to defend or carve out a space for the accommodation of their specific needs within an extant social formation. The latter takes place when subaltern groups develop new meanings and values, new practices, new relationships and kinds of relationship around emergent structures of radical needs and capacities (Nilsen 2007a) – that is, sets of needs and capacities that have developed but cannot be fully satisfied and deployed within the confines of extant structures (Heller 1976). The conflictual processes through which needs and capacities and the social organization of these develop constitute the kernel of the following definition of social movements: *a social movement is the organization of multiple forms of materially grounded and locally generated skilled activity around a rationality expressed and organized by (would-be) hegemonic actors, and against the hegemonic projects articulated by other such actors to change or maintain a dominant structure of entrenched needs and capacities and the social formation in which it inheres, in part or in whole*[16] – for example, when India's new social movements and postcolonial elites struggle over the direction and meaning of development (Nilsen 2008).

This definition does not restrict the referent of the term social movement to the collective action of subaltern social groups. Rather, it seeks to take account of how dominant social groups engage in collective action based on their superior access to economic, political and cultural power resources. More specifically, a social movement from above can be defined as the organization of multiple forms of skilled activity around a rationality expressed and organized by dominant social groups, which aims at the maintenance or modification of a dominant structure of entrenched needs and capacities in ways that reproduce and/or extend the power of those groups and its hegemonic position within a given social formation (Nilsen and Cox 2006; Nilsen 2009). In this study, the concept of social movement from above is put to work in Chapter 2, which presents an analysis of how the distributional bias of the costs and benefits associated with the SSP and MHP constitutes a case of 'accumulation by dispossession' (Harvey 2003, 2005), and inserts this in a wider conceptualization of how India's postcolonial development project has been shaped by the collective action of dominant social groups.

Social movements from below, such as the Narmada Bachao Andolan, can be defined as the organization of multiple forms of skilled activity around a rationality expressed and organized by subaltern social groups, which aims either to challenge the constraints that a dominant structure of needs and capacities impose upon the development of new needs and capacities or to defend aspects of such a dominant structure that accommodate their specific needs and capacities (Nilsen 2009).

Now, subaltern groups:

> experience deprivation and oppression within a concrete setting, not as the end result of large and abstract processes . . . it is the daily experience of people that shapes their grievances, establishes the measure of their demands, and points out the targets of their anger.
>
> (Piven and Cloward 1977: 20–1)

Yet, those experiences are not merely isolated instances or singular episodes of deprivation and oppression. Rather, they are 'clues to underlying structures and relationships which are not observable other than through the particular phenomena or events that they produce' (Wainwright 1994: 7). Furthermore, these structures and relationships can come within the cognitive and practical reach of movement participants if they combine and extend their 'fragmented knowledge' in ways which enable them to develop 'a better understanding of the social mechanisms at work, so as to direct their efforts in order that their intentions might be more efficiently fulfilled' (ibid.: 108; see also Kilgore 1999; Barker and Cox 2002). This, in turn, means that the character of the grievances, the demands, and the targets of the anger of social movements from below may change in an expansive way from forms of oppositional collective action that are bounded in scope and aims to a specific, situated and local experience towards more encompassing and radical counterhegemonic projects in which situated struggles 'shift gears, transcend particularities, and arrive at some conception of a universal alternative to that social system which is the source of their difficulties' (Harvey 2000: 241; see also Cox 1998). I shall refer to the realization of this potentiality as a movement process, and propose the concepts local rationality, militant particularism, campaign and social movement project as tools with which to make sense of different facets and phases of movement processes.[17]

A local rationality is a formal characteristic about the way subaltern social groups make sense of and engage with the world, at the heart of which lie needs and capacities that are constrained or encroached upon by the hegemonic projects of dominant social groups (see Cox 1999a: 113; Cox and Nilsen 2005; Nilsen 2009). Local rationalities can be understood as those oppositional ways of doing, being, and thinking that people develop in their situated, everyday efforts to cope with, negotiate, and resist such constraints and encroachments. However, local rationalities do not exist in 'hermetically sealed sites of autonomy', hidden from hegemonic ways of doing, being and knowing, but in 'relational spaces of connection and articulation' (Moore 1998: 347). They are, in Gramsci's (1998: 328) terms, '[the] healthy nucleus that exists in "common sense", the part of it which can be called "good sense" and which deserves to be made more unitary and coherent'. And if they are made more unitary and coherent, local rationalities may give rise to overt acts of defiance, opposition and confrontation, the character of which can be effectively grasped through the concept of militant particularism (Williams 1989; Harvey 1996, 2000; see also Cox and Nilsen 2005; Featherstone 2005; Nilsen 2009). This concept refers to how the oppositional collective action of subaltern groups 'is always embedded in 'ways of life' and 'structures of feeling' peculiar to places and communities' (Harvey 2000: 55), and hence also bear the imprint of this specificity. In other words, militant particularism refers to the struggles that emerge when a subaltern group deploys the ways of being, doing and thinking that define a local rationality in open confrontation with a dominant social group over a particular contentious issue or situation. In Chapters 3 and 4 of this book I show how the movement process in the Narmada Valley was predicated upon the transformation of local rationalities in the dam-affected communities through conflictual encounters with local agents of oppression mediated by urban, educated activists rooted in the new forms of grassroots politics that flourished in India in the 1970s.

If lines of communication and connection are established between militant particularisms activists may come to define common strategies, solidarities and identities that are opposed to what is perceived to be a common adversary. I propose the term *campaign* to define the organization of a range of local responses to specific situations in ways that connect people across multiple such situations and construct a generic challenge to such situations (see Cox 1999a: 109; Cox and Nilsen 2005; Nilsen 2009). Chapters 5, 6 and 7 of this book present an analysis of the processes through which a pan-state anti-dam campaign emerged from the militant particularist struggles that had emerged in the communities that stood to be affected by the SSP in the late 1980s, and trace the trajectory of the campaign against the SSP from 1990 to 2000, as well as its extension to the communities affected by the MHP.

Campaigns are typically constructed in field-specific terms – that is, they are oriented towards a specific policy-field or a specific kind of issue – and do not automatically, or for all their participants, bring into question how the field in which they organize is linked to an overarching social totality. Joining the dots between specific fields and the wider totality is, however, an inherent potentiality of movement processes. As activists discover the links between different fields of mobilization and different groups within those fields, and as they criticize the structural constraints that cause their problems or frustrate their campaigns, they may come to move beyond specific fields of contention and move towards a form of movement activity which posits the social totality as the object that is to be challenged and transformed. The outcome may be the construction of a social movement project – a form of collective skilled activity which is defined by (a) the articulation of a challenge to the social totality, which (b) aims to control the self-production of society, and (c) possesses or strives to possess a capacity for hegemony that would render (b) and thus (a) possible (see Cox 1999a: 102; Cox and Nilsen 2005; Nilsen 2009).[18] In Chapter 8, I show how the Narmada Bachao Andolan has constructed a social movement project around the politics of alernative development that joins the dots between the campaign against the Narmada dams and the way in which dominant proprietary classes have shaped India's postcolonial development project to their advantage, and how they have joined hands with other social movements in order to advance this project.

The movement process in the Narmada Valley presents a complex picture of mixed experiences. On the one hand, there are considerable achievements ranging from the enablement of local communities to assert themselves against local oppressors, to the politicization – both nationally and globally – of large dam projects and the role that international financial institutions play in advancing these projects, as well as the building of solidarities between the movements of subaltern groups across India. On the other hand, there is the undeniable failure to vindicate the key objective of stopping the construction of large dams on the Narmada. Now, to paraphrase William Morris, I believe that it is in pondering all these things, how movements fight and lose their battles, that we may also move towards an understanding of how the things they fought for may come about despite their defeat, as and when other movements come to fight for what they meant under another name. It is my hope that this study will contribute to the extraction of generic lessons and insights from the movement process in the Narmada Valley that may serve as a source of inspiration and instruction for the movements that are currently crystallizing in India in opposition to the increasingly aggressive and violent forms of dispossession which are constitutive of capitalist development.

2 Losing ground

Accumulation by dispossession in the Narmada Valley

'Before submergence, we would eat four *rotis* four times a day; now we eat two *rotis* two times a day' – this is how Chetram Narte, a Gond adivasi peasant, described the impact of the Bargi dam on the livelihoods of the villagers of Piparya on the upper reaches of the Narmada River in eastern Madhya Pradesh.[1] Prior to the coming of the dam, Chetram and his family used to farm five acres of land. Now, however, they are left to eke out a living from two acres. For many households in the submergence zone, the loss of land to the reservoir of the Bargi dam that was completed in 1990 has compelled one or several family members to migrate to regional urban centres such as Jabalpur, Bhopal, and Indore – and sometimes as far afield as to Surat and Delhi – to find work. In the urban centres, people often work on construction sites, although it is not unusual to find oustees from the Bargi reservoir area pulling rickshaws in Jabalpur. In the cities, they squat on pavements and in the mornings they all line up – sometimes as many as five-to six-hundred of them – in designated places referred to as labour *chowks* (squares). Labour contractors working for construction firms will turn up and select the workers they need. Being paid 50 to 60 rupees a day, they usually work for two or three consecutive days. Sometimes, if they are lucky, they will be able to work until a house is done. Most often, though, jobs are few and far between for the migrants (field notes, February 2003).

In Chetram's village, I came across a particularly harrowing example of the depredations the migrant workers in the area find themselves faced with. When I asked a group of villagers to tell me about their experiences of labour migration, Thakur Singh, a Gond peasant who had lost most of his land to submergence, told me that his son and some of his friends had gone all the way to Hyderabad to find work. He proceeded to tell me that a labour contractor from the neighbouring village had contacted his son and several others to offer them well-paid work. When they arrived in Jabalpur, they were packed into trains that took them to Hyderabad; once they arrived in Hyderabad they were crammed onto the loading planes of trucks and taken to a remote sugarcane-processing factory. At the factory they would work 12-hour shifts, earning around 18 rupees per day. Their wages, however, were not paid and the management kept them locked in behind the factory gates. When they got in touch with the police in order to have them force the management to let them go, the management told the police that the boys had taken an advance payment on their wages and could not leave the factory. The police, the boys reckoned, had been bought off by their employers. Thakur Singh only came to know about these conditions when some of the boys managed to run away and return to the village. The villagers decided to take legal action to get the boys back home safely, but before the matter wound up in court, rains wreaked havoc on the sugarcane harvests, and they were fired. After five months of work they were left with hardly 1,000 rupees each (field notes, February 2003).

In mainstream academic discourse there is a term for the experiences of the villagers in the submergence zone of the Bargi dam: 'development-induced displacement'. In the work of Michael Cernea, a leading expert in the field, development-induced displacement is posited as 'a *class* of socio-demographic events' that are inevitable and unavoidable in the sense that 'development cannot occur if existing patterns of human settlement remain forever frozen' (Cernea 1999: 2). The problem with development-induced displacement, on this view, is not its occurrence per se, but rather the fact that more often than not 'physical resettlement unfortunately occurs without rehabilitation' and therefore results in 'abject and dramatic impoverishment' for the affected groups (ibid.: 4). Displacement is thus conceived of as 'the social cost of development', and it is argued it has to be properly conceptualized with adequate methodologies which will allow for the incorporation of displacement 'into the routine economic analysis of development interventions' (ibid.: 7).

This perspective is, in my view, fundamentally flawed. The basic problem is that within this framework 'the lived social relations of people whose lands are being submerged and those who benefit from increased irrigation and electrification' are lifted out of their actual historical context 'onto an overall balance sheet that is an abstraction from the relations of production and exchange within which people find themselves enmeshed' (Whitehead 2003: 4225). When displacement is posited as a ubiquitous and inevitable aspect of human existence, we lose sight of the ways in which the loss of access to certain resources for some groups – typically subaltern groups – and the gaining of access to certain other resources for other groups – typically dominant groups – actually constitute moments in historically specific processes of change in social relations in which definite social groups are differentially positioned in terms of 'the extent of their control of social relations and . . . the scope of their transformative powers' (Sewell 1992: 20).

The notion of development-induced displacement also obfuscates the ways in which such processes of change are decisively shaped by dominant social groups who consciously and collectively deploy their greater transformative powers relative to subaltern groups so as to enhance and extend their control of social relations in a given spatio-temporal location. Another flaw in this perspective, closely related to the points already raised, flows from its designation of the impacts of displacement as 'common and fundamental risks of impoverishment' (Cernea 1999: 18). This designation in effect amounts to a definition of poverty as 'a *condition* . . . a negative attribute into which people fall, or from which "exit routes" can be designed' (Mosse 2007: 5; italics in original). An alternative which takes seriously the insistence upon viewing displacement in relational and historical terms would conceive of the impoverishment experienced by people such as the villagers in the submergence zone of the Bargi dam 'as arising from the operation of existing social relations and the adverse terms of inclusion in socio-economic systems' (ibid.: 5) – in particular the operation of processes of capitalist accumulation, and the ways in which subaltern groups are adversely integrated into these processes as casual labourers as a consequence of losing access to means of subsistence and production (see Mosse 2007: 9–18; Mosse, Gupta and Shah 2005; Breman 1996; Harriss-White 2005).

In this chapter I develop a perspective that seeks to avoid such ahistorical reifications of displacement and its impacts by analyzing the Narmada dams in terms of how the unequal distribution of benefits and costs that attach to the project constitute a case of 'accumulation by dispossession' (Harvey 2003, 2005). Accumulation by dispossession refers to the continued relevance in contemporary capitalism of the practices of what Marx referred to as 'primitive accumulation', namely the dual transformation 'whereby the social means of subsistence and production are turned into capital, and the immediate producers are turned into wage labourers' through the separation of 'the producer from the means of production' (Marx 1990: 875).[2]

The central contention of my argument is this: the distributional bias of the Sardar Sarovar Project (SSP) and the Maheshwar Hydroelectric Project (MHP) is expressive of a 'dual transformation' where (a) property rights in water and electricity, as well as profitable investment opportunities, are concentrated in the hands of regional, national and global propertied elites, and (b) the displacement of peasant producers from their land without adequate resettlement and rehabilitation (R&R) generates pressures towards proletarianization. The dynamics of accumulation by dispossession in the case of the SSP is the focus of the first part of the chapter, whereas the second part of the chapter turns to an analysis of the specificities of accumulation by dispossession in the case of the MHP. Furthermore, my analysis seeks to link accumulation by dispossession in the Narmada Valley to a crucial feature of the political economy of capitalist development in India, namely the way in which the central development strategies of the state have systematically resulted in the transfer and concentration of productive resources to and among 'dominant proprietary classes' in agriculture and industry, whilst simultaneously abrogating the access of subaltern groups to such resources – the effect of which has been to extend and entrench capitalist relations of production in postcolonial India. This argument is developed in the third and final part of the chapter.

Accumulation by dispossession in the Narmada Valley

Accumulation by dispossession 1: The Sardar Sarovar Project

Understanding how accumulation by dispossession unfolds in the case of the SSP on the one hand revolves around understanding how the dam is part and parcel of a 'built environment for production' (Harvey 1999) the purpose of which is to provide agroindustrial capitalism in South and Central Gujarat with irrigation and electricity, and, on the other hand, understanding how the construction of this built in May 1990. This was an important achievement, as the Japanese government 'in addition to being a major shareholder in the World Bank . . . was also co-financing the Sardar Sarovar Project through the Overseas Economic Cooperation Fund' (ibid.: 212). The activists had thus succeeded in making a significant chink in the SSP's financial armour.

Success in Japan in turn added momentum to the formation of the Narmada Action Committee (NAC), described by Jai Sen (n.d.: 17) as 'a loose grouping, or virtual committee – more a process than an institution – of Narmada campaigners in the North who were working to support the NBA campaign in India'. Drawing on, but also developing and strengthening the already extant transnational infrastructure of contention that had developed around the militant particularist struggles for resettlement and rehabilitation, and more recently the emergence of the anti-dam campaign, the NAC's activities focused on the 'dissemination of information on what was happening, particularly in the Narmada Valley, but also in parliaments throughout the world', thus rendering possible 'immediate action and follow-up' with the coordination of 'what were in fact a whole series of *national* campaigns engaging in what were in fact *domestic* politics' (ibid.: 17). The NAC thus 'operated simultaneously in local space, in national space, in international space, and also in transnational space, with a large array – or webs – of horizontal and vertical linkages' (ibid.: 17). And as we shall see, its multiscalar operations yielded dividends.

The independent review

Simultaneously with the intensification of transnational advocacy, pressure was building up in the Valley as the *Sangharsh Yatra* unfolded in December and January 1990, and partly in response to this, the World Bank gave private assurances to the Andolan that an independent review would be announced. In the wake of the wind-up of the *Sangharsh Yatra,* in April and May 1991, NBA activists Shripad Dharmidhikary and Kisan Metha went on a tour throughout Europe to meet with the press, politicians, and Western NGOs, so as to build further pressure on the World Bank to stick to its word. Finally, on 17 June, 1991 the World Bank declared that an independent review would be instigated to scrutinize the resettlement of the dam-affected communities, and the amelioration of the environmental impacts of the project. Headed by Bradford Morse and Thomas Berger, the Morse Commission as it came to be known, officially started work in September 1991. When the Morse Commission's report was published in 1992, its conclusions were unequivocal and harsh:

> We think that the Sardar Sarovar Projects as they stand are flawed, that resettlement and rehabilitation of all those displaced by the projects is not possible under the prevailing circumstances, and that the environmental impacts of the projects have not been properly considered or adequately addressed.
>
> (Morse and Berger 1992: vii)

Accordingly, the Morse Commission recommended that the World Bank should 'step back' from the SSP until a series of changes had been effected (see Dwivedi 2006: 247).

Whereas the report was greeted with elation by the NBA and its activists it was denounced by the state governments of all three riparian states – cutting across party-boundaries between the BJP, Congress, and Janata Dal – and subjected to severe criticisms from dam-supporters such as the ARCH Vahini.[8] The World Bank on its part sought to resist the recommendations of the report with various kinds of stalling tactics. Eventually, however, what Udall (1995: 220) calls 'a "face-saving" deal' was worked out between the Bank and the Government of India; the Indian government would ask the World Bank to discontinue its funding of the SSP, while the Bank would announce that it still believed in the project and the authorities' capacity to achieve the benchmarks: 'On March 30, 1993, the executive director for India made the expected announcement to the Board that the Indian government would complete the project on its own' (ibid.: 220). The NBA commented on the withdrawal by labelling it 'a triumph for thousands of struggling farmers and tribals in the Narmada Valley and a shot in the arm for the wider struggle against advancing neo-imperialism and the form of the World Bank-IMF sponsored structural adjusting programme and General Agreement on Tariff and Trade (GATT)' (cited in Dwivedi 2006: 250).

Commenting on the outcome of the transnational campaign to stop World Bank funding of the SSP, Jai Sen (n.d.: 20) argues that 'given the nature and duration of the multiple campaigns that had taken place, and also the stubborn resistance of the governments concerned and of the Bank, this was a historic victory for civil movements'. Indeed, the international Narmada campaign has been celebrated as an example of how 'transnational advocacy networks' can successfully combine 'information politics' – that is, 'the ability to quickly and credibly generate politically usable information and move it where it will have the most impact' – and 'accountability politics' – that is, 'the effort to hold powerful actors to their previously stated policies or principles' – so as to 'plead the cause of others or defend a cause or proposition' (Keck and Sikkink 1998: 16, 9). Khagram (2004: 137), for example, argues that the international campaign against World Bank funding of the SSP 'was effective in stalling construction on the Sardar Sarovar Project . . . by linking an ever more organized and sustained domestic social movement with transnationally allied advocacy efforts to a combination of transnational (international and domestic) norms on resettlement, tribal peoples, human rights . . . and especially the environment'. However, we now know that the actual impact of this 'historic victory' in terms of advancing the ultimate goal of the NBA – the permanent cancellation of the SSP – was far less significant than what was expected, both by activists and commentators in and beyond the academy. To unearth the reason why this is so, it is necessary to return to the movement process in the Narmada Valley and the way in which this process encountered the constraints that certain determinate structures of class power imposed upon the workings of the state system, and thereby also the strategic viability of jury politics.

Jury politics revived and revisited

Towards the five member group

When the World Bank withdrew from the SSP in 1993, the NBA made the following statement: 'We are happy that the fight is within our nation-state even if this might mean more repression' (cited in Dwivedi 2006: 250). Despite the cautionary note about repression,[9] the overall tone was one of optimism: the critique levelled at the SSP by the Morse Commission and the consequent departure of the World Bank had bolstered the NBA's case against the project and delivered a considerable blow to the legitimacy of the SSP: 'A new phase began, with the NBA now face to face with the Indian state' (Palit 2003: 88).

This new cycle of struggle ignited by the World Bank's withdrawal was marked above all by the revival of the demand for a review of the SSP by the Indian government. There were of course good reasons for doing so: the report of the Morse Commission and the consequent withdrawal of the World Bank lent credibility to the NBA's critique of the SSP and added weight to its counter-expertise, which in turn lent credence to the claim that a review of the project was justified and necessary. However, a familiar scenario repeated itself as state and central governments failed to respond to the NBA's demands. As in the first cycle of struggle, this can be linked to how Chimanbhai Patel was able to exercise his leverage over the central government: In July 1991, a new Congress government was installed in Delhi, with P.V. Narasimha Rao as Prime Minister. Prior to Congress's electoral victory, a merger was effected between Janata Dal and Congress in Gujarat, which secured the influence of Patel and the pro-dam lobby at central level. Indeed, both the Minister of State for Environment and Forests, Kamal Nath, and the Minister of Water Resources, V. C. Shukla, made statements in favour of the Narmada projects when they assumed their respective offices (Jayal 2000: 178).

As a reaction, an indefinite fast was launched in Mumbai in June 1993. After two weeks, the fast was called off when the government promised a review of the SSP. However, tangible follow-up actions were glaringly absent. Simultaneously, the water levels started to rise in the Narmada Valley, and in early July, houses in Vadgam (Gujarat) were being submerged. The waters reached Manibeli on 16 July and the Andolan declared the threat of *Jal Samparan* for the first time. If a review of the SSP was not declared by 6 August, a band of activists would drown themselves in the Narmada (Sangvai 2000a: 64). Pressure mounted on the union government as 6 August drew nearer. On 5 August, the Centre finally announced that a Five Member Group (FMG) would initiate discussion on all aspects of the SSP and submit a consensus report to the central government within three months (Dwivedi 2006: 251. After securing that the FMG's membership was balanced and its terms of reference broadened in a satisfactory way, the Andolan called off its threat of *Jal Samparan* and agreed to join the review process (Jayal 2000; Khagram 2004). With the revival of the demand for review, the NBA had once more placed the strategy of jury politics at the forefront of its struggle against the SSP. However, whereas the establishment of the FMG might at first sight be viewed as a concession to the NBA, the events that followed quickly contradict such impressions.

The interventions of both the central government and the governments of the riparian states seriously undermined the FMG's work. On 10 August, in a question-answer session in Parliament, the Minister of Water Resources made it clear that the Tribunal ruling of 1979 ruled out review of the SSP until 2024. Following this, on 30 September, Shukla sent a letter to the FMG that made it plain that 'the Narmada Projects were not under review and implementation would continue' (Khagram 2004: 133). The committee still went ahead with its work. Various experts and organizations, including the NBA, made presentations, but among the riparian states only the Government of Maharashtra co-operated with the FMG[10] (Dwivedi 2006: 251). Moreover, the final report of the FMG was withheld from the public as the Gujarat High Court claimed that the Tribunal Award was final and binding, and hence could not be reviewed: 'It was only with the Supreme Court's intervention a few months later that the report was made public and copies provided to all involved parties for comment' (ibid.: 251–2). And when the report was finally made public in December 1994, its impacts on the SSP were few, if any, despite the facts that the death of Chimanbhai Patel in 1994 had deprived the SSP of one of its most ardent and powerful advocates, and the electoral victory of Digvijay Singh (Congress) had given MP a Chief Minister who had expressed both his reservations about the proposed height of the SSP as well as certain sympathies with the cause of the NBA.

The turn to the Supreme Court

In February 1994, the sluice gates of the SSP were closed. This was in complete disregard of the Minister of State for Water and Forests' declaration that such an action would constitute a violation of NCA decisions. This scenario became the backdrop for a substantial strategic move on behalf of the NBA.

In May 1994, the NBA submitted two cases to the Supreme Court: the first demanded the overruling of the High Court of Gujarat's decision to withhold the FMG's report, whilst the second and more significant case claimed that the execution of the SSP constituted a violation of people's basic right to life and livelihood. The Andolan invoked several articles of the Indian constitution to justify their case, including Article 32, which grants all Indian citizens the right to approach the Supreme Court to defend the enforcement of basic rights, as well as international norms, agreements and procedures on R&R and environmental concerns. The SSP was also questioned in terms of its adverse benefit/cost ratio and how this negated the contention that the project was in the national interest. The petition consequently asked that the Supreme Court order a stop in construction to allow a new body of experts to review the process, and also to secure the participation of local people at all levels in the decision-making processes associated with the projects (Khagram 2004: 134).

Following this, in July of the same year, the movement held a major rally demanding immediate compensation to those that had been affected by submergence in 1994, and the public release of the report of the FMG. The FMG's report was finally made public in December 1994. Whereas its evaluation of the SSP was less critical than that of the Morse Commission, and refrained from recommending stoppage of work on the dam, it still contained findings that lent support to many of the NBA's claims about the project: it questioned the official estimates of water availability in the river; it suggested a reordering of the allocation of water between the implicated regions, giving priority to the needs of Kutch and Saurashtra; it criticized the encouragement of sugarcane cropping in the regions in the immediate command area; it demanded an expansion of the official definition of Project Affected Persons; and it made implicit provisions for the pursuit of alternative approaches to water management not centred on big dams (Khagram 2004; Jayal 2000; Dwivedi 2006).

The Supreme Court first took up the cases filed by the Andolan in August and September of 1994. However, it was only in January 1995 that it first took action when, after hearing the arguments of the petitioner and the respondents, the court ordered that the FMG should prepare another report on the Narmada's hydrology, the height of the SSP, and the status of resettlement/rehabilitation and environmental impacts. The group submitted its report in April, stating that the SSP could only be completed if the studies and plans on R&R and environmental impacts were completed, if the local people where allowed full participation in and information about the implementation of the project, and if the dam bureaucracy was restructured so as to ensure efficiency and accountability during implementation. In May, the Supreme Court imposed a stay on the construction of the dam while it examined the FMG's report.[11] In July, the Supreme Court called upon petitioners and respondents to submit additional materials before the full hearings, and ordered a suspension of the dam-work. The FMG was also ordered to submit a further report on the hydrology of the Narmada river, the height of the SSP, and the impacts of the dam in terms of resettlement and environment (Khagram 2004: 134; Dwivedi 2006: 260). When the report was submitted in April 1995, the majority conclusion stated that the SSP could only be implemented given the completion of studies on R&R and environmental issues, the securing of participation of dam-affected communities in the project process, and the reorganization of the dam-bureaucracy to secure efficiency and accountability (Khagram 2004: 134–5; Dwivedi 2006: 260).

Following the submission of some 30 volumes of material from both parties, hearings began in November 1995 and were then resumed in January and April 1996 (Khagram 2004; Jayal 2000). In a hearing held in June 1996, the Supreme Court focused on the differences that had emerged between the GoG, which argued for the completion of the project, and the GoMP, which, under chief minister Digvijay Singh, had come to argue for a reduction in the height of the dam.[12] Yet another round of Supreme Court hearings were inaugurated in August 1996, where the court expressed that there was little doubt that the fundamental rights of the people of the Valley as guaranteed in the constitution were under threat by its implementation, and that the failure on behalf of the project authorities and government officials to comply with a range of environmental agreements constituted a clear violation of Indian and international law. Furthermore, the Supreme Court declared

– against the argument of GoG that the Tribunal's award could not be reopened until 2024 and that there were no legal grounds for Supreme Court readjudication – that the NWDT could not have conceived of the vast changes in the institutional context of R&R in 1979, and that the Supreme Court could pass judgement on the project (Khagram 2004: 136). In fact, in 1997, the Supreme Court decided that a constitutional bench should be set up in order to decide on the issues that related to the court's jurisdiction (Rajagopal 2004: 31).

Now, let me pause for a moment to investigate the combination of factors that led the NBA to pursue its strategy of jury politics through the Supreme Court. 'The decision to follow the path of litigation', Jayal notes,

> was not the outcome of unanimous agreement within the Andolan, which has a long tradition of debate on the issue of whether the battle should be fought exclusively in the public arena, or also taken to courts at various levels.
>
> (2000: 194)

The stakes in such a move were high indeed, and activists were conscious that a negative judgement would severely constrain the future of the campaign. The fact that the strategy of judicial activism was applied nonetheless has to be contextualized in terms of the presence of 'opportunity structures' (Tarrow 1998) that created a favourable environment for seeking legal redress, as well as emergent constraints on the Andolan's capacity to mobilize in the communities of the Narmada Valley.

In terms of opportunity structures, what stands out the most is perhaps the status that India's Supreme Court had obtained in the 1990s as an institution that often backed the claims made by social movements and other actors in civil society through judicial activism, in particular on environmental issues (Jayal 2000: 222; Randeira 2003a: 307). Chittaroopa Palit singles out this feature of the judiciary as an important factor animating the move towards judicial activism, and links it to an overall crisis of legitimacy in the transnational institutions promoting policies of neoliberal restructuring:

> . . . I think that in ninety-four, when we went to the court and that, I mean, I believe it was a different court from the court that [delivered] the judgement in 2000, because the political-economic circumstances have gone through a change . . . you see, [in] the late eighties there was a crisis in the world institutions . . . because of the failure of the recipes of the World Bank, the IMF and so on. And they were under siege . . . there was a withdrawal, there was a retreat, so there were partial victories for the people . . . I think it's important to understand that the Supreme Court [was] also working in the wider atmosphere of the World Bank having withdrawn just the year before . . . There was far more autonomy . . . I wouldn't say that it was an autonomous institution, but there was a degree more of autonomy than there is now.
>
> (interview, May 2003)

Palit (2003: 93) reiterates this line of argument elsewhere, arguing that the Supreme Court that the NBA approached in 1994 was characterized by 'a more activist judiciary . . . which allowed for a tradition of public-interest litigation that gave access to the poor and dispossessed . . .'. Indeed, the contention that the judiciary was not simply a ruling class institution rings especially true in the case of the PIL against the SSP in that, as I dicussed earlier, the Supreme Court repeatedly asserted its independence vis-à-vis supporters of the project in in parliament and government and refused to lift the stay first imposed in 1995. As Jayal (2000: 223) puts it, the schism between Parliament and the Supreme Court had 'obviously not been expressed for the first time, but the Narmada case certainly reinforced fears of judicial activism that . . . have been vexing politicians'.

In addition to this, the move to judicial activism – certainly a form of 'jury politics' where a body of 'experts', in this case legal experts, is asked to deliberate over and pass judgement on a certain body of evidence – was encouraged by the mounting expert knowledge that discredited the project. Chief among these was arguably the Morse Commission's report of 1992, but the body of evidence against the project authorities' claims about the benefits of the dam had kept growing with the partial critiques of the FMG, as well as several critical reports resulting from reviews carried out by state-appointed teams in MP, all of which offered support to the Andolan's critique of the project (see Jayal 2000).

Expressive of this faith in 'the weight of the evidence' is the argument of NBA activist Sitaram Patidar that the filing of a case to the Supreme Court was rendered possible by the fact that the NBA had accumulated a vast body of information, and that they had garnered the support of a brilliant lawyer. There was much enthusiasm in the communities during the early days of the hearings, because the project authorities were unable to counter the arguments made by the Andolan and its lawyer (interview, April 2003). In addition to this, as I noted earlier, the unity of the riparian state governments was starting to show signs of fissure and weakening. Taken together, these factors were undoubtedly perceived by activists as a favourable opportunity structure, where the costs of engaging in legal action – the time and effort that would have to be diverted to court proceedings at the expense of actual mobilization – seemed to be outweighed by the possible benefits that could be reaped, namely a conclusive judgement from the pinnacle of the country's judiciary.

However, we cannot fully understand the turn to the Supreme Court unless we also take into account certain constraints that bedevilled the movement process in the Narmada Valley. Earlier in the chapter, I noted how, in the aftermath of the stand-off at Ferkuwa, many people from the adivasi communities shifted to the resettlement sites in Gujarat. It is crucial to recall that this was not a one-way tendency; as both Jayal (2000: 192–3) and Dwivedi (1997: 19) have noted, a significant number of people also returned to their original communities due to the dismal conditions they found in the resettlement sites. Still, the overriding tendency from the mid-1990s seems to have been towards an incipient disintegration of the Andolan's mass base and an increasingly evident resistance fatigue. Dwivedi observes on the status of the mass base in 1994:

> From a majority of villages in Maharashtra and [a] few in M.P., there has been a steady flow of people to resettlement and rehabilitation sites with the perception gaining ground among a large section of the population that . . . the dam could not be stopped.
>
> (1997: 16)

The tendency towards disintegration was reflected in the *satyagraha* of 1994, which was held up by 35 activists spread throughout several villages; the activists were quickly removed from the area by the state administration. It never came close to the previous year's action, which had elicited significant attention outside the Narmada Valley and indeed important concessions from the Central Government. According to Dwivedi, the Andolan's activities were profoundly affected by this in the sense that, in the latter part of the nineties, '[t]he events and activities undertaken by the NBA . . . demonstrates its efforts to circumvent this problem of an eroding mass-base' (ibid.: 17). Whereas mass mobilization and jury politics had always existed side by side in the Andolan's strategic repertoire of contention, the turn to the Supreme Court can be understood as representing the supersession of the former by the latter, marking a strategic turn which was 'consonant with the very real fatigue and consequent impatience of a prolonged mass mobilization' (Jayal 2000: 222; see also Dwivedi 1997: 19).

The twin effect of positive incentives and negative compulsions was to create a scenario where a strategic shift was perceived as a necessary step if the campaign was to survive, and in this scenario judicial activism appeared to be the movement's best bet. Judicial activism is of course a risky business; as Randeira (2003a: 307) argues, it has its 'costs in terms of protracted legal battles with uncertain outcomes and the risk of depoliticizing an issue in the legal arena'. It seems clear to observers like Jayal and Dwivedi that the Supreme Court hearings in fact contributed to the constraints on the movement's capacity for mass mobilization. Referring to the emergence of a favourable opportunity structure, Jayal (2000: 195) writes: 'It is ironical that just as the tide has begun to turn in favour of the NBA, its momentum has tended to falter'. With the Supreme Court nominated 'as the final arbiter and having secured a stay from it, the NBA has deprived itself of opportunities to mobilize and of government targets to assail' (ibid.: 195; see also Dwivedi 1997: 18).

Irrespective of constraints upon mobilizational activity, the NBA's initial experience with the Supreme Court had been encouraging, as the court showed considerable sympathy with the NBA's case, and actively resisted attempts by the central government and the GoG to circumscribe and undermine its jurisdictional powers. However, from 1998 onwards, ominous signs suggested that changes were afoot in the Supreme Court's approach to the case. First, the court dispensed with the need to settle the jurisdictional questions that in 1997 had been assigned to a constitutional bench. Moreover, the Supreme Court limited its assessment of the case to the question of R&R rather than a comprehensive review of the project in totality (Rajagopal 2004: 32–3). Then, in the 1999 hearings, the GoG filed for a lifting of the stay on the construction of the dam with reference to the need to secure foreign investment in order to push the project forward (Randeira 2003a: 318; Rajagopal

2004: 33). The Supreme Court granted an interim lifting of the stay on the dam in February, and further concessions were given to the GoG in May of the same year. Then, on 18 October 2000, the Supreme Court delivered its verdict on the case of *Narmada Bachao Andolan versus Union of India and Others*. In a two to one majority judgement, the Supreme Court established that the construction of the SSP 'will continue as per the tribunal'; the building of the dam was to proceed *pari passu*, that is, after a given increase in height, R&R would have to be implemented before construction could be resumed upon the granting of permission from the NCA (cited in NBA 2000a: 7).

The Supreme Court ruling was indeed a blow to the NBA's case. Consider these elements from the judgement: against the NBA's claim that the SSP would negate the national interest by constituting a drain on public funds, the Supreme Court established that when projects are funded with public money, 'individual or organizations in the garb of PIL cannot be permitted to challenge the policy decision after a lapse of time' (cited in NBA 2000a: 2); against the Andolan's assertion that the project constituted a violation of rights, the Supreme Court ruled that '[t]he displacement of tribals and other persons would not per se result in violation of their fundamental or other rights' (ibid.: 2), and, furthermore, while displacement 'would undoubtedly disconnect them from their past, culture, custom and traditions . . . it becomes necessary to harvest a river for the larger good' (ibid.: 3); against the idea that India's judicial system should be an arena for reviewing development projects, the Supreme Court ruled that '[t]he conception and decision to undertake a project is to be regarded as a policy decision . . . Once such a considered decision is taken, the proper execution of the same should be taken expeditiously. It is for the government to decide how to do its job . . . It is now well established that the courts, in the exercise of their jurisdiction, will not transgress into the field of policy decision' (ibid.: 3–4); against the claims of the Andolan that the dam would not serve developmental purposes, the Supreme Court found that '[t]here is and has been in the recent past protests and agitations not only against Hydel Projects but also against the setting up of Nuclear or thermal Power plants . . . But the electricity has to be generated and one or more of these option exercised. What options to exercise in our constitutional framework, is for the government to decide keeping various factors in mind' (ibid.: 6). Concluding its judgement, the Supreme Court stated that '[e]very endeavour shall be made to see that the project is completed as expeditiously as possible' (ibid.: 9). In short, the Supreme Court verdict put a definite end to the struggle to stop the SSP.

How can the Supreme Court verdict be explained? Rajagopal (2004: 37–48) has argued that the verdict has to be understood in terms of how several intersecting 'scripts' that are intrinsic to legal discourse and reasoning framed the assessment of the disputed facts that the Supreme Court was presented with, and in terms of how these scripts led the court to delegitimate the case that the NBA sought to make. Whereas Rajagopal's perspective aptly delineates the limitations that legal discourse imposed upon the Supreme Court's deliberations, it fails to connect the verdict with a more encompassing analysis of how the political economy of the Indian state imposed constraints upon the viability of judicial activism against the SSP. On this point, Randeira's (2003a/b) analysis is closer to the mark when she argues that with the onset of global neoliberal restructuring there has been a realignment of the relationship between the executive, legislative and judicial branches of the Indian state in which the relative autonomy of the latter has been constrained, thus producing a more closely sutured state apparatus which engages in selective implementation of neoliberal policies, whilst referring to the increasing power of global markets and transnational institutions in order to justify its actions. In relation to the SSP, the Supreme Court verdict then dovetails with the increasing turn towards market-oriented solutions, such as the attempt to attract foreign investment, the floating of bonds on national and international markets in order to obtain the needed funds for completing the project, as well as the prominent role that the SSP plays in Narendra Modi's attempts to position Gujarat as a haven for global capital. However, in order to truly understand the Supreme Court decision – and thereby the failure of the NBA's campaign against the SSP – in relation to the political economy of the state, it is necessary to bring into view the full trajectory of the anti-dam campaign and the premises upon which it was conducted from 1990 to 2000. I take up this discussion in the following section.

The limits of jury politics and the political economy of the state

In Chapter 4, I showed how when militant particularist struggles for resettlement and rehabilitation emerged in the Narmada Valley in the mid-1980s, they assumed the form of rightful resistance – that is, a form of political practice which revolved around a rationality which sought to hold state and project authorities accountable to laws and provisions related to the resettlement of project-affected people. This rationality was reproduced in the practice of jury politics, which was the strategic hinge upon which the anti-dam campaign turned.

Now, for some academic observers, when such a strategy is pursued in a democratic context, the likelihood of a successful outcome is substantial. Khagram, for example, writes:

> . . . big dam critics and the range of tactics they employ are likely to be much more effective in democratic institutional contexts. These regimes offer greater opportunities to organize and gain access to decision-making processes, and significantly reduce the ability of big dam proponents to violently repress contestation.
>
> (2004: 3)

According to Khagram, campaigns against large dams in India have been 'greatly facilitated by the presence of democratic institutions' in combination with 'the gradual institutionalization of globalizing norms on the environment, indigenous peoples, and human rights domestically' (ibid.: 34). The empirical basis for Khagram's claim is precisely the campaign against the SSP, and the proof he offers is the withdrawal of foreign and World Bank funding from the project and the Supreme Court's imposition of a stay on construction of the SSP. However, this proof does not hold up to scrutiny at all. As the analysis of the trajectory of the anti-dam campaign from 1990 to 2000 presented in this chapter has shown, the strategy of jury politics enjoyed far less access to decision-making processes than Khagram's claims would have one believe, and, of course, its final deployment in the sphere of judicial activism yielded a conclusive defeat for the NBA – a fact which is glaringly absent from Khagram's study.

Now, I am of course not arguing that the state operated as a behemoth during the decade from 1990 to 2000. Indeed, it is quite possible to tease out cracks and fissures in the process, for example in the apparent willingness of various Chief Ministers and indeed a Prime Minister to inaugurate reviews, or the resurgence of differences between Gujarat and Madhya Pradesh as to the height of dam. Nevertheless, the significant dynamic is ostensibly that of the closing of the ranks which occurred at every juncture where the push of the dominant proprietary classes and their representatives came to shove, and the consequent abrogation of activists' access to decision-making processes. This is also true of the NBA's engagement with the Supreme Court. Whereas activists were prompted onto the judicial path by the Supreme Court's track record on public interest litigation, and encouraged by the Supreme Court's refusal to lift the stay on the dam as well as its refusal to yield to parliamentary efforts to circumscribe the domain of its jurisdiction, all this was effectively brushed aside with the Supreme Court verdict of October 2000 – a verdict which explicitly stated that the Supreme Court was not to serve as an arena for contesting state development strategies. Once again, the ranks of the state-system were closed at a crucial juncture, and the closure went in the favour of dominant social groups. The character of this trajectory contains crucial insights about the limits of jury politics, and to unearth these insights we need to probe deeper into the political economy of the state.

If we look again at the case of the KMCS and its mobilization around customary rights and citizenship, it certainly testifies to the potential for empowerment which resides in subaltern appropriations of the 'state-idea' – i.e. the representation of the state as a coherent body external to society which neutrally arbitrates in conflicts between equals. It also demonstrates that the 'state-system' – i.e. the 'palpable nexus of practice and institutional structure centred in government' (Abrams 1988: 82) – is not a tightly sutured leviathan, and that it may well be 'made to do the bidding of India's lower orders' (Corbridge and Harriss 2000: 239). However, in the case of the Andolan's struggle for review of the SSP and its turn to the Supreme Court the state-system appears more as 'a committee for managing the common affairs of the bourgeoisie', and the state-idea as an ideological veil which 'contrives to deny the existence of connections which would if recognised be incompatible with the claimed autonomy and integration of the state' (Abrams 1988: 77).

The explanation for these divergent outcomes requires a conceptualization of the nature of state power which balances two crucial propositions that follow from the assumption that the state is not 'a substantial entity separate from society' (Abrams 1988: 61) but rather 'a complex social relation that reflects the changing balance of social forces in a determinate conjuncture' (Jessop 1982: 221). On the one hand, this entails that state power is not 'a fixed sum of resources which can be appropriated by one social force to the exclusion of others' (ibid.: 225). Just as social power is conjunctural and relational, vacillating in accordance with the outcomes of struggles between dominant and subaltern social groups, so too is state power, and this means that it cannot serve simply as a monolithic vehicle for the execution of the designs of dominant social groups. On the other hand, state power and its structuration into institutions and forms of representation and intervention will have 'unequal and asymmetrical effects on the ability of different social groups to realise their interests through political action' (ibid.: 224). Whereas social power is relational and conjunctural, the structures in which it is embedded nevertheless exhibit considerable durability as they are 'consistently reproduced over extended periods of time' (Sewell 1996: 842); this reproduction in turn reflects the privileged command of dominant groups over resources that enhance their capability to reproduce their hegemonic position, and one such resource is precisely state power. Thus, whereas access to the institutions of the state-system, and thereby state power, is not unilateral, the mutually constitutive relationship between 'political and non-political power' (Abrams 1988: 82) entails that a particular configuration of state power will, lest it collapses under the weight of its internal contradictions, underpin the reproduction of the basal structural framework of the social formation in which it is embedded and of which it is congealed.

These abstract arguments assume relevance for the comparison between rightful resistance against everyday tyranny and jury politics in the anti-dam campaign for the following reasons. Whereas the KMCS offensive against the everyday tyranny of the local state was highly significant for the communities involved, it was nevertheless centred on claims to which the higher echelons of the state-system could concede without undermining its own authority and without going against the interests of extra-local proprietary elites, or, for that matter, basal structures of proprietary power. Indeed, ceding to the KMCS' demands can be seen as an exercise in bolstering the state-idea as such. The NBA's campaign against dam-building, however, was pitted directly against the vested interests of the proprietary elites of south and central Gujarat, whose capacity to influence the workings of the state-system outshone that of the adivasis and petty-commodity producers mobilized by the NBA in Madhya Pradesh and Maharashtra. This can of course be read as testimony to Corbridge and Harriss's (2000) argument that the extent to which subaltern groups can make claims on the state is subject to conjunctural fluctuations related to regional and state-specific balances of class power. However, I would argue that in the case of the NBA's anti-dam campaign it is also possible to detect constraints to subaltern claims-making on the state which are of a more structural character. This is so because the campaign was not only directed against one particular dam-project. It was deeply embedded in a generic opposition to dam-building as a development strategy, as well as a critique of the wider model of development of which this strategy was a part and concerted attempts to constitute a nation-wide alliance of social movements around this critique (see Chapters 5 and 8). In short, the campaign against the SSP struck against 'the permanence of existing structures and relations' (Kamat 2002: 158) as it in effect levelled a challenge against the way in which the postcolonial state and its development strategies have functioned as key modalities in the reproduction and extension of capitalist relations and capitalist accumulation in India's passive revolution. In doing so it transcended the limits to the possibilities for movements from below to act through the state, its agencies, and its ideologies.

Thus, the NBA's campaign against the SSP throws up important clues regarding the limits to the possibility for movements of acting through the state and its agencies, and this in turn calls for a re-engagement with questions concerning the extent to which social movements from below can and should pursue their campaigns and projects via the state. In Chapter 3 I made a 'first cut' at this question by discussing the trajectory of the KMCS in light of, on the one hand, Corbridge and Harriss's claims that subaltern politics is best pursued via the democratic process of the state, with social movements putting pressure on political parties and governing elites to improve the lot of poor and disadvantaged groups, and, on the other hand, Sangeeta Kamat's argument that a politics centred on demystifying the state to subaltern groups occludes the structures of power upon which the state rests and which it is instrumental in reproducing, and therefore also moulds the praxis of social movements from below in such a way as to reproduce the status quo. In relation to the case of the KMCS I argued that Kamat's critique was misplaced as enabling the making of rights-based claims by subaltern groups in a context of everyday tyranny is in fact a radical political project, and, more importantly, that the development of more radical political projects may be predicated on an initial rupturing of local rationalities of submission and deference through rightful resistance. The case of the NBA's campaign against the SSP, however, suggests that Kamat's arguments do carry relevance for those phases in a movement process in which it is the relations of power upon which the state itself is based that come to be challenged.

As I argued earlier the process of radicalization through which the anti-dam campaign emerged actually articulated a challenge to the relations of power from which the postcolonial Indian state is congealed and which it has been instrumental in reproducing. This, however, was not reflected in the NBA's strategic rationality: the campaign was pursued through a strategy which was moored in the assumption that the state could be held accountable to democratic principles (see Nilsen 2007b, 2008). Thus, as a 'second cut' at the question of the extent to which movements from below can use the state to pursue their oppositional projects I would argue that whilst, on the one hand, it is indeed called for to acknowledge 'the possibilities for empowerment that might exist within India's polity' (Corbridge and Harriss 2000: 238), it is, on the other hand, equally imperative to give serious thought to the limits that might exist to those possibilities and what this entails for social movements from below in contemporary India. If we fail to do so, we run the risk of abrogating the strategic repertoire of social movements from below at a conjuncture in which subaltern groups are under increasing pressure from social movements from above that seek to expand the power of dominant proprietary classes through ever more aggressive forms of accumulation by dispossession. I return to this question and its strategic ramifications in the concluding chapter of the study.

Concluding remarks

In this chapter I have analyzed the trajectory of the NBA's campaign against the SSP from 1990 to 2000. I focused on how this decade-long trajectory can be understood as a succession of cycles of struggle animated by processes of collective learning, as well as on the theoretical and political ramifications of the eventual failure of the campaign in terms of the debate over the extent to which social movements from below in contemporary India can and should pursue their political projects in and through the state.

In the first part of the chapter I engaged with the cycle of struggle that unfolded from 1990 to 1991, when the Andolan first launched the demand that the state should organize a review of the SSP and brought non-violent direct action to bear on this demand. I showed how the strategy of demanding a review of the project was rooted in the body of counter-expertise that had been produced about the SSP, and how this kind of 'jury politics' rested on a rationality similar to that which guided rightful resistance in the early phase of mobilization. Furthermore, I showed how the choice of non-violent direct action was informed by both ethical and tactical considerations. The trajectory of this cycle of struggle started with abortive attempts to get the state governments of Madhya Pradesh and Maharashtra to implement a review of the project, continued with a failed attempt to persuade V. P. Singh's government to hold a review, and it ended with the *Sangharsh Yatra* and the stand-off at Ferkuwa on the border between Madhya Pradesh and Gujarat and yet another failure to compel the central government to implement a review. The refusal on part of the central government to engage with the NBA's demands was a direct outcome of the interventions of Chimanbhai Patel, Chief Minister of Gujarat and leading representative of the agroindustrial lobby in the state, and as such it revealed the constraints imposed upon the workings of the state by structures of class power.

The second cycle of struggle was marked by the adoption of a set of deeply symbolic methods of protests centred on the dam-affected adivasi villages rather than direct action aimed at state authorities. I argued that non-cooperation with project authorities and the annual monsoon satyagrahas could be understood as symbolic-communicative practices of resistance – the former representing a popular reclaiming of 'eminent domain' and the latter representing an enactment of sacrifice and resolve – which drew on a particular construction of collective memories of the anticolonial struggle to convey certain messages about the NBA and its politics to different audiences. In terms of the dynamics of the movement process, this cycle of struggle is ambivalent. On the one hand, it can be viewed as an indicator of a resilient and creative movement which is capable of reinventing itself in the face of strategic dead ends, and which chose to do this by adopting a strategy which sought to consolidate its identity and project. On the other hand, it can be interpreted as a strategy that was adopted in order to circumvent emergent constraint on the Andolan's capacity to mobilize people in the dam-affected communities after the stand-off at Ferkuwa.

In the third part of the chapter I focused on the international campaign against World Bank funding of the SSP. I showed how the activities of the transnational advocacy network that had emerged around the militant particularist struggles in the Narmada Valley in the mid-1980s intensified its activities and radicalized its objectives. I traced the evolution of the campaign from a series of Congressional hearings in the USA, via the successful campaign against Japanese funding of the SSP, to the appointment of the Morse Commission in June 1991 and the eventual withdrawal of World Bank support for the SSP in 1993 as a result of the devastating judgement passed on the project by the Commission's report. Undoubtedly, the international campaign against World Bank funding of the SSP is an example of the potential power of transnational advocacy networks and the way in which such networks can deploy information and accountability politics across spatial scales. However, I think it is justifiable to question the most exuberant assessments of the campaign against World Bank funding: victory in the transnational arena did not impact as one might have expected in terms of advancing the campaign against the SSP, and this calls for further engagement with the relationship between movement strategies and structures of class and state power at national and regional scales.

The fourth cycle of struggle in the campaign against the SSP was set in train with the departure of the World Bank, and was marked by the NBA's return to the practice of jury politics; the demand for a review of the project was resuscitated and directed squarely at the central government. Eventually, the central government announced the appointment of the FMG, which would look into the controversial aspects of the project. I showed how the efforts of the FMG were stymied both by dam-supporters at central level, and by the refusal of several of the riparian states to co-operate with its activities, and how the publication of its report was withheld as a result of pressure from the GoG. The impasse of the FMG in turn became the context for another strategic shift by the NBA as in 1994 the movement came to resort to judicial activism via the Supreme Court to stop the SSP. This turn, I argued, was the outcome of both positive incentives and negative compulsions, the former being related to a perceived opportunity structure in terms of the Supreme Courts's positive approach to public interest litigation and the latter being related to an erosion of the capacity for mass mobilization in the Narmada Valley. In spite of the fact that the initial engagement with the Supreme Court was a positive experience for the NBA, the initial outcome of the process was disastrous: in October 2000, the Supreme Court ordered that the SSP should be completed as quickly as possible, thus putting an effective end to the NBA's anti-dam campaign.

In the final part of the chapter I sought to explain the trajectory of the NBA's campaign against the SSP by discussing the rationality that underpinned the strategy of the campaign and the nature of its objectives in relation to the political economy of state power in postcolonial India. Contrasting the NBA's jury politics with the KMCS's relatively successful engagement in rightful resistance, I argued that the different outcomes of the two struggles had to be understood in terms of how they pursued different objectives: the KMCS was engaged in a local struggle, the ramifications of which did not threaten basal structures of proprietary power, neither at a regional nor at a national scale, whereas the NBA was engaged in a campaign which not only militated against the vested interests of powerful regional elites, but which also challenged dam-building at a generic level, as well as the postcolonial development project of which dam-building was a constituent element. In other words, the NBA in effect levelled a systemic challenge against the fundamental dynamics of capitalist development in postcolonial India and the role of the state in reproducing and extending this process, and in doing so it transcended the boundaries of what it is possible for social movements from below to achieve by acting in and through the state, its agencies, and its ideologies. This in turn led me to revisit my arguments about the extent to which the state constitutes a site for empowerment for social movements from below in contemporary India. The imperative, I argued, is to seek to steer a cause between committed state-centrism and principled anti-statism – a point which I argue more fully in the concluding chapter of the book. In the next chapter I investigate some of the internal challenges that activists face in developing the collective skilled activity of subaltern social groups through an analysis of the campaign against the MHP.

environment leads to the expropriation of subsistence peasants and petty commodity producers in Madhya Pradesh.

The SSP and agroindustrial capitalism in south and central Gujarat

Commenting on how the recommendations for river basin development in the Narmada Valley made in the 1960s dovetailed with Gujarati interests, Dwivedi (2006: 74) points out how the construction of 'a high-storage dam at Navagam implied a substantial reduction in water scarcity in the state' as it 'could make productive use of this water with the high-level canal . . . running through the heart of Gujarat right up to south Rajasthan, with no burden of displacement and rehabilitation as the villages to be submerged were largely in MP'. As was pointed out in a World Bank appraisal document from 1985, the SSP is 'the largest Indian irrigation system planned and designed as one unit', and the project has been designed to make a major contribution to increasing the extent of agricultural land under irrigation in Gujarat; the irrigated command area of the SSP covers some 20 per cent of the total cultivable area in the state (cited in Dwivedi 2006: 100). It is for this reason that the project has been dubbed 'the lifeline of Gujarat' by state authorities and dam-builders. The SSP is a multi-purpose project which is also designed to generate electricity: a riverbed powerhouse and a canal-head powerhouse will have installed capacities of 1200 MWs and 250 MWs respectively.[3]

Yet, according to critics of the SSP, the plot is much thicker than this. First, they challenge the claim that irrigation from the project will have a drastic impact on agriculture in the state. As late as the 1990s, the 13 agro-climatic zones of the command area were yet to be assessed in terms of suitability for and need of irrigation. When the Morse Commission carried out such an assessment as part of its review of the project in 1992 they found that in many of the regions, intensive irrigation would actually result in soil degradation, waterlogging, and salinization, and argued that the SSP was 'likely to perpetuate many of the features that the Bank has documented as diminishing the performance of the agricultural sector in India in the past' (Morse and Berger 1992: 321). Moreover, many of the agro-climatic zones of the command area were already sufficiently irrigated (D'Souza 2002: 104). Second, critics also maintain that the irrigation potential of the SSP is highly overstated due to the NWDT's overestimation of the Narmada's water flow in the 1970s.[4] Indeed, when the dam stood at 110 metres in 2004, only 57,000 hectares of land received irrigation, compared to the 550,000 hectares that were supposed to be irrigated according to official claims (Bavadam 2007). As for electricity, critics point out that the installed capacity of 1450 MW should not be mistaken for firm power, which will be 425 MW at most, and which will then decline towards zero over a period of 45 years as water is diverted for irrigation purposes (Sangvai 2000a: 99).

However, the most significant point of criticism in relation to the present analysis relates to the distributional bias of the irrigation and electricity benefits that are actually generated by the dam, and specifically the argument that elite groups in central and southern Gujarat will corner these benefits.[5] This bias is clearly brought out by Dwivedi's (2006: 123–7) mapping of who stands to gain the most from the SSP, in which industry and agriculture emerge as the main beneficiaries of the project in terms of irrigation and electricity. The percentage distribution of power benefits to industrial consumers is estimated at 55 per cent, and a water supply of 0.2 MAF is also expected to benefit the industrial sector. Indeed, industry has responded favourably to the SSP in the form of concentrated industrial development: by 1995, Rs. 75,000 crore has been invested in the so-called 'Golden Corridor' on the Delhi–Ahmedabad route; another major industrial estate is being developed near the dam site in Gujarat; and water and electricity are also expected to benefit industrial estates in Kutch and Saurashtra. This has in turn impacted back on the design of the SSP: 'The location of these estates has been a major consideration in finalising the alignment of the two major branch canals of the project' (ibid.: 124). Furthermore, the SSP is expected to boost sugarcane cultivation in the command area, and this has in turn impacted on agro-processing as sugar co-operatives and factories have sprung up in Ahmedabad and Baroda. This in turn feeds back to industry in a beneficial way by increasing the demand for agricultural inputs. Dwivedi makes the crucial observation that whereas it is claimed that the benefits of irrigation and electricity will accrue to more than 3,000 villages in the command area, this impact will be highly uneven as 'farmers in [Bharuch], Baroda and Ahmedabad districts, at the head of the command, will be the first to benefit from the project' (ibid.: 124). Agriculture in this area is already capital and energy intensive, and it is generally unlikely that the project authorities will be successful in their intended efforts to discourage the farmers in the command area from cultivating water-intensive crops such as sugarcane as the lobby which has sprung up around sugarcane cultivation in central Gujarat enjoys significant power and clout in the state (ibid.: 125). Finally, farmers are expected to benefit from a reliable electricity supply that facilitates a shift from costly diesel pumps to cheaper electric pumps to irrigate their fields.

This distributional bias is more than merely a quantitative misallocation of benefits in an inevitable process of change in land and water use patterns. What occurs, rather, is a *de facto* concentration of property rights in water and electricity in the hands of the classes at the apex of a system of agroindustrial capitalism in central and southern Gujarat. And rather than being a singular event of enclosure of means of production, this concentration of property rights is best understood as a moment in a process of change centred on capitalist transformation and class formation in agriculture in central and southern Gujarat that dates back at least to the second half of the nineteenth century.

The state of Gujarat came into being in 1960, and the districts of Surat, Valsad and Bharuch form the southern part of the state. The central plain of south Gujarat that 'it is one of the regions in India where the process of modernization has pushed forward most rapidly in recent decades' (Breman 1985: 3).[6] Focusing his research on the district of Surat, Jan Breman traces the historical roots of the transition towards capitalism in South Gujarat to the 1870s, when the district emerged at the helm of Indian cotton-production. Throughout the last decades of nineteenth century, commercialization gathered momentum and resulted in incremental changes in caste and class relations in the region as Kanbi Patidars – middle peasants who tilled the land and lived like common Shudras – started to challenge the economic and social predominance of high-caste landlords. After Independence the central plain of South Gujarat emerged as a 'mini-Punjab' and the 'upper stratum of the population living in the central plain' rapidly came to the fore as fully-fledged capitalist farmers (Breman 1985: 25).

Agricultural transformation was significantly boosted by the construction of dams on the river Tapti: in 1953, the Kakrapar dam was constructed and ten years later the Ukai dam emerged upstream from Kakrapar, providing irrigation to large parts of Surat as well as some parts of Valsad, and a concurrent strengthening of the commercial orientation of regional cropping patterns. Furthermore, the capital intensity of farming operations increased and this in turn attracted banks that were willing to finance investments and handle farmers' savings. Finally, marketing came to be controlled by farmers' co-operatives rather than merchant capital, thus boosting the power of the new class of capitalist farmers (Breman 1978–79a: 42).

The Patidars consolidated their social and economic ascent in the postcolonial period as they were among those owner-tenants who benefited from the Tenancy Act of 1957. Moreover, to the extent that they were already landowners at the time, their dominance within the Congress Party enabled them to avert land reforms from impacting adversely on their command over land (Shah 1990: 82). The Patidars have also been the primary beneficiaries of the Green Revolution and the spearheads of rural industrialization in the region (Breman 1985: 75). Labour arrangements have changed as bonded labour gave way to free wage labour.[7] This process has also been driven by the influx of labour migrants from the tribal hinterlands of eastern Surat: displaced by dam building on the River Tapti, adivasis have came to join the ranks of what Breman (1996) calls 'the footloose proletariat' – i.e. 'an enormous mass of men and women, adults and children, who possess little if any means of production of their own and who lead a circulatory existence in the lowest rungs of the labour system' (ibid.: 243).

Similarly, Kheda district in central Gujarat displays an economy of advanced, intensive agricultural operations which originate in 'a long-term process of agricultural commercialization and economic development, a process which accelerated after independence and which stimulated the trend towards diversification of the rural economy' (Rutten 1995: 69). Indeed, the three first decades of the twentieth century were marked by unprecedented growth in cash crop farming, accommodated by further intensification of production. Agricultural growth remained high during the first one-and-a-half-decades after independence, and in the 1960s, the onset of the Green Revolution came to accelerate this process: the production of foodgrains almost doubled and the total output of cash crops increased fourfold (ibid.: 68–79). Rutten notes 'the rise of a new class of well-to-do farmers from among the ranks of former self-cultivating middle-peasants' as the distinguishing trajectory of change in Kheda over the past two centuries (ibid.: 91). As in South Gujarat, this class of well-to-do farmers overwhelmingly consists of Patidars.

Furthermore, again mirroring developments in South Gujarat, the advance of the Patidars in Kheda dates to the middle of the nineteenth century, but was consolidated in the aftermath of independence, when the Patidar community emerged as a class of proprietors due to land reforms: as the 1960s drew to a close, they were the dominant landowners in the district. They also reaped the benefits of the Green Revolution, and 'the speeding up of agrarian modernization in the 1960s and 70s has turned this group into rich farmers, well-provided with capital' (Rutten 1995: 105). Farming in the district is characterized by the use of wage labour. All in all, the changes from 1960 onwards have thrown up a form of farm management among the most substantial landowners which dovetails 'with the characteristics of capitalist farming . . . appropriation of surplus value generated by wage labour, along with the sale on the market of a high proportion of surplus value in order to generate more surplus on an ever-expanding scale' (ibid.: 167).

Gujarat also 'occupies a prominent position on the industrial map of India' (Shah 1990: 93). Surat, for example, emerged as 'one of the most important industrial growth poles in Western India' (Breman 1996: 49) between 1971 and 1981 through the development of diamond-cutting and the production of artificial silk, as well as the emergence of a substantial petrochemical industry related to the extraction and processing of natural gas from the reserves of the Bombay High Plateau in the Arabian Gulf. However, more important in relation to understanding the link between economic change in Gujarat and the class interests that attach to the construction of the SSP is the emergence of agroindustry. Much as in agriculture, the high caste groups that once dominated in the industrial sector of Gujarat have increasingly been challenged by Patidars who have diversified their economic operations on the basis of their agrarian prosperity: 'Rich and middle *patidar* peasants who prospered in agriculture have diverted their surpluses to industry and invested in agro-based industries' (Shah 1990: 94). This is a tendency also noted by Breman in his studies of Surat, where he argues that the district has witnessed 'the rise of larger, much more capital-intensive and technically more advanced agro-industries for processing the produce of the new irrigated crops' (Breman 1978–79a: 44). Furthermore, the cultivation and cropping of sugarcane are highly co-ordinated activities; production, processing and marketing takes place on a co-operative basis (ibid.: 49). Similarly, Rutten (1995) in his study of Kheda notes that Patidars dominate the sugar industry, the groundnut oil mills, and the dairy co-operatives. 'Moreover', he adds, 'rich cultivators have invested their surpluses in the industrial sector by buying company shares' (ibid.: 94). These processes of economic change have laid the basis for powerful and effective collective action among the agroindustrial elites of South and Central Gujarat.

Agroindustrial elites, collective action and the SSP

T. J. Byres (1981: 425) has argued about 'the rich peasant stratum' that crystallized in parts of India from the mid-1960s onwards that it came to constitute a 'powerful class in itself, eminently capable of class-for-itself action'. This is certainly true in terms of the transition towards agroindustrial capitalism in south and central Gujarat, where the socioeconomic ascent of the Patidars, and in particular their control of the agricultural co-operative societies, has underpinned their emergence as 'a powerful lobby which, thanks to its co-operative form, is sure of having easy access to the local, state and central authorities at any time' (Breman 1978–79a: 49). Similarly, Shah (1990: 88) notes that 'the rich and middle cultivators have built up active organizations to protect and advance their economic interests'. Moreover, members of these organizations have been active both inside the parliamentary realm, through such formations as the Khedut Sangh in the 1950s and the Swatantra Party in the 1960s, and as extra-parliamentary pressure groups, such as the Khedut Samaj which was formed in 1972 to oppose the Land Ceiling Act and other forms of land-related legislation that were perceived to be anathema to the interests of the new agrarian elite. In the industrial realm, organization has occurred around several chambers of commerce and industry-owners' organizations aligned to the non-left parties in the state. The leaders of these organizations maintain close ties to government committees and the bureaucracy at district and state levels (ibid.: 96).

This capacity for class-for-itself action among the rich farmers of Gujarat has in turn had a significant impact on the trajectory of the SSP. When the preparations for the investigations of what was to become the SSP got under way in 1947, this was with the strong support of Sardar Vallabhbhai Patel – India's first Home Minister after independence and a key representative of the Patidars of south and central Gujarat, for whom bringing Narmada waters to the region was a central aspiration (D'Souza 2002; Fisher 1995). Government efforts to secure a large dam at Navagam in the 1960s were bolstered by extensive farmer support for the project. Indeed, when the conflict between Gujarat and Madhya Pradesh was at its most heated in the late 1960s, '[t]here was a short-lived but important movement among the farmers in South Gujarat . . . to pressure the state not to weaken its resolve' (Sen 2000a: 1). As the project has progressed, farmers' organizations have also invested heavily in security bonds and debentures issued by the SSNNL (Dwivedi 2006: 124).

The nexus between farmers, industrialists and politicians in support of the project has been maintained through the 1970s and 1980s until the present. In particular, this has been evident in the political trajectory of Chimanbhai Patel from the early 1970s to the mid-1990s. When Chimanbhai Patel first became Chief Minister of Gujarat in 1973 his political base was precisely 'the affluent farmers of the dominant Patidar landowning caste' (Frankel 2005: 523). He actively tried to resolve the deadlock between Gujarat and Madhya Pradesh, but was eventually ousted from power due to the Nav Nirman uprising of 1974 (Jones and Jones 1976: 1018). When he was re-elected as Chief Minister in 1990, he quickly emerged at the helm of the forces pushing for the implementation of the SSP by circumventing the NBA's efforts to force the central government to implement a full review of the SSP (see Chapter 6). Patel passed away in 1990, but his mantle has been taken up by subsequent chief ministers. Most recently, the SSP has consistently been fronted by the present BJP Chief Minister, Narendra Modi, as part and parcel of his efforts to attract foreign direct investments to Gujarat by projecting it as the 'business state of India'.[8] These efforts have in turn been endowed with Hindu communalist meanings in several public actions staged by Modi in support of the project (see Bavadam 2004a).

Displacement and resettlement in Madhya Pradesh

Whereas there seems to be consensus on the number of villages that will be affected by the submergence caused by the SSP reservoir – 245 – and their distribution among the three riparian states – 193 villages in Madhya Pradesh (MP), 33 villages in Maharashtra, and 19 villages in Gujarat – there does not exist an exact and uncontroversial official estimate of the number of people that stand to be displaced by the SSP (D'Souza 2002). Moreover, official estimates of the number of dam-affected communities do not correspond with realities on the ground as these have been documented by successive independent inquiries. In the first half of the 1990s, this was one of the central shortcomings of the project identified by the independent review of the Morse Commission, which stated that '[t]he Bank and India have both failed to carry out adequate assessments of human impacts of the Sardar Sarovar Projects' which in turn 'led to an inadequate understanding of the nature and scale of resettlement' (Morse and Berger 1995: 371). Furthermore, the official definition of project-affected person and/or project-affected family has come in for harsh criticism as it only recognizes individuals with formal title deeds to their land; this neglects how the SSP reservoir impacts on boatsmen, fisherfolk, riverbed farmers, sand-quarry workers, landless labourers, and adivasis without formal title deeds to the land they occupy and use as a source of livelihood. Moreover, critics maintain, displacement is not only a reservoir-phenomenon: people will also be displaced by the canal network attached to the dam, as well as secondary displacement related to resettlement, afforestation, and catchment area treatment. Fisherfolk and other groups dependent on a regular flow of water downstream from the dam will be affected by the project, and so will a motley crew of hawkers, shopkeepers and artisans whose livelihoods are dependent upon the dam-affected villages. If these groups are taken into account, the potential number of people who stand to be affected by displacement arguably reaches 1,000,000 (see Sangvai 2000a: 103–4).

Whereas the stipulations for resettlement and rehabilitation (R&R) laid out in the Tribunal Award were extensive and could potentially have formed the basis for successful R&R, the ground realities in the Narmada Valley have persistently confirmed the Morse Commission's assessment that 'resettlement and rehabilitation of all those displaced by the projects is not possible under the prevailing circumstances' (Morse and Berger 1992: vii). In flagrant violation of the stipulations of the Tribunal Award, a master plan for R&R has not been put in place, there are wide discrepancies between the R&R policies adopted by the riparian states, and, perhaps most importantly, both Maharashtra and Madhya Pradesh have admitted that they are unable to find land to resettle the displaced communities (Fisher 1995: 31; Dhagamvar*et al.* 1995: 51).

The record on the actual practice of R&R of SSP oustees only adds to an already dismal picture. In western Madhya Pradesh 193 villages stand to be affected by the SSP reservoir. Some 26 of these are adivasi communities located in the hills of Alirajpur tehsil (administrative sub-district) in Jhabua district, whilst the majority of those affected by the dam are caste Hindu farming communities located in the Nimad plains.[9] Deficiencies in R&R were pointed out as early as 1992 by the Morse

Commission, which highlighted several policy and implementation failures in the R&R policy of the Government of Madhya Pradesh (GoMP).[10] The prospects for successful implementation of R&R 'have always been, and continues to be severely limited' as the project authorities have failed to gather necessary data about the dam-affected communities and had also not consulted these communities about the impending process of submergence, displacement and R&R (Morse and Berger 1992: 194). Thus the report concludes:

> large numbers of Madhya Pradesh oustees cannot expect to regain their standard of living as a result of resettlement and rehabilitation . . . many oustees can expect to experience a substantial loss of economic status; the expectation is that they will go from having land to being landless.
>
> (ibid.: 196)

Ten years later, the Housing and Land Rights Network of the Habitat International Coalition who reviewed the impact of submergence in 2002 passed a scathing verdict on the implementation of R&R in Madhya Pradesh. When the height of the SSP was raised from 90 to 95 metres, crops and houses in dam-affected villages were submerged, and personal property and livestock were washed away; villagers were left without food supplies to see them through the year, and even after the water had receded they would be unable to cultivate their lands due to the silt that covered their fields (Housing and Land Rights Network 2002: 10–12). Yet, even in this context, the resettlement sites provided by the GoMP lacked cultivable land for agriculture and alternative livelihood provisions, as well as adequate housing, infrastructure and civic amenities, disputes over land and plots were rife, and a significant part of the land that was being allocated for R&R would be submerged as the height of the SSP was increased further. This scenario was compounded by the widespread non-recognition of land rights in tribal areas, and, not least, a lack of information about displacement and R&R in the affected communities (ibid.: 20). Indeed, the scenario in 2002 constituted a blatant violation of the Supreme Court's stipulation that the height of the dam should be increased *pari passu* with R&R.[11] In March 2006, when the NCA gave clearance for the height of the SSP to be raised from 110 metres to 121 metres, things had not improved much: following a visit to the dam-affected areas in the state, a team of government ministers submitted a report which condemned the state of R&R in Madhya Pradesh, labelling official claims that oustees would be resettled by late June 2006 as 'a cruel joke' (cited in Bavadam 2006). Indeed, at this point the UNHCR issued a press statement expressing its grave concerns about the non-availability of adequate resettlement sites in Madhya Pradesh, and the fact that this was likely to leave affected villagers homeless when submergence set in (UNHCR 2006).

Adivasi livelihoods in Alirajpur

The peasant economy of the Bhil and Bhilala adivasis of Alirajpur is characterized by subsistence production and 'dependence on [the] immediate natural environment for material sustenance' (Baviskar 1995: 91). The economy is centred on agriculture and livestock, as well as the gathering of various forms of forest produce. What sets cultivation and the use of livestock in the adivasi communities aside from peasant households in the Nimad plains is the degree of self-sufficiency and restricted interaction with markets. Moreover, in contrast to the hierarchical structure of the caste Hindu villages in the plains, these communities are fairly egalitarian: 'All households in the village have access to land and almost equal guarantee of subsistence' (ibid.: 91). Landholdings are worked collectively through various institutions that co-ordinate labour-sharing practices (ibid.: 93).

Agriculture in the adivasi communities is based on the utilization of two forms of land. In between the clusters of huts that make up a village hamlet, the revenue land – i.e. 'legally owned land for which revenue is paid to the state' (Baviskar 1995: 137) – is located. Among the hill slopes that constitute the backdrop to the hamlets, one finds the *nevad* lands – that is, fields that have been cleared illegally in the forest. The lion's share of the cultivation takes place on the plots of land bordering the huts. However, this land is not of such fertility that it can satisfy the livelihood requirements of a family; thus the cultivation of *nevad* fields complements the yield gained from the revenue land. Clearing and cultivating *nevad* is of decisive importance to adivasi livelihoods, but it is also a problematic practice as these fields 'encroach upon land belonging to the Forest Department' (ibid.: 149). With the commodification of forest resources from the colonial era onwards, wide-ranging legislation was put in place which effectively outlawed the traditional ways in which adivasi communities had made use of the forests – i.e. not just cultivation, but livestock grazing, collecting building materials, fuel, medicines and edible gums (see Chapter 3).

Despite the overall subsistence characteristic of the adivasi peasant economy, there is also a degree of interaction with the regional market economy. Surplus agricultural produce along with minor forest produce is sold in local markets to obtain cash to buy such commodities as tobacco, cloth and medicines. The markets are an arena where adivasis find themselves in a disadvantageous position vis-à-vis caste Hindu traders, merchants and moneylenders: people typically face 'unfavourable terms of trade for their produce' (Baviskar 1995: 158) and usurious interest rates on debts incurred to moneylenders and traders. In addition, labour migration, which is likely to increase dramatically due to displacement, constitutes a mode of interaction with the regional market economy.[12]

Not much is known about the pre-colonial history of the adivasi communities of Alirajpur, but Baviskar (1995) argues that by the end of the eighteenth century the Bhils and Bhilalas had been displaced from their original habitats in the plains to the nearby hills by Rajput invaders. Further processes of change occurred in the nineteenth century as the British gradually came to exert a stronger hold over the region: Kanbi Patidars were encouraged to settle as agriculturalists in the plains, settled agriculture was promoted among the adivasis, and, crucially, the forests that the adivasi communities depended on for their livelihoods were commodified: 'Adivasis were being increasingly excluded from the forest and their customary use rights restricted. . . . Land was leased to contractors whose activities turned vast tracts of forest into semi-barren land' (ibid.: 70). This process of commodification is evident in such facts as the three-fold rise in revenue from Alirajpur between the beginning of the twentieth century and the 1930s. The sale of timber yielded Rs. 11,000 in 1901–2 and Rs. 113,564 in 1937–38 – an increase of no less than 1,032 per cent (ibid.: 75). The revenue system came to link villages closer to the district headquarters, a process which was crucially linked to the upshot of market towns which 'served as nodes which channelled regional surplus into a national market' (ibid.: 76).

Following Independence in 1947, Alirajpur entered the Indian republic as part of the state Madhya Bharat.[13] Jhabua district itself was constituted in 1949, and Alirajpur was made as a tehsil of Jhabua: 'Almost the first act of the new regime was to order a detailed land survey for permanent settlement. Titles to land were issued, soil types were assessed, and regular rates of land revenue were fixed' (Baviskar 1995: 80). In 1950, the districts of Jhabua, Khargone and Dhar were declared Scheduled Areas and Bhils and Bhilalas residing there were designated as Scheduled Tribes by 1956. Such designations were intended to secure the areas and their populace access to certain welfare measures, but the reality was – and continues to be – quite different, as 'most government programmes consisted of handouts in times of distress . . . which failed to address the underlying causes of adivasi impoverishment. Tribal rights to the forest remained unrecognized; their continued alienation from the land base upon which they depended for a sustenance precluded any opportunity for genuine gains in power and prosperity' (ibid.: 81).[14] The state's developmental neglect of the adivasis of Alirajpur is mirrored in and closely related to their systematic exclusion from the arena of parliamentary politics. As I bring out in the next chapter, adivasi interaction with the state revolved around subjection to coercion and extortion by local state officials in the police, forestry and revenue departments; the skilled practice of positing demands and asserting claims on the state on the basis of constitutionally defined rights and entitlements had to be built through a process of mobilization and resistance.

Petty commodity production in Nimad

The caste Hindu farming communities of Nimad exhibit very different socioeconomic characteristics from the adivasi communities of Alirajpur: in place of subsistence production we find 'petty commodity production' – that is, a form of peasant production in which peasants 'are unable to reproduce themselves outside the relations and processes of capitalist commodity production' and 'the latter [comes] to constitute the conditions of existence of peasant farming and are internalized in its organization and activity' (Bernstein 1994: 55).

In Nimad, this is evident in terms of how agriculture is characterized by private ownership of land and all other major means of production, the existence of a class of wage labourers, and the thoroughly commercial and intensive nature of agricultural operations.[15] Farmers make extensive use of the biochemical and mechanical inputs that were introduced with the adoption of new technologies associated with the Green Revolution. This has in turn increased the intensity of the cropping pattern. In the 1980s, this resulted in a substantial acceleration of the annual growth of the gross value of agricultural output (field notes, April 2003; Shankar 2005).

The Nimadi peasantry is an internally differentiated category: small or marginal farmers own and cultivate one to five acres of land, relying mostly, but not exclusively, on family labour, and take up work as agricultural labourers in order to sustain a livelihood; medium farmers own and cultivate 5 to 15 acres of land, relying on family labour in most of their farming operations, but hire additional hands during peak seasons; large farmers cultivate 15 acres or more, and their agricultural operations are totally dependent on both regular and casual wage labour (field notes, April 2003). Interviewees in the Nimadi villages tended to place the majority of landowners in the category of medium farmers, but judging by overall trends for Madhya Pradesh this is a rapidly diminishing group: Shankar (2005: 5017) notes that small and marginal landholdings are proliferating in the state, and 'an increasing number of small and marginal landowners, operating low productivity holdings are being forced to enter the labour market'. The character of farming operations vary considerably between the different categories of farmers. Small farmers' operations are often labour-intensive – several small farmers reported that they hired a considerable number of labourers during the harvest – and geared towards cash crop cultivation, yet farmers would typically report that profits would be used to cover household expenses, and that this in turn severely restricted their capacity to expand their activities. Loans from co-operatives and village moneylenders are taken up to fund new crop cycles, and in some cases farmers had been forced to sell off land in order to pay back their debts. Larger farming operations tend to exhibit a greater degree of economic dynamism and a greater capacity for expansion into agroindustrial processing and the service sector (field notes, April 2003).

At the opposite end of the social spectrum is the regional proletariat, which is broadly made up of three groups: landless Nimadi villagers, small and marginal Nimadi farmers, and migrant labourers; the latter group is largely made up of adivasis from Dhar and Badwani districts, where the resource base has been depleted to the extent that subsistence agriculture is no longer a viable livelihood. There are two broad categories of labour regimes – regular and casual labour. Regular labourers enter into an annual contract with a landed household. Their wage – according to the farmers – is 50 rupees per day, which makes for an annual income of 16–17,000 rupees. The demand for labour peaks with planting, weeding and harvesting operations; this is when farmers resort to casual labour. Labourers are paid on a daily basis or according to various piece-rates, in cash or in kind; wages were generally reported to range between 30 to 40 rupees per day for male workers and 20–25 rupees for women (field notes, April 2003).

It is commonly noted that Patidars have come to constitute a powerful and prosperous community in the Nimad region (e.g. Baviskar 1995; Dwivedi 1997). Interestingly, during the post-independence era, the Patidars of Nimad seem to have gone through a similar trajectory to that of the Kanbi Patidars in central and western Gujarat. The Patidars have emerged from the status of tenant farmers and a fairly inferior caste status to the position of dominant and prosperous landholders enjoying substantial ritual purity throughout much of Nimad. Concurrently, the upper-caste feudal landlords have experienced a process of relative decline (field notes, April 2003).

The emergence of Nimad's peasant proprietors is linked to the impact of land reforms that were initiated in the 1950s. Parallel with the creation of the state of Madhya Pradesh after Independence, there have been successive rounds of land reform legislation. Tenancy reforms started in 1951 when the Madhya Pradesh Abolition of Property Rights Act came into force, abolishing 'all proprietary rights in estates and *mahals,* which now [became] vested in the state' (Land Reforms Unit 2002: 123). Subsequent legislation simplified land tenures, protected the rights of sub-tenants and vested the right to the intermediaries' estates in the state government (ibid.: 113–14). Legislation imposing ceilings on the size of landholdings was first introduced in 1961 when the Madhya Pradesh Ceiling on Agricultural Holdings Act came into force. However, implementation of these provisions proved to be difficult: legal disputes delayed the acquisition of surplus land, absentee landlordism continued, and large farmers circumvented the land ceiling (ibid.: 114–15; see also Gupta 2005: 5095).

Whereas the implementation of land reforms in the aftermath of independence and the later introduction of high yielding varieties and irrigation created a space in which petty commodity production could flourish with peasant proprietors at the helm, the agricultural economy of Nimad is not characterized by expanded reproduction and diversification beyond agriculture on the scale witnessed in southern and central Gujarat. Rather, Nimadi agriculture seems to be predominantly characterized by 'simple reproduction' and only limited diversification into industry and other branches of the economy. Moreover, judging by farmers' narratives, the last decade has been marked by tendencies towards 'a simple reproduction "squeeze" on [peasants'] capital, labour or both' (Bernstein 1994: 56), a situation which was attributed on the one hand to ecological degradation due to intensive farming which had reduced the fertility of the soil, and, on the other hand, reductions in input subsidies following the implementation of neoliberal reforms in the early 1990s (interviews and field notes, April 2003). These narratives dovetail neatly with state-wide tendencies in the agricultural sector in Madhya Pradesh as a whole, where the accelerated growth in output that marked the 1980s has given way to slowdown and stagnation, and where the size of landholdings is decreasing, resulting in a scenario where 'an increasing number of small and marginal landowners, operating low productivity holdings are being forced to enter the labour market' (Shankar 2005: 5017).

Finally, it should be noted that the political position of Nimad's peasant proprietors very much parallels the limitations of their socioeconomic base. Whereas the Patidar farmers to a large extent dominate politics in the region, and enjoy 'close associations with the local administration and politicians' (Dwivedi 2006: 286), they have not been able to constitute themselves as a dominant class-in-itself at the state level in the same way as the agroindustrial elite of south and central Gujarat. This in turn has to be understood in the wider context of political dynamics in Madhya Pradesh: constituted as 'a collection of left-out portions of different states combined into one heterogeneous unit' (Wilcox cited in Gupta 2005: 5094), with a far higher proportion of Scheduled Tribes than Gujarat, the state has not witnessed the rise of a social group which could assert political hegemony at a pan-regional level (see Kela 2003: 5).[16]

In the case of the SSP accumulation by dispossession is enacted through 'the forceful expulsion of peasant populations . . . [and] the conversion of various forms of property rights . . . into exclusive private property rights . . . and the suppression of alternative forms of production' (Harvey 2003: 145). The concentration of property rights occurs through the ways in which the construction of the dam provides access to irrigation and electricity to the class of agroindustrial capitalists that have emerged as a hegemonic social force in south and central Gujarat in the postcolonial era. Indeed, it is precisely the conscious exercise of collective agency by agroindustrial capital in south and central Gujarat which explains the distributional bias of the SSP in its favour, and this in turn is part of a longer historical trajectory in which this regional elite has mobilized to shape the workings of state development strategies in its favour. The expulsion of peasant populations and suppression of alternative forms of production takes place through the displacement of adivasi subsistence peasants and caste Hindu petty commodity producers which, due to the thoroughgoing weaknesses of policies and practices related to R&R will generate pressures towards proletarianization.

Just as the concentration of property rights in water and electricity in the hands of agroindustrial capital in south and central Gujarat is part of a longer historical process of class formation, the displacement of the adivasi communities of Alirajpur have to be viewed as a moment in a process of dispossession and alienation from means of production that stretches over centuries. The adivasi communities of Alirajpur have emerged in their present state through several rounds of dispossession from colonial times onwards, and the current submergence and displacement can arguably be understood as a crucial moment in which this process reaches its conclusion by bringing about a radical and absolute abrogation of access to means of subsistence and production such as land and forests. In this context, they are left with few options but to sell their labour power in order to survive. Indeed, more than a decade ago, Baviskar (1995) argued that the adivasis that stood to be displaced by the SSP reservoir were likely to join the ranks of the footloose proletariat of south and central Gujarat. Today, that prediction stands vindicated as a steady flow of families affected by submergence make their way towards the urban centres of Gujarat in search of work.

The workings of accumulation by dispossession in Nimad have to be conceived in terms of the 'continuous destruction and (re)creation' of petty commodity production that is characteristic of capitalist development (Bernstein 1994: 55; see also Harriss-White 2006). Again we are dealing with a moment – arguably a conclusive moment – in a more long-term process in which the space created for petty commodity production in the early postcolonial era is being increasingly constrained by reforms which put petty-commodity producers at a disadvantage in relation to wider market forces. As much as the differentiated social structure of Nimad is likely to translate into differentiated impacts of displacement, dispossession due to the construction of the SSP will undoubtedly intensify the processes through which an increasing number of peasants in the region are compelled to turn to wage labour in order to sustain a livelihood.

Accumulation by dispossession 2: The Maheshwar Hydroelectric Project (MHP)

The dynamics of accumulation by dispossession in the case of the Maheshwar Hydroelectric Project (MHP) exhibits both similarities and differences with the SSP. In terms of the distributional bias of costs and benefits, the burden of displacement is borne by petty commodity producers in Nimad. However, in terms of the benefits, what we find in the case of the MHP is not so much the concentration of property rights in water and electricity through the modality of a state-directed development project shaped by the collective action of regional agroindustrial elites, but rather the provision of profitable investment opportunities for domestic and transnational industrial and financial capital via the modalities of privatization and liberalization. It is this latter element which constitutes the chief focus of this part of the chapter.

Displacement and resettlement in Nimad

According to official estimates, the reservoir of the MHP will submerge approximately 5,000 hectares of agricultural land spread across 61 villages in Khargone district. When the German government withdrew its support from the MHP in 2000 (see Chapter 1) this was the outcome of the presentation of evidence that suggested that the extent of submergence and displacement caused by the project was highly underestimated, and that the provisions for R&R were highly inadequate (Schücking 1999). Moreover, as with the SSP, the estimates of people to be submerged are highly unreliable, and the project authorities operate with a very narrow definition of project-affected families (ibid.: 1; see also Bissell *et al.* 2000: 3). Moreover, Schücking (1999: 2) found that the physical infrastructure of the Nimadi villages has been consistently underestimated.

When the MHP was granted clearance by the Ministry of Environment and Forests in 1994, this was done on the condition that the dam builders could document that there was land available for R&R. However, it has been documented that the availability of land for R&R is highly questionable. Several studies have established that land listed as available for R&R 'will fall into the submergence zone of either the downstream Sardar-Sarovar dam or Maheshwar itself' (Schücking 1999: 3). It should be noted that this is happening in a state whose government has publicly declared that there is not enough land available for securing R&R for the oustees of the SSP. Indeed, mirroring the fate of the oustees of Kevadia Colony in Gujarat, the 50 families that were displaced so that the MHP project colony could be built have yet to be resettled on adequate land. Thus, the Independent Review of Bissell *et al.* (2000: 9) concludes in terms of the viability of the R&R plans that 'the resources to carry out R&R in accordance with the stated policy and conditions of clearance, do not exist'.

Industrial and financial interests in the MHP

The primary justification of the MHP is the provision of electricity: according to the claims of SMHPCL, the project will deliver 400 MW of power (see Chapter 1). However, critics maintain that this claim conceals the fact that the MHP will only be capable of delivering peak power during the four monsoon months of the year, and far less during the remaining eight months of the year (Mahalingam 2000). With considerable escalations in the costs of the project, critics also maintain that the costs of the electricity actually produced will be far higher than what is postulated by the SMHPCL, and thus out of reach of average rural households (Mahalingam 2000; NBA 1999). Indeed, what is striking about the MHP in contrast to the SSP is that it has not been promoted by regional political and economic elites craving electrification so much as private corporations, both domestic and transnational, and, more recently, domestic and transnational financial institutions, for whom the project constitutes an investment opportunity. And what is crucial to understand in this respect is that the MHP has emerged as an investment opportunity at the confluence of two key processes of neoliberal reform: the privatization of India's power sector and the liberalization of its financial sector.

The privatization of the MHP in 1994 was the first case of privatization of a hydropower project in India, and as such it foreshadowed many of the changes that were to take place in the Indian power sector as the decade unfolded. On the eve of Independence, power generation in India was largely in private hands. However, the Electricity Supply Act of 1948 established that all further developments in the power sector were to take place under state control. States and territories constituted their own vertically integrated entities or State Electricity Boards (SEBs). By the early 1990s, SEBs were in control of more than 70 per cent of India's power generation, and virtually all of its distribution. In some important respects, this was a very successful strategy in that 'the pre-1991 institutional arrangements were remarkably effective in accelerating the development of electricity services in India' (Dubash and Rajan 2001: 3). Nevertheless, India's power sector was in severe trouble in the early 1990s. In spite of the increased capacity of the power sector, there was still a lag relative to demand and energy consumption was also inefficient. Maintenance and modernization of power plants were neglected, and so were distribution and transmission mechanisms. Most importantly, the SEBs were in serious financial trouble due to the ways in which electricity was subsidized so as to benefit agrarian elites (Bosshard 2002: chapter 1.3; Dubash and Rajan 2001: 5).

By the late 1980s, there was an emerging consensus that something had to be done about the structural inefficiencies of the power sector. Reflecting the neoliberal climate of the time, the crisis came to serve as a lever for developing and demonstrating 'nimbleness, to show the world, but particularly foreign capital, that India was a good place to do business. The power sector was chosen to be at the forefront of the new liberalizing India' (Dubash and Rajan 2001: 9). In October 1991, the Indian Power Ministry embarked on an offensive to encourage private capital to enter into power generation. Private corporations were allowed to 'establish, operate and maintain generating power plants of virtually any size and to enter into long time purchasing agreements with SEBs' (ibid.: 10); tax holidays and guaranteed returns were introduced to speed up the process, and the response from domestic and international investors was overwhelming.[17]

S. Kumars, a business group that originated in the textile sector, but later branched out into power generation, tyre manufacturing, infrastructure development, financial services and information technology, was at the forefront of this process when, in 1994, it established the Shree Maheshwar Hydel Power Corporation Limited (SMHPCL) to take up the concession for the MHP (Ghosh 2006b). The SMHPCL sought foreign equity for the MHP from the very outset, but as shown in Chapter 1, this proved to be a difficult undertaking. By 2001, at least 10 foreign investors had pulled out of the MHP, by and large as a result of the concerted resistance of the NBA, and the project was at an impasse (Bosshard 2002: 8).

The solution to the problem was sought in Indian financial institutions, and by early 2002 a veritable financial maze had emerged around the MHP. S. Kumars was to put up 20 per cent of the equity, while the Industrial Development Bank of India (IDBI) and the General Insurance Corporation of India were to fill the 15 per cent gap left by Siemens' withdrawal from the project. The Industrial Finance Corporation of India (IFCI) was to coordinate a lenders' consortium consisting of IDBI, the Power Finance Corporation (PFC), IFCI, the State Bank of India (SBI), Dena Bank and Punjab National Bank. The Madhya Pradesh State Industrial Development Corporation extended 45 crore rupees in inter-corporate deposits. The PFC, the Frankfurt Branch of SBI and the Bank of India supplied foreign currency loans. Importantly, the GoMP played a key role in facilitating interaction between the SMHPCL and the financial institutions; in March 2003 a meeting was organized between state and union ministers, funders, and representatives of the SMHPCL in order to 'tie up the finances of the Maheshwar project to the extent of Rs. 2.233 crores through loans and debentures to be financed by the Indian financial corporations' (Ghosh 2003: 4). The meeting was a success, with the financial institutions, lead by the Life Insurance Corporation of India, agreeing to put up the needed funds for the project.

At this point, however, financial irregularities temporarily caught up with the project. As both Bavadam (2004b) and Ghosh (2003, 2006b) point out, S. Kumars and SMHPCL have a long string of defaults on loans attached to them. One of these loans, amounting to Rs. 103 crores, was taken from the Madhya Pradesh State Industrial Development Corporation (MPSIDC), and when S. Kumars defaulted on these loans the GoMP attached the project properties and initiated criminal proceedings against the company in 2004. PFIs also stopped providing finance for the project at this point.

However, the Madhya Pradesh state government again intervened in order to help the project along: in September 2005, the land for the project property was released, the state government waived the security that S. Kumars was originally required to give to the MPSIDC, the amount returnable to the state was reduced, and the rate of interest on the project loans was drastically reduced (Bavadam 2006; Ghosh 2006b). The project could thus be resumed in 2006, with SMHPCL approaching IDBI, LIC and GIC for equity amounting to Rs. 90 crores and Bharat Heavy Electricals Limited for equity worth 70 crores. IFCI was asked to convert unpaid front-end fees into equity amounting to Rs. 19.5 crores, and substantial loans were taken from the Rural Electrification Corporation, the Housing and Urban Development Corporation and the Power Finance Corporation (Bavadam 2006). Further aid came the project's way in early 2007, when the credit rating agency CARE gave a Triple A rating to debentures worth 400 crores issued by the SMHPCL.[18]

The strategy of turning to Indian financial institutions to find funding for the MHP was rendered possible due to the liberalization of India's financial sector – a process which had been underway since the second half of the 1990s. India's financial sector was originally structured to address postcolonial developmental imperatives, and the state played an active role in directing the activities of financial institutions towards the promotion of social goals. Indeed, most of India's financial institutions were either created by the government after Independence or nationalized between 1955 and the 1970s (Bosshard 2002: 1.4). The financial sector was roughly divided into two overarching categories of institutions: commercial banks that mobilize short-term deposits from retail savers and focus on meeting the short term needs for finance in industry trade and agriculture, and development finance institutions (DFIs) that provide a channel for the flow of long-term funds from public and government sources to fund industrial and infrastructure development. Political influence has been exercised through direct ownership and regulation of these institutions.

Whereas this created a potential for the promotion of social goals, it also created a space for vested interests and political cronyism in terms of influencing lending decisions. The consequence was a high frequency of lending to uneconomic projects, which in turn left the financial institutions with substantial non-performing assets. Frequently, due to corruption and the political clout of important corporations, loans were diverted into new projects and affiliated companies, which meant that the projects the loans were supposed to fund were left high and dry, and in turn that debts were not serviced (Bosshard 2002: 20–1). The end result of all this was that the capital adequacy of India's financial institutions plunged and the government had to bail them out. This, as Bosshard correctly notes, amounted to 'a large-scale socialization of private risks and losses. Like the power sector, the Indian financial sector involves huge transfers of wealth from society at large to a privileged elite' (ibid.: 21).

When India first embarked on its programme of neoliberal restructuring in the early 1990s financial reforms 'were slow to gather pace, but significant changes were introduced in the second half of the 1990s' (Corbridge and Harriss 2000: 154; see also Chandrasekhar and Ghosh 2002: 27–9, 97–112). Some of the crucial changes were as follows: new private banks and insurance companies could enter the market; interest rates were deregulated; foreign exchange operations were deregulated; directed credit was rolled back; banks could open and close branches on their own accord; a private capital market was created; banks and development finance institutions could raise private equity capital; the government announced that it would cease its bailouts of finance institutions; and there was a reduction of government ownership in the public sector banks (Bosshard 2002: 22). Liberalization constituted a challenge to DFIs in the form of competition from commercial banks and insurance companies that provided long-term loans and who had cheaper access to funds in the form of household savings. This in turn engendered greater pressure on the margins and profit rates of the DFIs.

Moreover, the strengthening of capital markets entailed that most creditworthy companies and institutions could raise equity and place bonds on the market directly rather than taking costly loans from financial institutions. All this has led to a loss of customers for the DFIs, who have responded by measures such as increasing their financing of projects for private infrastructure so as to move away from the financing of loss-making industries, implementing new business activities, and raising equity from private shareholders so as to make up for the reductions in government support for their capital base (Bosshard 2002: 22).

Bosshard (2002) documents how the recently liberalized financial institutions have moved into the recently privatized power sector, and in particular hydropower. This move has in turn been underpinned by the activities of international financial institutions. Whereas the World Bank has discontinued its financing of individual power projects, it has come to focus on state-level restructuring programmes. Central features of the programmes that the Bank supports are: unbundling of generation, transmission and distribution of power; privatizing power distribution; private involvement in the generation and transmission of power; and increases in power tariffs for agricultural and domestic consumers (ibid.: 79). The International Finance Corporation supports 'what it believes to be innovative technologies and projects' in the power sector (ibid.: 83). The IFC takes its cue from the World Bank by funding private companies who engage in such technologies and projects (ibid.: 83). Furthermore, the Asian Development Bank (ADB) is a significant official donor to India and focuses in particular on the restructuring of the power sector; one of the states it is currently involved in is Madhya Pradesh. Moreover, bilateral institutions such as Japan Bank for International Cooperation, the Canadian International Development Agency, USAID, and the Swedish International Development Agency also participate in funding the process of restructuring. Export credit agencies such as Norway's Eksportfinans are crucial in financing the participation of foreign contractors (ibid.: chapters 3.3–3.5). Finally, the restructuring of India's power sector is also based on loans and bonds from the international capital markets (ibid.: 103).

The crucial feature of accumulation by dispossession in the case of the MHP is how it has been propelled forward by a constellation of domestic and transnational corporations and financial institutions for whom the project constitutes a profitable investment opportunity, and how the emergence of this constellation has in turn been predicated upon the privatization of India's power sector and the liberalization of its financial sector. Thus, the MHP exemplifies two of the hallmarks of accumulation by dispossession in the neoliberal era. Privatization, Harvey (2005: 160) argues, is crucial in opening up 'new fields for capital accumulation in domains hitherto regarded off-limits to the calculus of profit-availability' by releasing public assets onto the global marketplace as commodities. It is of course precisely this that has happened in the case of the MHP and, more widely, in relation to the restructuring of India's power sector. The privatization of the Indian power sector was in turn closely related to the wider fiscal crisis which rocked the Indian economy in the early 1990s, which lends support to Harvey's (2003: 149–52) argument that the management of fiscal crises is intimately related to accumulation by dispossession as it creates opportunities both for devaluing public assets and for releasing them onto the market where capital can seize hold of them. Furthermore, the web of financial institutions that was spun around the MHP as a strategy to circumvent the dearth in funding that resulted from popular resistance testifies to how deregulation has 'allowed the financial system to become one of the main centres of redistributive activity through speculation, predation, fraud, and thievery' (Harvey 2005: 161).

Now, it is my contention that accumulation by dispossession in the Narmada Valley is not an idiosyncrasy but rather an example of how capitalist relations have been deepened in the postcolonial era through state development strategies that have concentrated productive resources in the hands of dominant social groups, and that this is linked to the ability of these groups to set limits and exert pressures on the articulation and implementation of these strategies. It is to an examination of this dynamic in postcolonial capitalism in India that I now turn.

Accumulation by dispossession and the political economy of postcolonial capitalism in India

Large dams and river valley development schemes were constructed as 'built environments for production' (Harvey 1999) that would contribute to the ambition of the Nehruvian state to overcome the limited structural transformation of the Indian economy and to surge ahead with the desired 'catch-up . . . with the Industrial Revolution that occurred long ago in Western countries' (Nehru cited in Chatterjee 1993: 202). As such, dam-building can be said to be representative of how the postcolonial state sought to define 'its distinctive content' in 'the universal function of "development" of national society as a whole' (Chatterjee 1993: 203).[19]

However, as much as the construction of large dams was ostensibly posited at the forefront of the postcolonial development project as 'an intervention carried out in the name of the public good' (Singh 1997: 21), the actual distributional consequences of large dams negate such claims. A recent comprehensive report on India's experience with dam-building passes a harsh judgement on the capacity of dams to boost irrigation. The authors point out that the area actually irrigated by large and medium dams falls below the projected area, actual increases in yields fall below anticipated yield increases, actual changes in cropping patterns deviate from projected changes in cropping patterns, and price assumptions tend to be overly optimistic (Rangachari *et al.* 2000: 56). Thus, the actual impact of large dams 'as far as irrigation benefits are concerned, is therefore almost entirely distributional' (ibid.: 57), with benefits accruing to dominant farmers and industrialists in the command area, whilst the financial and social costs of dams are borne by tax-payers and dam-affected communities. Moreover, the financial performance of dams started off badly and has gotten progressively worse as capital outlays and financial losses have increased simultaneously, and whilst losses on dam projects increased, financial allocations and the actual number of projects instigated increased (ibid.: 62–5).

If we turn to the converse side of the equation – displacement and loss of land and livelihood – we encounter a familiar level of uncertainty as to the actual number of people who have been displaced. Estimates vary from between 21 million to 33 million people, but regardless of such variations, there is no doubt that 'the magnitude in which displacement should be estimated is in the tens of millions' (Rangachari *et al.* 2000: 116). Now, what is particularly important about these tens of millions of people is the fact that their social profile is far from neutral. As Whitehead (2003: 3) points out, 'the marginality of the scheduled tribes in India stands in contrast to their predominance in the populations displaced by dams and other development projects': adivasis constitute eight per cent of India's population, but as much as 40 to 50 per cent of those who have been displaced in the post-colonial era,[20] and an additional ten per cent of those displaced are dalits (see also Singh 1997: 190).

As in the case of the Narmada dams, the nationwide record on R&R in India is dismal. This is in turn related to the fact that whereas the Indian state is endowed with formidable powers of expropriation through the Land Acquisition Act of 1894, there is as of yet no national legal framework guaranteeing the rights of oustees and laying down guidelines for the conduct of R&R (Parasuraman 1999; Cernea 1999).[21] Moreover, the reality of the conduct of R&R is characterized by the fact that 'much of what is promised, however inadequate it may be, is also not delivered' (Rangachari *et al.* 2000: 117). As a consequence, the vast majorities of those displaced by large dams have ended up swelling the ranks of the reserve army of casual migrant labour that fuels the fires of capital accumulation throughout India.

In sum, the chief effect of large dams have been to redistribute already extant inputs by concentrating property rights in water in the hands of an emergent class of agroindustrial capitalists whilst disproportionately dispossessing subaltern social groups from access to means of production and thus generating pressures towards their proletarianization.

Now, the process of resource transfer that has been engineered through the distributional bias of big dams is not a singular case of a flawed development strategy. Rather, it is a generic feature of the workings of the major development strategies of the postcolonial Indian state, and illustrates how these strategies have served to extend and entrench capitalist relations in postcolonial India. In order to understand this dynamic, it is necessary to interrogate the processes of political struggle through which the Nehruvian developmental state came to be constituted, and in particular how the trajectory of the postcolonial development project came to be shaped by a social movement from above that was capable of setting certain limits to and exerting certain pressures on the articulation of state development strategies. Furthermore, this dynamic must be traced beyond the unravelling of Nehruvian developmentalism towards an engagement with the advent of structural adjustment in the 1990s, and the increasingly aggressive implementation of neoliberal accumulation strategies that is currently taking place in India.

On the eve of independence 'there was no question of doing away with private property . . . almost all the [Congress] High Command realized that the foreseeable future would be a capitalist future' (Chibber 2003: 223). This scenario is in turn rooted in the dialectic of mobilization from above and below that unfolded during the last decades of the struggle for independence in India. The point of departure for understanding this dialectic has to be the recognition that the Indian National Congress (INC) originated as an elite pressure group and in its early years exhibited 'a studied distance from popular mobilization and mass organization' (ibid.: 113). Even after mass mobilization was adopted in the 1920s, elites remained in control of the upper echelons of the organization, and peasant masses never achieved direct access to the organization (Frankel 2005: 28–9). When mass mobilization set in, it did so under Gandhi's tutelage, who had earned the trust of right-wing elements of the Congress due to 'his own particular brand of elite paternalism' and 'his staunch defence of property and wealth' (Chibber 2003: 113; see also Bose 1997). Moreover, Gandhi's leadership found expression in the entrenchment of a political programme which separated social and political issues and sought to win independence in the shortest possible time by harnessing the energies and aspirations of all social classes whilst sidelining internal, exploitative divisions among the Indian people. Mass aspirations for social change were contained within boundaries that were acceptable to dominant social groups by a leadership that was determined 'to avoid the political costs of a direct attack upon the existing social order' (Frankel 2005: 5, 32–47).

Within the confines of this bias against transformative politics, social movements from below eventually failed to impart a radical direction to the anti-colonial struggle. The Communists tried to become hegemonic among the peasants organizations related to Congress. By 1936, the All-India Kisan Sabha (AIKS) had been formed, bringing together small landowners, tenants and landless labourers on a platform that challenged the dominance of the feudal elite in the countryside. Yet, as the AIKS was increasingly radicalized, a split emerged with Congress. Faced with an ultimatum from Gandhi, the conflict was resolved in favour of the moderate elements of Congress, and the AIKS were gradually marginalized from 'the mainstream of the nationalist movement' (Frankel 2005: 62). A similar trajectory characterized organized labour. After WWII there was a significant labour upsurge in India, at the helm of which was the All-India Trade Union Congress (AITUC) and the Indian Federation of Labour (IFL), both of which were beyond Congress control and headed by radical leaders.[22] The radical thrust of the labour upsurge, however, was stymied by labour legislation passed in 1947, which, whilst making some concessions to labour, drastically curtailed the power of trade unions to compel collective bargaining (Chibber 2003: 120–2). Moreover, Congress and its federation of labour organizations, the Indian National Trade Union Congress (INTUC), which favoured arbitration over strike action, came to sideline AITUC. As the influence of INTUC grew, labour was eventually effectively demobilized, thus stymieing 'the agent that could have been pivotal in giving the state more leverage than the business class' (ibid.: 126).[23]

This leverage could indeed have been needed, for the demobilization of movements from below contrasts sharply with the sustained mobilization from above in the final decades before independence – especially from Indian capital. In the aftermath of the First World War, the Indian capitalist class 'emerged not only as an economic category with a growing independent base but was also able to organize itself as a self-conscious "class-for-itself"' (Mukherjee 2002: 19). Organized by the FICCI, Indian capital was supportive of Congress's goals of decolonization and independence, but simultaneously focused its energies on maintaining bourgeois hegemony within the nationalist movement. In particular, Indian capital focused on shaping the industrial planning policy that would be so central to Indian import-substitution industrialization. In 1944–45, the Bombay Plan was published, calling for the state to 'exercise . . . a considerable measure of intervention and control' (cited in Mukherjee 2002: 397). Now, what has to be understood is that the issuing of the Bombay Plan was 'fundamentally a defensive maneuver' intended to 'forestall future socialist attacks on business by opening the way for *capitalist* planning' (Chibber 2003: 97). The Bombay Plan was thus a response to radical elements in the National Planning Committee and the radicalization of the Quit India Movement. In the wake of independence, this strategy was to prove successful.

As much as it was clear that the future of the Indian nation was to be a capitalist one, it was also clear that capitalism would not be brought about through the kind of social movement from above associated with bourgeois revolutions, where the old order comes under attack from 'a group in society with an independent economic base, which attacks obstacles to a democratic version of capitalism that have been inherited from the past' (Moore 1991: xxi).[24] Fundamental structural features of the postcolonial social formation militated against this. On the one hand, capital was not 'independently dominant in Indian society and state' and 'single-handed and unaided dominance in society [was] also ruled out for the other propertied classes' (Kaviraj 1997: 52). On the other hand, the democratic character of the Indian polity and the fact of universal suffrage ruled out the kind of forcible expropriation of direct producers that had been at the heart of primitive accumulation in western Europe (Chatterjee 1993: 208).

These constraints were overcome through a strategy of 'passive revolution' (Kaviraj 1997; Chatterjee 1986, 1993). Jettisoning ambitions of 'a full-scale assault on all pre-capitalist dominant classes' (Chatterjee 1986: 48),[25] a social movement from above emerged that sought to advance capitalist development in a more molecular manner, on the basis of a fragile and unruly coalition between the industrial bourgeoisie, the landed elites and rich farmers, and the politico-bureaucratic elites.[26] Conversely, the problem of how 'to effect the required degree of dissociation of direct producers from their means of production' (Chatterjee 1993: 210) was resolved by consigning the articulation and implementation of development strategies to the field of planning, which was construed as a field in which experts engaged in 'the technical evaluation of alternative policies and the determination of choices on scientific grounds' (ibid.: 201) and arrived at objective assessments of 'the "necessary costs" to be borne by each particular group and the necessary "benefits" to accrue to each' would be determined 'within a universal framework of the common good' (ibid.: 210). Albeit contradictory, uneven and sluggish, the result of India's passive revolution was 'to enhance the power of those who were the most important holders of property rights – in the first place, the industrial and commercial bourgeoisie and the rich peasantry – and of the bureaucratic office holders whose discretionary powers were increased with the greatly expanded role of the bureaucracy as a whole' (Corbridge and Harriss 2000: 65).

In the field of agriculture, the consolidation of proprietary power occurred through the curtailment of land reforms to the extent that, if these reforms impacted at all, the primary beneficiary was the extant stratum of rich peasants. The sidelining of the AIKS prior to independence had undermined much of the momentum for a radical programme of land reform. This trend continued after independence as reform efforts encountered resistance at state level, where landed elites reigned supreme and effectively controlled the Congress apparatus, resulting in what Frankel (2005: 190) has called 'defective legislation'. Whereas the position of the feudal ruling class, the large zamindars, was undermined to a substantial extent, it was medium and small landlords and in particular rich peasants who were able to mould the implementation of land reforms so as to establish themselves as independent proprietors and 'in many areas of India, the new dominant class in the emerging agrarian structure' (Byres 1981: 423). Poor peasants gained very little from land reforms, and were often adversely affected by their class bias. These patterns of stratification were further enhanced from the 1960s onwards, when Indian authorities substituted land reforms for the technocratic strategy of agricultural development known as the Green Revolution (Frankel 1971, 2005; Varshney 1995; Byres 1981). Again, the rich peasantry benefited from the introduction of the new technology because it was 'deliberately steered towards the regions where they were most in ascendancy, and within those regions towards them' (Byres 1981: 425). In addition to this, India's rich peasantry were very effective in exercising its collective power to avoid taxation, which in turn meant that they were absolved 'of all responsibility of financing development' (Patnaik 1986: 15). Dominant landed classes were also able to control Community Development projects so as to enhance 'their access to scarce development resources' (Frankel 2005: 102).

In the realm of industry, the coming of independence witnessed heightened opposition to the ambitions of a strong interventionist state from Indian capital articulated by the Economic Committee of the Congress (Chibber 2003: 106). The institutions that were supposed to constitute the cornerstone of planning for industrial growth – the Planning Commission and the Industries Bill – bore the imprint of the concerted counter-offensive mobilized by industry as they 'were both, in their final design, fashioned to accommodate business designs as much as possible' (ibid.: 146, see pp. 170–92). The Indian strategy of import-substituting industrialization shielded domestic industry from competition by means of tariff barriers and restrictions on imports, and supported industrial development through the transfer of public funds in the form of subsidies, incentives and credits. However, such measures of protection and support were not complemented by the kind of disciplinary mechanisms that would allow the state to 'regulate and monitor the flow of capital, to ensure it went into targeted areas, and that it was used efficiently' (ibid.: 33). With the state being too weak to monitor and direct investments, there was no way to ensure that public funds were being deployed in socially useful ways: 'Capitalists were able to initiate a half-century long primitive accumulation, socializing their risks and losses, while privately appropriating the gains. The end result was that there was development and growth – but at an enormous cost to the public' (Chibber 2005b: 239).

This dynamic of resource transfer to dominant social groups through state development strategies was underpinned by the way in which subaltern social groups were co-opted into the Nehruvian state while at the same time being blocked from direct access to the processes of electoral politics.[27] In the aftermath of independence Congress built its organizational network by 'adopting local power structures' which in turn meant that 'local notables' served as 'intermediaries in the relationship between the village and outside authorities in the administration and government' and 'controlled the "vote banks" built on the loyalties of local faction members' (Frankel 2005: 23). Thus, just as subaltern social groups had been deprived of direct access to the Congress organization during the anti-colonial struggle, they were deprived of direct access to electoral politics after independence, which resulted in the failure to convert 'the superior numbers of the poor into a powerful political resource' (Frankel 2005: 25).

Elite support for the postcolonial development project proved to be very resilient. As much as the Indian economy started to stagnate in the mid-1960s and remained mired by sluggishness until the 1980s, there was significant support for the strategy of state intervention among the country's dominant proprietary classes[28] (Corbridge and Harriss 2000: 102–3; see also Vanaik 2001; Chibber 2003; Kohli 2006a/b). Eventually, however, the internal contradictions of the postcolonial development project – and in particular the inability of the state to tax propertied elites (Frankel 2005: 512; see also Byres 1981: 445–6) – came home to roost. When the Indian economy recovered from stagnation in the 1980s, this happened due to 'a big increase in the fiscal stimulus to the economy provided by government spending' (Chandrasekhar and Ghosh 2002: 9) which was financed in large part by external commercial borrowing. By the beginning of the 1990s, this had created an untenable fiscal situation: the public coffers were drained of foreign exchange and the state's credit ranking was so low that further loans from foreign banks were not forthcoming (Frankel 2005: 590). Underpinned by loans from the IMF, the World Bank and the Asian Development Bank, reforms to redress the crisis were introduced in the 1991/92 budget presented by Finance Minister Manmohan Singh of Narasimha Rao's Congress government in June 1991.

However, whereas the fiscal crisis of the early 1990s created a conjunctural opening for market reforms, it does not by itself explain why elite resistance had given way to elite support for neoliberal restructuring. Neoliberal reforms were being pushed ahead by a social movement from above that reflected 'the emergence of new business groups, which saw the regime of internal controls as an impediment to their own ascent to power' and as 'a formidable barrier to entry into increasingly lucrative markets' (Chibber 2003: 249, 252; see also Corbridge and Harriss 2000: 137–45; Chandrasekhar and Ghosh 2002: 31–7). Reflected in the formation of the Confederation of Indian Industry,[29] these new business groups explicitly sought 'to work toward a globalization of Indian industry' and to promote 'deregulation, de-control, and de-licensing in all areas' (Pedersen 2000: 270). Crucially, the changes in the attitudes of sections of Indian capital to liberalization intersected with the growing influence of a segment of the politico-bureaucratic elite which nurtured 'close links with the IMF and the World Bank' and whose inclinations naturally veered 'in the direction of the Fund-Bank policy regime' (Chandrasekhar and Ghosh 2002: 37). This constellation of political-economic elites came to constitute the bedrock of the social movement from above for neoliberal reform in India.

The adjustment policies that were implemented in the early 1990s had a fourfold aim: (i) to reduce state-imposed controls on capacity creation, production and prices; (ii) to open up the economy to international competition; (iii) to roll back the presence of the state in production and trade; and (iv) to thoroughly liberalize the financial sector (Chandrasekhar and Ghosh 2002: 22). Observers have eagerly pointed out the partiality and unevenness of neoliberal reforms in India, as well as the lack of leverage on part of the state in terms of pushing the reform agenda into a second stage (see Corbridge and Harriss 2000; Vanaik 2001; Frankel 2005). However, the early 2000s arguably witnessed a more assertive implementation of neoliberal accumulation strategies in India.

This was evident from the increasingly aggressive approach to privatization of public sector undertakings. The initial and relatively careful attempts at disinvestment in the public sector that characterized the early and mid-1990s came to give way to increasingly higher targets of disinvestment as well as more lucrative deals for potential takers (Chandrasekhar and Ghosh 1999; 2002: 88). First, the prices of equity were lowered. Second, the prime assets of the public sector were offered up for sale. Third, the government had to offer managerial control to investors from the private sector, even in cases where they were minority shareholders (ibid.: 91–2). Still facing a lack of interest from the private sector, the BJP-led National Democratic Alliance government in 2001 opted for accelerated and time-bound disinvestment, which further enhanced the bargaining position of private sector investors in relation to the state (ibid.: 93). By 2003, this had led to a scenario in which several key public industries were up for grabs for the corporate sector. The disinvestment drive came to a temporary halt in 2006, when the Congress encountered opposition from the left parties which lent support to the UPA government, but with the sidelining of the left in the general elections of 2009, an aggressive programme of disinvestment of public sector undertakings is once again on the agenda.[30]

A more recent example of the increasingly aggressive implementation of neoliberal accumulation strategies is of course the Special Economic Zones (SEZs) policy which was introduced in 2005 and became operative in 2006. Seeking to redress the lag in foreign direct investment, the policy offers a range of incentives for capital to invest in the establishment of Special Economic Zones, ranging from a single-window clearance mechanism for SEZ proposal, via strict control of labour to fiscal incentives that are so generous that both the Indian Finance Ministry and the

Asian Development Bank have warned against serious revenue losses as a consequence of the policy (Ramakrishnan 2006; Aggarwal 2006). In early 2007, state governments had notified more than 260 SEZs, the establishment of which would require in excess of half-a-million acres of land, yet neither had specific legal provisions for resettlement and compensation related to land acquisition been established, nor had responsible authorities carried out any research on the number of people that were likely to be affected by land acquisition (Chandra and Basu 2007; Shridar 2006). Indeed, the rush to establish SEZs, as Chandrasekhar (2006) argues, is clearly 'nothing short of a crude form of primitive accumulation of capital' (see also Sampat 2008) – a rush which recently received a shot across the bough as farmers' resistance eventually put a stop to the Maha Mumbai SEZ at Raigad (Bavadam 2009).

A decade and a half of reform in India, then, has done a lot to install the key modalities that according to Harvey (2005: 160–3) facilitate the workings of accumulation by dispossession in its neoliberal mode. Through the management and manipulation of a fiscal crisis, dominant proprietary classes have managed to push ahead reforms centred on privatization, liberalization and financialization. Moreover, neoliberal economic policies have undermined state redistribution of market-generated incomes through reductions of public expenditure related to the social wage and forms of subsidies which previously kept petty-commodity producers afloat in the Indian economy (see Patnaik 2003; Corbridge and Harriss 2000).

These modalities of dispossession are at work throughout India. In such cases as the Maheshwar dam in the Narmada Valley, and in the Special Economic Zones proliferating from Maharashtra and Haryana to West Bengal and Orissa, in the profound crisis of small and medium agricultural producers throughout India, and in the capillary mechanisms of dispossession evident in the attempts at corporate take-over of shoe-shining on Mumbai's metropolitan trains and street-vending on Delhi's sidewalks, productive resources are being transferred to propertied elites, be they of domestic or transnational origin, whilst the livelihoods of subaltern social majorities are undermined and abrogated. Increasingly, these processes of dispossession are also coming to be undergirded by state coercion and repression. Recent examples include the shooting of 12 Munda adivasis who were protesting their displacement due to the construction of a major steel plant at Kalinga Nagar in Orissa in January 2005, the killing of three people in Manipur on December 2005 as security forces opened fire on protestors raising demands for R&R for dam oustees, and in 2007 the killing of villagers protesting against the acquisition of land for the establishment of SEZs in West Bengal and Orissa (see Baviskar and Sundar 2008).

Concluding remarks

In this chapter I have argued that in the distributional bias of the impacts of dam-building on the Narmada River it is possible to discern a case of accumulation by dispossession which is intrinsically related to regional processes of class formation as well as the fundamental dynamics of capitalist development as it has been moulded by social movements from above in postcolonial India.

In the first part of the chapter, I showed how the SSP will concentrate property rights in irrigation and water in the hands of agroindustrial capitalists who have risen to dominance in south and central Gujarat in the postcolonial period. I also showed how submergence of land by the SSP reservoir will displace adivasi communities engaged in subsistence production and caste Hindu farming communities engaged in petty commodity production in Western Madhya Pradesh, and that due to a lack of adequate policies for R&R, displacement will generate pressures towards the proletarianization of these communities. In both cases, displacement can be understood as moments in more long-term processes of dispossession.

In the second part of the chapter I showed how, in the case of the MHP, accumulation by dispossession again occurs at the cost of petty commodity producers in Nimad, but favours different dominant groups in different ways and through different modalities. The chief beneficiaries of the MHP are national and transnational industrial and financial capital for whom the project constitutes a profitable investment opportunity, and as such, an outlet for surplus capital. This constellation has in turn been rendered possible by two key processes related to the introduction of neoliberal reforms in the Indian economy – financial liberalization and privatization of the power sector.

In the third and final part of the chapter I sought to embed accumulation by dispossession in the Narmada Valley in the fundamental dynamics of capitalist development in postcolonial India. I argued that the extension and entrenchment of capitalist relations in India has occurred through a 'passive revolution' in which a social movement from above has been able to set limits and exert pressures on the articulation and implementation of key state development strategies to the extent that such strategies have resulted in the concentration of means of production in the hands of dominant proprietary classes, and, conversely, the dissociation of subaltern social groups from their means of production. More recently, the advent of neoliberal reform – animated by a social movement from above rooted in domestic elite groups from whom state-led capitalist development had come to constitute a barrier to continued growth and expansion – has effected the installation of accumulation strategies which facilitate the appropriation of productive resources by industrial and finance capital, and intensify the abrogation of subaltern access to means of subsistence and production.

It is within this wider field of force – moulded by asymmetrical power relations and the conscious exercise of agency by dominant social groups – that the movement process in the Narmada Valley, to which I now turn, has unfolded.

3 Everyday tyranny and rightful resistance

The emergence of the Khedut Mazdoor Chetna Sangath

Early March, 2003 – beneath a makeshift shelter that had been put up outside the *tehsil* headquarters in the centre of Alirajpur town, some 150 adivasi activists from the Narmada Bachao Andolan had gathered for a *dharna* – a sit-down demonstration – to protest the imminent submergence of their villages as the height of the SSP was being raised to 95 metres. Throughout most of the day, the activists compiled files of papers that confirmed the villagers' right to resettlement and rehabilitation (R&R), and discussed plans of action for the coming days; their efforts were centred on eliciting a commitment from the sub-divisional magistrate – the most senior administrative official in the *tehsil* – that he would deal with the complaints of the dam-affected communities.

Early one afternoon, as a response to the magistrate's protracted refusal to enter into discussion with the protesters, the decision was made to carry out a *gherao*[1] in which the activists would storm and lay siege to the *tehsil* headquarters and prevent the magistrate from leaving until he had addressed their demands. They crossed the road and approached a couple of officials who were hanging out around the doorstep on the ground floor, and demanded that the magistrate should come out and talk to them immediately. The magistrate, however, refused to step outside his office. The activists then made their way past the officials on the ground floor and filed up the stairs to the first floor where they sat down outside the door of the magistrate's office, chanting slogans and singing protest songs. The *gherao* eventually developed into something of a stalemate: the police arrived, but did not take any action; the activists stood their ground, and demanded a written list of names of the people whose lands were to be submerged; the magistrate persisted in refusing to meet with the protesters and eventually emerged from his office with a brief statement washing his hands of all responsibility for R&R of project-affected persons. The *gherao* was called off when the magistrate retreated to his office and exited out the back door (field notes, March 2003).

For many – perhaps most – of the activists who stormed the *tehsil* headquarters on that afternoon, it was only one of many – perhaps countless – *gheraos* they had taken part in through their involvement with the NBA; indeed, non-violent direct action such as that described here has been a mainstay of the repertoire of contention deployed in the anti-dam struggle in the Narmada Valley since its very inception in the late 1980s. Nevertheless, the very fact that the *gherao* actually took place is far from inconsequential.

Two decades earlier, activists coming to work in the adivasi communities in Alirajpur encountered communities that were subjected to severe forms of coercion and extortion at the hands of local state officials – a form of coercion that I shall refer to as everyday tyranny. Rather than openly opposing such coercion, the villagers practised a submissive deference that minimized the risks of violent retaliation by forest rangers, police officers and revenue officials. This relationship of dominance and subjugation, however, was ruptured when two former NGO workers intent to organize and mobilize in these communities arrived on the scene. After establishing links with the communities, they gradually started to confront state officials on specific cases of malpractice and extortion. Their challenge to the local overlords was eventually successful and this success became the starting point for a process of mobilization – a militant particularist struggle centred on defending the communities' customary use rights to forest resources, and the constitutional rights and entitlements they held by virtue of being Indian citizens as well as Scheduled Tribes – which resulted in the formation of the trade union Khedut Mazdoor Chetna Sangath (KMCS; The Peasants and Workers' Consciousness Union) in the *tehsil* of Alirajpur in the early and mid-1980s.

The KMCS organized more than 100 adivasi communities on issues of customary use rights to forest resources and administrative malpractice by state officials in the area. The SSP and its impacts entered into its purview when it became clear that 26 of the villages in which the KMCS was active would be affected by the SSP reservoir. In 1986, the KMCS came to collaborate with the social action groups that were emerging in the dam-affected adivasi communities in Maharashtra and Gujarat (see Chapter 4) and facilitated a survey of the 26 villages by the Delhi-based Multiple Action Research Group (MARG). The MARG survey clearly revealed the failure of state authorities to recognize the right of the communities to information about the impact of the project and their rights and entitlements as project-affected people:

> In none of the 26 villages, had the government of MP given any notices under Section 4 or Section 6 of the Land Acquisition Act (1894) . . . In no cases have the district authorities in MP informed the villagers about the dam.
>
> (MARG cited in Dwivedi 2006: 156)

From this point onwards, the KMCS, whereas it retained its separate organizational identity and structure, was a key player in mobilizing the dam-affected communities in Alirajpur – initially around demands for the right to information and the right to R&R, and later around the efforts to stop the SSP. The basic argument developed in this chapter is that the process of mobilization engendered a profound transformation of the local rationalities which guided people's perception of and engagement with the unequal and oppressive power relations that were constitutive of everyday tyranny. The fear and submission which had underpinned the coercive reign of local officials gave way to a perception that resistance was fertile rather than futile, and practices of deference were substituted for the practical skills of assertive and knowledgeable engagement with the state and its representatives. And this transformative process has been the cornerstone of adivasi participation in the struggle against dam-building on the Narmada.

The argument unfolds in three parts. In the first part of the chapter I describe everyday tyranny as a lived experience. I then trace its roots to the criminalization of customary use of state-owned forests and forest resources as well as adivasi cultural practices. I portray how the adivasi communities negotiated this extortion through a local rationality centred on deference and submission in daily life, and relate this to experiences of failed mobilization in the recent past. I also engage with everyday tyranny as a local state-society relationship, the signal features of which were a de facto absence of rights and entitlements in relation to the state among the adivasis and, concurrently, a de facto absence of accountability of the state and its officials to adivasis as citizens and members of a population with legally defined rights and entitlements. Finally, I show how a capacity for resistance was created in the adivasi communities through the intervention of urban, educated activists. I detail the character of the initial confrontations with local representatives of the state, how these confrontations in turn spiralled into a successful challenge to everyday tyranny, and how this eventually resulted in the widening and deepening of mobilization throughout the adivasi communities of Alirajpur. The second part of the chapter engages more briefly with the formation and politics of the KMCS. I focus on how mobilization spread throughout south and east Alirajpur through a series of successful confrontations with local state-officials, and how the KMCS came to promulgate a politics centred on the defence of customary rights and the claiming of citizenship and constitutional rights and entitlements by and for the adivasi communities. The third and final part of the chapter presents a detailed analysis of the transformation of local rationalities and how this transformation engendered a set of emotional dispositions, cognitive resources, and practical skills that underpinned a militant particularism centred on what O'Brien and Li (2006: 24) have referred to as 'rightful resistance'. Finally, the politics of rightful resistance in Alirajpur is discussed in light of divergent perspectives on the extent to which the state can be said to constitute an enabling space for the struggles of subaltern groups in India.

The contours of everyday tyranny

Living with everyday tyranny

Describing the attempts of activists to mobilize adivasis to take part in a protest against the cruelties of local state officials in Alirajpur town in some two decades ago, a KMCS activist describes how 'after much persuasion' they managed to organize 'a small rally of some fifty people'. However, the adivasi participants 'continually deserted the rally on being called by their *sahukars* to explain why they were participating in it' (Banerjee 2003: 16). The *sahukar* is a Hindu or Muslim moneylender, and alongside local state officials he constitutes a towering authority in adivasi life.[2] The disruption of the protest was a direct outcome of the immobilizing fear that was at the heart of the relationship between adivasis and powerful outsiders – be they moneylenders or local representatives of the state – throughout Alirajpur. The reasons for this fear were clearly brought out to me a couple of days after the siege of the *tehsil* headquarters described in the introduction to this chapter, when during a lull in the *dharna*, I got talking to Ratan, an adivasi activist from the village of Sugat, about how he came to be involved with the KMCS and the NBA. Gradually, the conversation turned to the relationship between the villagers and the local state officials prior to the mobilizational efforts of the KMCS and the NBA:

> In past times, Ratan claims, when his village was still under the reign of the prince in Mathvad, the villagers could freely enter and use the forest to clear plots of land for cultivation, to gather firewood and building materials, and to graze their livestock. However, with the end of the prince's reign came the end of these rights: the officials working for the forest department and the revenue department, as well as the local police, started to harass and extort the villagers. The fear of the officials was such that, if two brothers were caught working on a field in the forest, one of them would do the ploughing, and the other would stand guard to look out for the forest rangers. If they were caught ploughing their field, they risked being beaten up, or having their hand nailed to the trunk of a tree. Invariably, villagers that were caught cultivating their plots in the forest would be taken to the local police station, where they would be savagely beaten. A case would be filed against them for encroaching on reserved forests and this would be used as a means to extort money from the villagers – a handsome bribe would make the charges disappear. Ratan also recounts how, if a villager ran into the officials on the road, they would often demand that he or she carry their bags for them. If they refused – and even if they failed to greet the officials politely – they would be given a heavy bashing.
>
> (interview, March 2003)

Ratan's account of violence, coercion and extortion at the hands of local state officials is only one of many that I came across as I spoke to and interviewed activists from the adivasi communities of Alirajpur.[3] In these accounts, the officials of the forest department, revenue department, and the police were consistently singled out as agents of oppression.

Echoing Ratan's story of the violent extortion meted out by forest rangers, activists in the village of Kakrana recounted how villagers, if they were caught walking along the road carrying a sickle, they would be accused of going to collect fodder from the forest and beaten up; the officials would invariably demand money from them if they wanted to avoid criminal charges. Similarly, if people were caught with an axe, or if they were carrying firewood, they would risk beatings and extortion. If someone needed to cut down trees to get building materials for constructing a house, the forest guards demanded a bribe of 2,500 rupees, chickens and liquor. In fact, in Kakrana, it seems that the extortion of bribes was regularized in the sense that the forest guards would charge a fixed amount from the village for allowing people to use the forests for agriculture and grazing (various interviews, March 2003).

Officials would also crack down on various cultural practices related to festivals, marriages and indigenous forms of dispute settlement. There are a range of festivals in which home-brewed liquor plays an important role. However, the domestic brewing of liquor is illegal, so the local police outpost would make every household in the hamlet send them chickens as a bribe to turn a blind eye to these activities. Also, if the police came across someone brewing liquor, they would take the person to the police outpost, bash him up and demand a bribe of 1,000–1,500 rupees. For example, Indal is a major festival to celebrate good crops and good harvests. In order for the police to let the festival be carried out in peace, the villagers would go to the police station in Sondwa and pay a bribe of 500–1,000 rupees. If a person was found intoxicated during the festivals, the person would be bashed up, and a bribe would be demanded both from this person, and from the family that hosted him or her. The adivasi marriage system is different from the practice of arranged marriages found in caste Hindu communities. In the adivasi communities, men and women themselves choose to live together, and the woman then comes to live with the man and his family. If they got news of a marriage having taken place, the police would call the man's parents to their quarters to enquire whether the girl came to their house of her own free will. To 'prove' that this was the case, the family would have to pay a bribe of 1,000 rupees, five or six kilos of flour, onions and *ghee* (clarified butter). If there was a dispute in the village, informers were likely to report this to the police. The police would in turn call the implicated parties to the police station, where they would be beaten up and a bribe of 2,000 rupees would be demanded. If the village headman settled the dispute, as is the traditional practice of dispute resolution in the village, he would be called to the police station and a bribe would be demanded from him (interview, Kemat, March 2003).

Moreover, officials would often demand various services from the villagers; for instance, they could be forced to collect and deliver firewood to the officials, or to wash the officials' clothes – all free of charge. If officials came to their villages, they would demand to be given a cot to rest on and, furthermore that the villagers cook them a meal (field notes, March 2003). Indeed, as one of the urban educated activists that had been active with the KMCS put it, the local representatives of the state had imposed 'a feudal stranglehold' on the adivasi communities of Alirajpur (interview, Chittaroopa Palit, May 2003). I shall refer to this stranglehold as *everyday tyranny*, and in the next section I discuss its basis in forest legislation and caste ideology, its reproduction as an outcome of a prevailing local rationality of fear and submission, and, finally, its character as a state-society relationship.

The origins, dynamics and characteristics of everyday tyranny

Everyday tyranny was essentially predicated upon a two-pronged criminalization – first, the criminalization of indigenous use rights in relation to forests and forest resources; second the criminalization of indigenous cultural practices. When forest rangers filed charges against people who had been found tilling their fields in the forest, they did this with reference to Indian forest legislation, which establishes 'the right of the state to exclusive control over forest protection, production and management' (Gadgil and Guha 1993: 185). The lineage of this legislation can in turn be traced to the appropriation and commodification of India's forests by the British colonial state. To secure access to timber – initially for the building of ships and then for the expansion of railways – the colonial state resorted to legislation, culminating in the Indian Forest Act of 1878, which established 'the absolute proprietary right of the state' to India's forests, and thus abrogated 'by one stroke of the executive pen . . . centuries of customary use by rural populations all over India' (Gadgil and Guha 1993: 134; see also Prasad 2004; Singh 1986; Mahapatra 1993). The abrogation of customary use rights in turn entailed that clearing and cultivating fields in the forest – one of the key dimensions of adivasi livelihoods – as well as other customary uses of the forest came to be designated as 'encroachments' on state property (Prasad 2004: 32). Similarly, the criminalization of indigenous cultural practices such as traditional systems of arbitration administered by village elders similarly reflects the impact of state formation on adivasi communities.

Criminalization and the resultant coercion and extortion were mediated by and through caste ideology. Adivasis are located at the bottom of the caste hierarchy, and are commonly despised by non-adivasis as 'sub-human, as objects of contempt and ridicule mingled with an underlying current of fear' (Baviskar 2001: 10). Thus, the relationship between adivasis villagers and Hindu townspeople – *bazaarias* – is suffused with 'the brutal contempt of the Hindu bazaaria for adivasis because they eat meat and drink alcohol' (Baviskar 1995: 82). As is evident in the accounts cited earlier, this contempt clearly shaped the relationship between adivasis and the representatives of an administrative apparatus 'which is overwhelmingly manned by non-adivasis' (Baviskar 2001: 9).

The reproduction of everyday tyranny hinged upon two basic factors. On the one hand, criminalization did not translate into actual attempts by local state officials to end adivasi cultivation in the forest, home-brewing or conflict resolution by village headmen and elders. Rather, for the local state officials, the illegality of customary use of the forest and certain indigenous cultural practices served as a lever for unlawful extraction of money and services. As a former KMCS activist writes of instances where forest rangers come across adivasis cultivating their *nevad* fields or collecting timber for building materials: 'The tacit understanding . . . prevailing between the adivasi and the local staff of the forest department in such circumstances is for the forest guard to take a bribe and look the other way' (Banerjee 2003: 1). On the other hand, the extraction of bribes was not confronted and resisted by the villagers; it was, rather, something that they complied with: 'the constant transactions between the forest officials and the people made it apparent to the adivasis that the intention of the fines was not to *stop* nevad but, on the contrary, to make it possible by appeasing the state' (Baviskar 1995: 178; italics in original). The giving and taking of bribes, in short, had been woven into the fabric of daily life to such an extent that it became a guiding principle of how relations and interactions between adivasis and state officials were supposed to be conducted.

Compliance with extortion on behalf of the adivasi communities was rooted in their fear of and perceived powerlessness in relation to state officials. Activists throughout the adivasi villages of Alirajpur would point to how the capacity of state officials to dole out punitive sanctions in response to belligerence and defiance was well-known and widely feared in the communities, and effectively undercut any capacity for or propensity towards open resistance (field notes, March 2003). Fear was in turn interlaced with and underpinned by ignorance – first of the illegality of the exaction of bribes, and second of the fact that the adivasis were themselves bearers of rights and entitlements by virtue of being citizens of the Indian state and members of a Scheduled Tribe. As I discuss in more detail later, when urban educated activists or high-ranking politicians and bureaucrats pointed out that the local officials' coercion was in fact unlawful, this was news to most of the villagers. A former KMCS activist portrayed the scenario as follows: 'the Indian constitution was not known to these people; they used to think of this as a *raj*, and of the police and the ranger as a *raja*' (interview, Rahul Banerjee, April 2003).

However, the lack of a capacity for and propensity towards resistance has by no means been a constant feature of adivasi relations to external social groups and forces; rather, the history of Bhil and Bhilala adivasis in western India 'has been a chronicle of incorporation and resistance' (Baviskar 1995: 85). In the early nineteenth century groups would set out from the hills towards the plains to raid wealthy Hindu farming communities, and the adivasis also resisted the incursions of Kanbi Patidars from Gujarat under the auspices of the British; the British policy of pacification of the adivasi areas encountered large-scale adivasi resistance in the 1840s; and in defiance of the repression of the great rebellion of 1857, adivasi resistance continued for several years under the leadership of figures such as Nimlia Rutina, Bheema Naik and Khajya Naik – the names of whom live on in the collective memories of the communities (ibid.: 56–65). Nevertheless, it seems that it was precisely collective memories of involvement in resistance that were at the heart of the awareness of the punitive consequences of such involvement.

In the 1950s and early 1960s, Jhabua witnessed intense mobilization by the Lal Topi Andolan, a socialist movement championing the right of adivasis to access and use forest land. The movement was headed by Baleshwar Dayal Dikshit, whose political activity in the area dated back to the 1930s, when he spearheaded campaigns against adivasi *begaar* – forced labour – for the feudal princes of Jhabua and against the usurious practices of the *sahukars*. The Lal Topi Andolan gained significant momentum – reflected in the electoral victories of socialist candidates endorsed by the movement in Jhabua in state and general elections in the 1950s and 1960s – but eventually failed to extend its influence more widely in Madhya Pradesh and gradually ran out of steam in the 1960s. Movement leaders recruited from the adivasi communities were co-opted into the Congress Party, while those who chose to stay with the movement were subjected to violent beatings, arrests and false charges at the hands of the police (Banerjee 1999, 2003; Baviskar 1995: 83–4). Once bitten by repression, people were clearly and understandably twice shy of resistance.

As a state-society relationship, everyday tyranny was of course far removed from the liberal-democratic ideals of citizenship enshrined in the Indian constitution.

Drawing on the terminology of Corbridge *et al.* (2005), one could say that the local state in Alirajpur was not 'seen' or 'encountered' as a set of agencies and functionaries that provided services to and were accountable to the citizens of a political community.[4] On the contrary, adivasi 'sightings of the state' (ibid.: 5) were centred on seemingly all-powerful 'tyrants' who imposed a cruel regime of extortion upon their 'subjects' with a heavy hand, and who responded to defiance with violence and coercion. In the context of everyday tyranny, citizenship was undermined in two basic ways: first, through 'the absence of public enforcement of a universal legal order' and the engagement of the state in 'the violation of citizens' rights', and, second, through 'the absence of the social conditions that make possible the effective exercise of citizenship' due to 'the presence of sharp economic disparities and inherited social inequalities' (Jayal 2000: 26, 27). Indeed, the relationship between local state officials and the adivasi communities was in important respects reminiscent of the structural characteristics of slavery, serfdom, and caste subordination delineated by James Scott:

> Each represents an institutionalized arrangement for appropriating labor, goods, and services from a subordinate population. As a formal matter, subordinate groups in these forms of domination have no political or civil rights, and their status is fixed by birth . . . The ideologies justifying domination of this kind include formal assumptions about inferiority and superiority which, in turn find expression in certain rituals or etiquette regarding public contact between strata . . . An element of personal terror invariably infuses these relations – a terror may take the form of arbitrary beatings, sexual brutality, insults and public humiliation.
>
> (1990: x–xi)

Everyday tyranny exhibits all these features: the entrenched extortion of money, foodstuffs and services; the *de facto* absence of political and civil rights in interactions with state officials, compounded by the lack of awareness among the adivasis of their being bearers of *de jure* rights; the suffusion of interactions between adivasis and state officials by caste ideology; the underpinning of the relationship of domination and subjugation by the fear of violence.[5]

Yet, something changed; as activists typically put it in interviews and conversations, at some point they 'stopped being afraid' and came to participate actively in open resistance to the everyday tyranny of local state officials. The question, then, is a simple but important one: how could it be that adivasis who in the early 1980s had barely dared to gather in a public protest in Alirajpur town confidently marched past their former oppressors and laid siege to their administrative stronghold in 2003?

Confronting everyday tyranny

The capacity for resistance displayed in the *gherao* of the *tehsil* headquarters, and in countless other protest actions that the adivasis of Alirajpur participated in throughout the 1980s and 1990s, was forged in the process that would eventually lead to the formation of the KMCS. The origins of this process, in turn, can be traced to the arrival of two young men – Khemraj and Amit – in Alirajpur in the early 1980s, and their consequent engagement with everyday tyranny in the adivasi communities.

The decision made by Khemraj and Amit to go to Alirajpur to work among adivasis was attributed to their frustration with the apolitical character of the work they were doing through the NGO Social Work and Research Centre in Tilonia, Rajasthan (see Banerjee 1994: 813; Baviskar 1995: 176):

> . . . they had been working with an organization called the Social Work and Research Centre . . . they'd been setting up hand pumps and so on. And apparently the institution had said that our relationship is appropriate technology, and not of intervening in social structure, but after all that, when the hand pumps were put in, during the process, Khemraj and others found that it was really the more dominant groups who got all the hand pumps and the water, and, you know, the poorer people, the so-called low people, they didn't get access to that water. So it was obvious that it was not either caste or community neutral . . . So they decided that they wanted to work in an area that was so-called backward, where there were adivasis, they wanted to work with adivasis.
>
> (interview, Chittaroopa Palit, May 2003)

Other activists situate their own entry into the activities of the KMCS similarly in the changes that were occurring in Indian left politics in the 1970s:

> I was part of a Marxist student front and all that, and I at that point of time was a Marxist. The problem was that in Bengal, where I come from, in Calcutta, at that time in the late 1970s, the problem was that this whole Naxalite movement had splintered totally, so I was part of a group of one of these splinters, so I didn't see any scope for action . . . there was no party, you know, to give shape to this radicalism. So I was in a sort of 'what to do' and all that. This is when I went to this NGO in which Khemraj was working, which was a pretty famous NGO at that time, Social Work Research Centre . . . So I thought 'Ok, let's try this out, because there's nothing happening here. Let's see what can be done'. That's how I drifted into this whole thing.
>
> (interview, Rahul Banerjee, April 2003)

The phenomenon of young, radical people seeking out subaltern rural communities as the targets of their efforts in politicized grassroots organizing is expressive of a general trend in Indian oppositional politics in the 1970s, referred to by Kamat (2002) as 'the new grassroots movement' (see Chapter 1).

Within this wider context, Amit and Khemraj arrived in Alirajpur in October 1982. Their point of entry into mobilization in the adivasi communities was Khemla, a young man from the area who was known for his belligerent attitude towards state officials – a belligerence, some suggested, that was passed down from his father who participated in the Lal Topi Andolan (field notes, March 2003). Shankar, a KMCS activist residing in Alirajpur town, conveyed the story of the initial efforts at mobilization as follows:

> When they first met, Khemla explained the problems of the tribal communities of the area to Khemraj. The two of them then travelled to Khemla's village, Chhoti Begalgaon near Mathvad, where they would stick together, herding the family's goats. The irrigation department was constructing a pond in the area, and Khemraj and Khemla discovered that the workers were being paid only four rupees per day, which was well below the minimum wage. When they confronted the contractors with this, they responded by beating up Khemla. However, the news of this incident spread in the area, and Khemla and Khemraj were contacted by people from different villages throughout the area, who informed them about the atrocities that were being committed by state officials and contractors in the region. The two of them then started travelling and working throughout the area. In the village of Gondwani, people were terrified of the forest officials, and Khemraj and Khemla would have to enter the village after night had fallen so as not to be found out by the forest officials. The villagers would then tell them about the atrocities committed by the officials of the forest department.
>
> (interview, April 2003)

The news that this confrontation had occurred spread, and seems to have had 'a dual function of informing and mobilizing at the same time' (Guha 2002: 227). By sheltering the activists and introducing them to other aspects of everyday tyranny, villagers effectively contributed to the mobilizing efforts of the newcomers.

In a particular case, a villager had been picked up by the officials and taken to the forest department depot in Attha, where he was severely beaten up. Khemraj and some of the villagers went to the forest depot to intervene in the situation. The forest officials beat Khemraj to a pulp, and the villagers accompanying him had to take him to hospital. About a dozen of the villagers proceeded to sit on a *dharna* in front of the *tehsil* offices; press notes were circulated, and the incident became news. Arjun Singh of the Congress Party, who was then Chief Minister of Madhya Pradesh, responded by suspending six of the forest guards. This created a general feeling of confidence in the activists, and the news of their success spread rapidly. It was a crucial incident due to the fact that, up until then, the forest department and the forest guards had seemed invincible. More and more people gradually got into contact with Khemraj and Khemla, who then took the matter to Bhopal, where they met with Digvijay Singh, then president of the Congress Party in Madhya Pradesh, and the Chief Minister. The Chief Minister in turn then sent the Forest Conservator, the head of the forest department in the state, to Mathvad, where a huge crowd had gathered. Prior to this event, the villagers experience of the forest guards had been that of a group of people who dealt out bashings, took chickens and other food, and demanded bribes with impunity, and they asked the Conservator whether such practices were lawful or not. When he replied that it was illegal, the villagers argued that the forest guards were clearly not following his orders. In response, the Forest Conservator implored the villagers to file complaints if such incidents took place again (interview, Shankar, April 2003).

The struggles over the issue of minimum wages and the success of the challenge mounted to the Forest Department were decisive turning points in the sense that they engendered the first tangible crevices in the workings of everyday tyranny. With the confrontation with the Forest Department the dynamic of mobilization escalated. Whereas the challenge from the activists was once again met with violent repression, this did not entail defeat; rather, it spurred a resolve to take the matter further. By staging a *dharna* in front of the *tehsil* offices in Alirajpur the activists shifted the focus of defiance and challenge further up the administrative ladder. The subsequent intervention by the Chief Minister of the state further intensified this escalation, and this in turn fed back into the mobilization process by generating confidence among the villagers in the commitment and skills of the activists, and by showing that it was in fact possible to win concessions from the state. Yet another round of escalation took place when more people got in touch with the activists and they decided to take the matter to the state capital. The meeting with Digvijay Singh and Arjun Singh, which resulted in the Forest Conservator being sent to Mathvad to hear the people's complaints, might seem like an insignificant event, but it did in fact represent a resounding and quite spectacular success.

This becomes particularly clear if these events are seen in relation to how the collective memory of the defeat and subsequent repression of the Lal Topi Andolan constituted a veritable barrier to mobilization in the adivasi communities. This initial victory amounted to nothing less than a reversal of the 'grammar' of the local rationality of everyday tyranny and the collective memories of defeat. First, the fact that the activists managed to elicit responses in their favour from the Chief Minister, the leader of the Congress Party, and the Forest Conservator – not to speak of the fact that they dared to challenge the local agents of oppression in the first place – constituted a radical volte-face of the presence of the state as negation of citizenship, and, moreover, struck at the heart of the fear which maintained everyday tyranny as a local rationality. Second, the very fact that victories – no matter how small they might seem – could be won, contradicted extant memories of defeat, and demonstrated in a very tangible way that mobilizing against and challenging the state and its representatives could in fact make a difference. For example, Luharia, one of the central KMCS and NBA activists from the village of Jalsindhi recounted how prior to the KMCS coming to the village they were all scared of the officials. Almost all the villagers had cases registered against them for encroaching in government forests. Referring back to the *dharna* in Alirajpur in the aftermath of Khemraj's beating, he claimed that the effect of this action was to reduce the atrocities committed by the officials. The villagers learned how to get organized; whenever officials would come to the village, they would gather and prevent them from entering. They gained the courage to argue with the officials, and they learnt how to argue with them. Gulabia, Luharia's brother, also emphasized that they had learned 'how to speak' and who to speak to in order to put forward their grievances, claims and demands. Through their interaction with the activists, they had obtained a lot of information that helped them in dealing with the government officials (interviews, March 2003). Third, the fact that throughout this process, the activists who had come from outside to provide some sort of leadership had stuck to their word and had been willing to put themselves in harm's way to champion the rights of the adivasi communities, contrasted with the experience of co-optation, and a deep-seated fear of outsiders. According to a former KMCS activist, Khemla's beating was the moment when 'the ice broke' between the urban, educated activists and the villagers (interview, Chittaroopa Palit, April 2003). A village activist from Kakrana commented that the urban educated outsiders differed from the state officials in their conduct: whenever officials came to Kakrana, they would demand pillows and blankets to sit on, but the activists did not want this kind of treatment; they would sit on the ground, and eat whatever was cooked in the house. A warm and personal relationship developed, where activists would stay in the villages like members of the family (interview, Kemat, March 2003; see also Baviskar 1995: 176). These mutual bonds of trust, respect and friendship provided a vital base for building the KMCS.

The emergence of the KMCS

Towards the formation of the KMCS

Following these initial rounds of mobilization, the activists established a base in the village of Attha and the organizing gathered pace in the eastern and southern parts of Alirajpur. The dynamic of expansion was characterized by the continuation of confrontation with the coercive practices of local state officials and the transmission of the news that such confrontations were taking place.

Kinship often functioned as a modality of transmission: activists would go along when people in a village which had been organized visited their relatives in other villages, and they would talk to people there about what had been achieved in other communities.

> In Kakrana, people had heard of what had been achieved in terms of challenging the atrocities of the Forest Department's officials. Also, a year before Kakrana itself was organized, a dog had died in the neighbouring village of Jandana, and the police had demanded money for turning a blind eye to the matter. One of the villagers, Vaniya, who later became an activist with the KMCS and the NBA, contacted Khemla, Amit and Khemraj, who quickly put a stop to the attempt to extort money from the village. This success encouraged people in Kakrana to get organized. In another case, a fight had taken place in the village, and the police demanded a bribe. The villagers turned to the group of activists, and one of them came to the village. He wrote a letter to the police, asking why they demanded money, and what rules and regulations entitled them to do so. Recounting his personal experience of this event, Kemat explained that as he witnessed this, he thought that whereas before, the

villagers had been afraid to talk to the police, the police had now been made to apologize, and this was a significant change.

In order to tackle the issue of extortion in relation to disputes in the villages, the activists started spreading an awareness that villagers should not fight among themselves, because infighting provided the police with an opportunity to demand bribes. If they came across a case where an official had taken a bribe, they would confront this official and demand that the money be given back. If the official failed to comply with their demands, they would file a written complaint against him. This was a very successful strategy, and it boosted the confidence of the people that something could be done. For example, on one occasion, a person in the village had killed someone's goat. He gave his own goat as compensation to settle the matter, but the police at the outpost in Sondwa came to hear about the incident and came to the village. While walking back from Kakrana, the police officers beat up several villagers and demanded that they be carried on the villager's shoulders the fourteen kilometres to the police station. This infuriated the people of the village, and a group of them went with one of the activists to the police station to make it clear that they would take action against such atrocities from now on.

(interview, Kemat, March 2003)

Another familiar feature of the dynamic of mobilization that emerged from Kemat's narrative was the significance of those instances in which the activists would succeed in eliciting statements from high-ranking officials that local state functionaries who exacted bribes and manhandled villagers were in the wrong. For example, on one occasion, a visit by the Scheduled Caste/Scheduled Tribe Commissioner, B. D. Sharma, to Kakrana was organized. He came to the village and talked to the people there about their rights, and the villagers thought that if such a senior government official could support them in claiming that the abuses of forest officials and police officers are wrong, that means that until now, they have been cheating them. At another occasion, the entire village, along with the activists, went to the sub-divisional magistrate and asked to be shown the rules where it said that the police were allowed to bash them up. The magistrate had to admit that there were no such rules. People reckoned that if the highest official of the area says that there are no such rules, the atrocities of the police must surely be wrong. Such events, according to Kemat, were turning points in the awareness of people in the communities (interview, March 2003).

It was on the basis of this process that the KMCS was constituted as a trade union. A trade union is perhaps an unlikely organizational form for a movement of subsistence peasants, but it was chosen for pragmatic reasons: government officials and contractors are obliged by law to respond to the grievances and claims put forward by trade unions (Kela 2006b). At its height, the KMCS organized some 100 adivasi villages in southern and eastern Alirajpur. Most of its activities were carried out on a voluntary basis by villagers who took on the role as part-time activists, while leadership was provided by ten full-time activists – both adivasis and non-adivasis – working for very modest salaries (Baviskar 1995: 176–7). The activities of the

KMCS spanned a wide spectrum, from anti-corruption campaigns directed against the state to a range of constructive activities such as the setting up of a primary education system based on Bhilali language, implementing environmental regeneration programmes, organizing co-operative marketing, and rejuvenating labour-sharing institutions and traditional irrigation techniques (see Banerjee 1994). The movement also focused on gender issues and sought to facilitate women's participation in the KMCS (interview, Chittaroopa Palit, May 2003; see also Baviskar 1995: 182–3n).

Customary rights and citizenship in the politics of the KMCS

As is characteristic of militant particularist struggles, the politics of the KMCS evolved out of and in relation to determinate and situated experiences of oppression and exploitation, and a central feature of such experience in the adivasi communities of Alirajpur was of course the criminalization of the adivasi customary use rights to the forest and forest resources. Rahul Banerjee recounted how this became the first and most central issue on agenda of the KMCS:

> . . . when they went around holding meetings and all, so they came across this problem of access to forest resources. It was severely restricted for the adivasis. They had to pay bribes; they would get beaten up and things. So then the next phase of the movement was that . . . that the adivasis should have access to forest resources for their daily needs and even for agriculture . . . So the whole brunt of the movement was that these people should be allowed to do whatever they did in the forest without having to pay bribes. It was at that basic level.
>
> (interview, Rahul Banerjee, April 2003)

Customary use rights, then, were defended as legitimate and valuable against the practices of criminalization that underpinned the workings of everyday tyranny. Writing in 1995, Baviskar noted the success of this defence: 'Popular resistance has rendered the task of fining and eviction difficult and, for the last ten years, villagers in the Sangath have lived in comparative calm, free from government harassment' (1995: 187).

In his account of the evolution of the politics of the KMCS, Rahul went on to argue that in the initial phase of mobilization, there was no grand ideological scheme that animated the activities that were undertaken. Rather, the imperative was that of organizing the communities so as to render possible further collective action, consolidating the gains that had already been achieved, and trying to pry open cracks and fissures in the state apparatus that activists could use to their advantage:

> . . . you know, the work started in that kind of frame: 'ok, people have problems, and we should try to solve those problems by organizing them' . . . So they used tactics that have become quite common these days, you use your

> contacts outside, to help the initial organization process. So they had these contacts from their NGO days, with the high-level bureaucrats and politicians also . . . So they used these contacts and put pressure on the local bureaucrats and politicians and things to, you know, keep them at bay somewhat . . . And KMCS itself . . . was formed as a trade union . . . always it had been working at that trade union level of consciousness: you have this problem and you solve it, and if you can act in an organized manner you can solve it, or if you don't solve it, at least you get some purchase with the state. And you establish your identity as a sort of people who need to be satisfied if votes are to be taken. And this is how it has worked.
>
> (interview, April 2003)

However, the politics of the KMCS was also widened; this is evident in how the defence of customary use rights was developed. As activists gradually discovered the potentially harmful effects of nevad agriculture, the defence of customary use rights was imbued with an ecological dimension:

> By the time I came they had already raised the nevad issue, created an opposition to a certain extent, and in fact, when I came, just before that, two or three months before that, there had been a huge survey all over that, the area that the KMCS was working in, to ascertain what was the extent of nevad. And the slogan that they were giving was that . . . 'we won't leave our nevad, we won't break any new nevad'. And the organization was also grappling with the ecological imperative, because this area is very hilly, you know . . . [explains how the monsoon rains would wash away the soil] . . . so it basically meant that if people continue to break nevad at that pace, then soon there'll be no forest left, you know, which is also a great source of sustenance. And this nevad will be washed away in two or three years.
>
> (interview, Chittaroopa Palit, May 2003)

The defence of customary use rights and the imperative of ecological sustainability were in turn coupled with political demands for the devolution of forest management to community level. The basic demand was that the forest belongs to the communities, but simultaneously the argument was made that the communities also had an obligation to protect the forest. Whereas some people in the local communities argued that it was the government's duty to protect the forest, the activists claimed that the villagers could do it themselves. They also campaigned around the question of irrigation, trying to strike a balance between which claims could be made on the government, and what the communities could do for themselves, using the labour-sharing arrangements that prevailed in the villages as a basis for implementing local development projects. The activists pointed out how millions were spent on government forest management schemes, but in actual fact nothing was being done. The villagers then started a campaign imploring the authorities not to waste money on these projects, to let the communities themselves take responsibility for the preservation of the forest (interview, Kemat, March 2003).

One might call this an *innovative* defence of customary use rights. It was not merely a question of restoring and reclaiming the legitimacy and legality of usufruct rights and practices, but of renewing and reinventing their character in relation to changed circumstances – the potentially harmful impacts of nevad agriculture on soil erosion – and contemporary challenges – the need for greater local autonomy in developmental decision-making. A similar approach can be traced in the way the KMCS worked for the restoration of the traditional credit system – *uchna* – so as to undermine the power of the *sahukars.* Before it fell into disrepair, the system allowed people to borrow money, grain and pulses from others who had a surplus without paying interest. The only obligation was that the principal would have to be returned to the lender upon demand. However, debt could be re-scheduled by borrowing from a new lender to repay the previous until the borrower was in a position to pay back the debt with his or her own funds:

> Each family would contribute twenty kilos of grain each year at harvest time to constitute a grain bank and this would then be distributed among those that needed it at an interest of 25% annually. Similarly each family would contribute Rs. 10 every month and this money would then be advanced as short loans to those who needed it at the same interest rate as above. It was decided that once the grain banks and the credit funds increased to large values and were running well the interest rate could be brought down.
>
> (Banerjee 2003: 20)

The resuscitated credit institution was initially a success, but eventually ran into administrative problems as the KMCS did not manage to develop the capacity to manage the expanding system of records and files due to the pressure of day to day activism (ibid.: 20).

I showed earlier how a lack of awareness of civil rights and constitutional provisions and entitlements for Scheduled Tribes compounded the immobilization caused by the fear of violent reprisal by depriving the adivasis of the cognitive capacity to make rights-based claims on the state and its representatives. Speaking to adivasi activists, a consistent theme in their narrative of involvement with the KMCS revolved around how they had learned that the police, the revenue officials and the forest rangers were public servants, that they received a wage from the state and were not entitled to beat up and extort the villagers, and that adivasis – as all other citizens – were bearers of inviolable rights, as well as special entitlements, vis-à-vis the Indian state. This, in turn, was the direct outcome of the focus on the claiming of citizenship in the politics of the KMCS:

> . . . we were not working at the level of understanding, trying to build up an alternative to the state or something . . . We were saying that: 'Look, the state is there, it has a constitution, which provides a lot of benefits for the adivasis, which are not reaching the adivasis. So what you do is you organize and you try to see that those benefits reach you'. So it was at that level.
>
> (interview, Rahul Banerjee, April 2003)

One of the strategies for doing this was encouraging and organizing participation in *panchayat*[6] elections. In many of the areas where the KMCS was active, adivasi candidates won the elections unopposed. Moreover, in the struggle against the local bureaucracy and local exploiters, creating an awareness of political and civil rights was a pivotal task:

> As far as the KMCS was concerned, it was basically against the local bureaucracy and the local exploiters . . . Basically, our role over there was this: that the Indian constitution was not known to these people; they used to think of this as a raj, and of the police as a raja and the ranger as a raja. They didn't even have the idea of what they were doing with their voting; the power of the vote, whatever limited power is there, even that understanding was not there . . . So basically what the KMCS has done is that we made these people proficient enough to participate in the democratic system. And that is what they have done, and that is what they are doing now.
>
> (interview, Rahul Banerjee, April 2003)

As this account brings out, through the process of mobilization, the KMCS disseminated knowledge about constitutional provisions for adivasis, the workings of the state apparatus and the local electoral process, and political and civil rights. This in turn contributed to a profound alteration in the character of subaltern 'sightings of the state' in the adivasi communities in Alirajpur: 'the Sangath has effectively reiterated that power is not vested in an omnipotent, inaccessible state structure, but is reproduced through people's everyday actions of conformity and resistance' (Baviskar 1995: 195). I shall discuss the character and significance of this transformation further in the third and final part of the chapter.

Rightful resistance and catalytic work in subaltern politics

The politics of the KMCS and the form of the process through which it emerged can be understood as a case of what O'Brien and Li have called 'rightful resistance':

> Rightful resistance is a form of popular contention that operates near the boundaries of authorized channels, employs the rhetoric and commitments of the powerful to curb the exercise of power, hinges on locating and exploiting divisions within the state, and relies on mobilizing support from the wider public. In particular, rightful resistance entails the innovative use of laws, policies and other officially promoted values to defy disloyal political and economic elites; it is a kind of partially sanctioned protest that uses influential allies and recognized principles to apply pressure on those in power who have failed to apply pressure on those in power who have failed to live up to a professed ideal or who have not implemented some beneficial measure.
>
> (2006: 2–3)

The process through which the KMCS emerged exhibited most, if not all, of these features: the pursuit of claims and demands was conducted via the authorized channels of the state by confronting officials with the illegality of their actions, either in person or in writing; in their efforts to curb the coercive exaction of bribes, activists employed the rhetoric of the powerful by pointing out how government officials acted in breach of national law, violated basic constitutional rights, and conducted themselves in a way that negated the commitment of the Indian state to tribal integration and development; adivasi contention was of course fundamentally enabled by support from influential allies in the urban educated activists who commanded a set of key mobilizational skills; divisions within the state were located and used by taking local, village-specific claims higher up the political and administrative ladder and by couching the grievances in a terminology of law and citizenship 'that even unresponsive authorities must recognize, lest they risk being charged with hypocrisy and disloyalty to the system of power they represent' (ibid.: 5).

The result of the process, in turn, was a profound transformation in the character of subaltern 'sightings of the state' in Alirajpur: where adivasis had once seen state officials as well-nigh all powerful figures, they came to see public servants whose powers were legally circumscribed and who were accountable to them as citizens; where the villagers had once seen a state apparatus whose activities centred on the forceful exaction of tribute, they came to see an institution that was supposed to provide services and safeguard rights, an institution upon which they could make rights-based claims and demands, and an institution which they could participate in the running of. It was, then, a process through which formerly subjugated communities emerged as agents who could and would, competently and assertively, 'seek to engage with the state as citizens, or as members of populations with legally defined or politically inspired expectations' (Corbridge *et al.* 2005: 13).

The capacities by and through which subaltern groups may succeed in making the state do their bidding in Alirajpur were not given or intrinsic to these groups. Rather, they were the result of the development of skilled activity in and through conflicts over the character of given social relationships – in this case the local state-society relationship I have referred to as everyday tyranny – and the result of this development was a profound transformation of local rationalities. The starting point of this transformation was not hegemony of the Gramscian type, characterized by the giving of 'consent' by the subaltern majority to 'the general direction imposed on social life by the dominant fundamental group' (Gramsci 1998: 12). Everyday tyranny was ultimately underpinned by a fear of violent coercion that resulted in practices of deference and submission in interaction with the representatives of dominant social groups. This was a local rationality in which subaltern groups literally chose the path of least resistance and kow-towed to the tyrants so as not to upset their tempers, thus minimizing the risk of violent reprisal. The transformation of this local rationality was sparked by the intervention of urban educated activists who destabilized local power relations through what might be called *catalytic work* – a practical and conflictual process through which the received wisdoms of everyday tyranny were gradually subverted. The accounts of villagers reproduced earlier exhibit a consistent focus on concrete episodes where villagers and activists had confronted local officials about their coercive and extortive practices, pointed out the illegality of these practices, and threatened to take action, thus compelling the officials to admit to their wrongdoings, apologize to those victimized and withdraw demands of bribes. These narratives can be read as stories of 'showdowns' between oppressors and oppressed, where the power equations between the two parties are reversed: the claims and complaints of the oppressed are vindicated as being just and legitimate, the oppressor loses the air of invincibility and emerges as a culpable villain rather than the indisputable figure of unaccountable authority that he once was.

I would like to suggest that these episodes can be thought of as *catalytic events* in the transformation of local rationalities in the adivasi communities. With the term catalytic events I refer to confrontational episodes in and through which the received wisdom of subjugation and domination inherent in a given relationship of power is subverted by having its logic reversed or overturned, either momentarily or permanently. The received wisdom which is referred to here is that of knowing one's place in a relationship of power, knowing what behaviour is tolerated by the dominant party and what behaviour is not, being aware of the consequences of deviating from such behavioural patterns – i.e. punitive sanctions that may be enforced as a response to defiance – and thus conforming to the established 'codes of conduct' implied by this relationship of power, the consequence of which is the perpetuation of a given relation of domination and subjugation. The subversion of such a relation of power through a confrontational episode has a catalytic effect to the extent that it engenders a suspension of the received wisdom of everyday tyranny, and thus constitutes a tangible manifestation of the possibility that the tyrant can be challenged, and generating pressures towards a conception of resistance as something thinkable and doable. Indeed, when I asked villagers that had been involved in the mobilization process what they had learned from their participation in the KMCS, three themes stood out: first, that of losing their fear of the officials; second, that of learning that officials were not entitled to extort them; third, that of acquiring the skills that allowed them to challenge everyday tyranny. In sum, then, the transformation of local rationalities revolved around effecting changes in emotional dispositions, cognitive resources, and practical skills; it was these changes that rendered engagement in rightful resistance possible in the first place.

In extension of this, the urban educated activists that initiated and led the confrontations with the local state officials can be thought of as *catalysts* – that is, as a person or group of persons who introduce the ideas, skills and practices that are deployed in the articulation and execution of a challenge to powerful social groups, their practices and their institutions. Catalysts and catalytic events are of course closely linked in the sense that the ideas, skills and practices that catalysts introduce have to be put to the test through catalytic events in order to take root. The fact that activists put their actions where their mouths were, the fact that they led the confrontations, the fact that they risked and suffered beatings and other forms of repression, and not least the fact that these confrontations yielded results, seem to have been instrumental in convincing villagers that resistance was a viable alternative to acquiescence and deference, and, not least, crucial in building the bonds of trust that enabled more long-term organization and mobilization through the KMCS.

In effecting these transformations in and of local rationalities and thus curbing the repressive excesses of local state officials, the trajectory that led to the formation of the KMCS resonates with a range of recent perspectives on the role played by the discourses and institutions of the postcolonial Indian state in contemporary 'subaltern politics' (Corbridge and Harriss 2000: Chapter 9). In contrast to those who claim that these discourses and institutions have not been woven into popular common sense in India or that the postcolonial state offers little to subaltern groups by way of empowerment,[7] Corbridge and Harriss argue that the currently unfolding contention over the future form and direction of Indian development – what they call 'the reinvention of India' – is characterized by multiple strands of assertion from below, ranging various forms of 'empowerment from without' – i.e. dalits and adivasis using state reservation policies to get ahead in the spheres of employment, education and state administration – and 'empowerment from within' – i.e. the active participation of lower caste and lower class groups in electoral politics[8] and the successful formation of political parties representing dalits[9] – to the advancement of subaltern interests by left of centre regimes in states such as West Bengal and Kerala. Crucial to their argument is the assertion that subaltern opposition to elite dominance in contemporary India is conducted by means of discourses and institutions that 'these elites once claimed for themselves' and, consequently, that state power should not be viewed simply as 'an instrument of repressive governmentality' but rather as an instrument that 'might yet be made to do the bidding of India's lower orders' (ibid.: 210, 212, 227, 239).[10]

For Corbridge and Harriss, their observations on the characteristics of subaltern politics in India translate into the argument that subaltern empowerment in contemporary India is a project that is best pursued in and through the framework of the postcolonial state: 'it is misleading to suppose that citizens' movements, NGOs and community organizations . . . provide an alternative to the state' (Corbridge and Harriss 2000: 203). Rather, the role of such movements and organisations should be that of putting pressure 'on the state to take the part of the poor, or to protect the poor from some of the abuses heaped upon them' (ibid.: 203). Indeed, the case of the KMCS and the process of rightful resistance through which it emerged might be read as lending credence to this line of argument, and, conversely, the experience of adivasi empowerment in Alirajpur might be understood as one of multiple examples of how, in India, 'power is leaching steadily, and in some respects ineluctably, to [subaltern groups], and has been claimed by them in terms which often resist the presumptions of a benign and disinterested state' (Corbridge *et al.* 2005: 83). This, however, is not an unproblematic proposition.

In her study of mobilization among tribal communities in Maharashtra, Kamat (2002) discerns a similar scenario to that which I have described as everyday tyranny, and portrays the strategy devised to counter it in similar terms to what I have done with the KMCS:

> The immobilizing fear of the tribals was identified by the activists as caused by their ignorance of their own powers (rights) as citizens within a democratic

> nation, and the legally circumscribed powers of political institutions . . . This . . . translates into a pedagogy directed at demystifying the state, empowering the *adivasis* with knowledge of the laws of the nation and their own rights so as to not only challenge the arbitrary nature of power exercised at the local level, but also to challenge those laws which are unjust and sustain domination.
>
> (ibid.: 122)

Now, the pedagogy of demystifying the state is a strategy which Kamat finds fault with in that it implies that 'politics (power relations) emanates from the state agents as it were, and not from the state structures'. Therefore, the 'juridico-legal' rules of the state 'are seen as binding on everyone equally, or ideally should be' and the praxis of social movements thus becomes centred on making 'the latter possible' without subjecting those very rules 'which represent the formal discourse of the state' to critique (ibid.:124). In such a form of praxis 'a distinction is maintained between state as practice and the state as structure, where the former is vigorously attacked and the latter is left untouched', which in effect means that movements from below end up promoting 'the 'illusion' of a state which exists for the interests of all people, including that of the poor' (ibid.: 125–6).

Whereas Kamat's critique is theoretically cogent, I nevertheless believe that it is flawed in that it lacks sensitivity to how a strategy of empowering subaltern social groups in relation to the state can in fact be radical relative to the context in which that kind of strategy is adopted. It is also flawed, I would argue, due to its lack of appreciation of the processual nature of social movements. When we are dealing with the mobilization of subaltern social groups in the context of everyday tyranny – i.e. a context in which domination is in large part underpinned by the absence of democratic principles and citizens' rights – then the strategy of claiming citizenship amounts to nothing less than the articulation of a set of radical need and capacities which, if realized, holds the potential to decisively rupture this tyranny (see Kela 2006). Furthermore, I am less than convinced that her assertion that the pedagogy of demystifying the state that lies at the heart of rightful resistance entails disciplining the will towards transformative praxis to a form of political action that is incapable of going beyond the parameters of liberal democracy. In fact, I think Kamat here confuses the *form* and *content* of rightful resistance. Surely, the mobilizational process that unfolded in the adivasi communities in the early and mid-1980s entailed the development of a form of knowledge and skills centred on the principles and procedures of the liberal democratic state, but the content of the experience seems to me to be more profoundly related to the realization that that overlords could be overthrown and, consequently, that resistance is a viable option. Here we do well to remember that social movements first '*mobilize* people who were not necessarily previously active' and second '*radicalize* people who were previously content with a view of the world designed for situations of relative quiescence' (Barker and Cox 2002: 21–2), and, consequently, the argument that mobilizing around the ability to make claims on the state locks in place activism in a form that underpins the status quo loses, if not its theoretical cogency, at least a substantial part of its analytical purchase. Put slightly differently, in cases where subaltern mobilization takes place in a context of everyday tyranny, the very possibility of the development of a radical form of political agency that transcends the parameters of liberal democracy might well be predicated upon an initial rupturing of local rationalities of submission and deference through rightful resistance. As such, the profound achievement of the KMCS was of course that it 'engendered a change in political consciousness, and . . . provided an experience of organization that will stand in good stead wherever adivasis stay or go, whether in the hills or in the plains' (Baviskar 1995: 195).

This, however, should not be read as a wholesale denunciation of Kamat's arguments about the limits to the pursuit of subaltern empowerment in and through the state. As Geoghegan and Cox (2001: 7) have argued, interaction and negotiation with the state should not be posited as 'the be-all and end-all of movement activity', and at certain conjunctures social movements from below may pursue forms of praxis which explicitly or implicitly challenges what Kamat refers to as the state-as-structure. As will become clear in Chapters 5 and 6, this is precisely what happened in the Narmada Valley when the militant particularist struggles that had crystallized around demands for R&R in the dam-affected communities in the riparian states coalesced into a pan-state anti-dam campaign. This aspect of the movement process in the Narmada Valley, and its ultimately unsuccessful trajectory, brings back into question, and lays the basis for a thoroughgoing critical engagement with, the limitations of a subaltern politics centred on redressing the state-as-practice.

Concluding remarks

In this chapter I have analyzed the character and dynamics of the process of mobilization that laid the foundation for participation in the anti-dam campaign in and among the adivasi communities of Alirajpur.

I started by describing how these communities were subjected to a coercive regime that I referred to as everyday tyranny at the hands of local state officials, and how villagers' ways of engaging with these forms of exploitation and oppression were mediated through and moulded by a local rationality of fear, deference and submission so as to minimize the risks of being subjected to violence and other forms of coercion by local overlords. Everyday tyranny was a local state-society relationship fundamentally at variance with the basic principles of liberal democracy, and characterized by the total undermining of the rights and entitlements typically associated with democratic citizenship.

I then showed how everyday tyranny came to be challenged through the intervention of two former NGO-workers who were intent on mobilizing the communities in the region. A series of confrontations with local state officials took place, which culminated in a substantial success as activists and villagers had their grievances against local state officials addressed and confirmed by the upper echelons of the state. This was a crucial moment in the mobilization process as it proved that organized, collective resistance was a viable option: victories could be won, oppressors could be defeated, and the outsiders that had initiated the process could be trusted to stand by their word and practice what they preached. From this basis in turn, the KMCS was constituted as an organizational vehicle for further mobilization. I showed how the KMCS – as is typical of militant particularisms – develop a politics that responded to local circumstances and situated experiences, and in which the innovative defence of customary use rights and conscientization of the communities in terms of how they possessed constitutional rights and entitlements, and how they could exercise these rights and claim these entitlements, were particularly central elements.

Finally, I designated the mobilizational process that ruptured the fabric of everyday tyranny and led to the formation of the KMCS as a form of rightful resistance. I presented an analysis of how the capacity for rightful resistance emerged from a process of catalytic work which transformed local rationalities. The politics of rightful resistance in Alirajpur was in turn discussed in terms of the extent to which the state constitutes a space of and for subaltern empowerment in India. I showed how, on the one hand, the trajectory of adivasi mobilization in Alirajpur lent credence to claims that the Indian state is a relevant site of subaltern empowerment, while, on the other hand, it can be criticized for relying on a strategy of demystifying the state which ultimately contrives to obfuscate the structural limits to empowerment via the state. This critique, I argued is flawed as it fails to appreciate how the claiming of citizenship is a profoundly radical project in a context of everyday tyranny, and in that it fails to appreciate how the actual experience of successful engagement in rightful resistance and the skills and forms of consciousness engendered through this experience may be vital to the future development of more radical forms of oppositional politics. Throughout the book, I will develop this discussion about the relationship between social movements from below and state power, in particular in relation to the trajectory of the NBA's anti-dam campaign. Now, however, I shift my focus to the emergence of militant particularisms in the dam-affected communities in Maharashtra, Gujarat and Nimad.

4 Discovering the dam

Militant particularist struggles for resettlement and rehabilitation

The revolt against everyday tyranny in the adivasi villages of Alirajpur was paralleled, and gradually came to be closely intertwined with, the emergence of militant particularist struggles for resettlement and rehabilitation (R&R) in the dam-affected adivasi communities of Maharashtra and Gujarat, as well as the caste Hindu farming communities in Nimad, Madhya Pradesh. This chapter is devoted to chronicling and analyzing that process.

In the first part of the chapter I focus on the emergence of the Narmada Dharangrasta Samiti (NDS) in the dam-affected tribal communities in Nandurbar district, Maharashtra in the mid-1980s. I start by detailing how the interaction between action researcher Medha Patkar and the dam-affected communities in Nandurbar resulted in the emergence of the NDS. I focus on how this process shared many of the features delineated in the trajectory through which the KMCS emerged, in particular the transformation of the local rationalities spawned by everyday tyranny and the creation of the practical, cognitive and emotive skills necessary for engagement in collective action. Next, I focus on the construction of a multiscalar infrastructure of contention which enabled the building of unity between dam-affected communities within and between states and the levelling of claims and demands at responsible authorities from the level of state agencies to a transnational institution like the World Bank.

The second part of the chapter focuses more briefly on how the ARCH Vahini (AV) came to articulate demands for land rights among the dam-affected communities in Gujarat. I trace the trajectory of the AV from the initial efforts at creating an awareness of the necessity and utility of collective mobilization to claim the right to R&R, and their efforts to pressure the Government of Gujarat (GoG) to recognize the rights of "encroachers" to land-for-land compensation. I focus on how this struggle gained crucial momentum through its relationship with the World Bank, which put pressure on the GoG to broaden its R&R policy, and how this strategy was ultimately succeeded – a result that was to have a decisive impact upon the AV's relationship to the other organizations in the Narmada Valley as contention over information and R&R intensified in 1987–88.

The third and final part of the chapter shifts the focus of attention to mobilization in the caste Hindu farming communities of the Nimad region in Western Madhya Pradesh. I chronicle the trajectory of mobilization in the 1970s and show how the experience of the ultimate failure of this mobilization gave rise to a local rationality of disillusionment and a vacuum of political skill in the Nimadi communities. I then move on to show how a new organization – the Narmada Ghati Navnirman Samiti (NGNS) – emerged to contest the impact of the SSP in the 1980s, but lacked the organizational structure necessary to energize actual mobilization in the dam-affected communities. I show how this changed as interactions started between the NGNS and NDS activists in the mid-1980s: popular confidence in mobilization was resuscitated and an infrastructure of contention capable of animating local collective action was constructed, thus drawing the Nimadi communities into the intensifying contention around the SSP.

The Narmada Dharangrasta Samiti (NDS)

Discovering the dam: Keshuvbhai's story

Keshuvbhai is one of the most senior activists from the adivasi communities of Maharashtra. Laying out the story of how the communities in the area had mobilized around and against the SSP in great detail, Keshuvbhai started by describing how villagers had once lived in fear of the officials, and how they had been kept in the dark about the ramifications of the SSP for their livelihoods and lifeworlds:

> As early as 1980, when the Narmada Valley Development Authority was carrying out surveys in the village, they had come to hear that there was a big dam – one of the biggest in Asia – coming up on the Narmada, in the neighbouring state of Gujarat. They were told that they would get compensation in the form of land for land, and that their lives would improve. They were told that the Sardar Sarovar would bring great benefits: it would yield massive gains in electricity and irrigation; thousands of villages that had been in darkness would be lit, and villages without proper water supplies would now have water. They didn't question these claims, nor did they inquire about how the dam would impact their community in particular. Prior to Medha's arrival, they conceived of the government as an ultimate power; the government was like a parent, there would be no questioning of the government officials. They were used to the abuses of the state officials: the police would come to the villages and get drunk; if they found a household brewing *mahua* [liquor], they would confiscate it and demand a bribe of between 3,000 to 4,000 rupees from the household. The forest officials would beat them up, file false cases of encroachment against them, and demand bribes to let them access their nevad fields. Also, in Nimgavhan, the district administration had set up a school, but this only existed on paper, as the teachers never showed their faces in the village.
>
> (interview, March 2003)

This is of course a familiar scenario by now; what Keshuvbhai was recounting was a local rationality in which the state was 'seen' by subaltern groups as being unaccountable and all-powerful.

Keshuvbhai's narrative also made it clear that this way of 'seeing the state' extended to how people conceived of the various projects and interventions of the state. The abuse and extortion he refers to are well-known facets of what I have called everyday tyranny, and the workings of everyday tyranny are also closely related to the activities of the dam bureaucracy. For example, he pointed out that the government's surveying teams would conduct themselves much as the police: when a team of 30–40 people came to the village, the villagers would have to provide pots of *mahua* and give up their chickens for meals. The team would also demand that every household give them 40 to 50 rupees (interview, March 2003). Non-disclosure of information about the impacts of the SSP was another way in which the state in practice denied the rights of citizenship to the dam-affected adivasi communities. What this situation amounts to is not one where citizens who face expropriation for allegedly public purposes are granted the right to information about the consequences of this expropriation, nor is it one of a state making any serious effort to reach these communities with that information. Rather, it is one where the adivasi communities are de facto treated as subjects that shall have to conform to the undisputable right of an absolute authority to confiscate their commons (see Parasuraman 1997: 39–40).

Keshuvbhai proceeded to tell me about the events that followed after action researcher Medha Patkar arrived in the Valley:

> In 1985, he recalled, Medha and a colleague came to the area and went around the villages, inquiring about the awareness of the dam and its impacts, and then returned to the city. When the government teams started their surveys, they were working their way upwards from the beginning of the submergence zone. By this time, Medha had returned, and was conducting her own survey, but moving in the opposite direction. While doing her survey, she also interacted with the villagers and enquired about their problems. Keshuvbhai himself was sceptical of Medha in the beginning; he couldn't understand what she was doing, and why she was asking so many questions. However, he gradually came to trust her and her intentions, and the villagers started telling Medha of their problems with the police and the atrocities they would commit in the villages.
>
> (interview, March 2003)

Here, another familiar feature crops up, namely the encounter between villagers and urban, educated activists – or in this case, an action-researcher. Keshuvbhai's remark about his initial scepticism testifies to the general distrust among the adivasi towards outsiders; the gradual overcoming of this distrust is also a familiar theme, namely that of realizing that the outsider arrives with good intentions and genuine commitment. Keshuvbhai was amused when he recounted an episode through which people came to appreciate and trust Medha's genuine commitment:

> On one particular occasion, a government surveying team was in Sikka, a nearby village. As usual, they had collected fifty rupees from every household, and demanded that the villagers cook them a chicken curry. What is more, they

> had gotten roaringly drunk. Medha showed up in Sikka and took photographs of the ill-mannered officials. They got scared by this and ran away (interview, March 2003).

This episode resonates with the notion of catalytic events in that the commitment and thus also trustworthiness of the outsider is demonstrated by her readiness to defy and confront officials that until then had only been known and feared as everyday tyrants. The fact that the outsider in this case was a woman probably strengthened the perception of genuine dedication and courage.

The establishment of a rapport between the outsider and the villagers in turn became the basis for mobilization and organization:

> After the incident, Medha went away, and then returned after two or three months. Upon her return, she called two or three representatives from all the villages that would be affected by the project. In that meeting she explained to them that there was a big dam coming up on the Narmada in Gujarat, and that as a result, their houses and fields would be submerged. 'How do you feel about that', she asked, 'are you getting land for land compensation?' Some people said 'Yes, the government will give land', but Medha insisted that this might be more difficult than what the state officials made it seem like, and that therefore, they would have to form an organization to raise their voice and put pressure on the government. She picked up a thin stick and snapped it, then picked up a bunch of sticks, and showed them how it couldn't be broken – unity would make them strong, she argued. People were impressed with Medha's actions and the way she spoke, so they decided to form the Narmada Dharangrasta Samiti. (interview, March 2003)

Again, it is possible to discern how the intervention of the outsider instigated a process of catalytic work through which local rationalities were transformed: what had previously been accepted as a fact, as an impending fate that could neither be questioned or avoided, and promises that had been, if not believed, at least accepted, was now constituted as problematic and as something that could be contested through mobilization and organization. And by facilitating the development of a critical awareness about the impacts of the dam and what rights and entitlements the villagers were in possession of, the skills and knowledge necessary to engage in such contention gradually crystallized. On the basis of this initial round of catalytic work, the process of building an organizational structure through which to pursue demands for information and R&R. I shall elaborate further on the character of organization-building later, where I refer to what emerged as an infrastructure of contention, but first I briefly investigate the outsider's view of the initial mobilization process.

Discovering the dam: Medha's Story

Early June, 2003: The *Andolan* is holding a *dharna* in Nasik in order to put pressure on the Government of Maharashtra to provide rehabilitation for the adivasi communities facing immediate displacement due to the raising of the height of the SSP. On the evening of the third day of a hunger strike, Medha Patkar recounted her version of the development of the NBA to me. She explained the background for her coming to work with the dam-affected communities in Maharashtra as follows:

> I was working in the tribal areas . . . in whole of the north-east tribal belt, and that was with the small action groups of the adivasi people. I did action research on the Dang, forty action groups in Dang district. Then I was working with the eight co-operative societies which were coincidentally on the draw-down land of the dam in the Banaskantha district. So, actually I left Bombay and came to Gujarat, because I was selecting [organizations] all over. I had been to Madhya Pradesh and looked at many organizations. Once I decided I would leave Bombay, then I left the slum development work there, and then decided to come to the rural areas. I wanted to be as much interior as possible. So I selected this organization SETU. SETU did not have any field work at that time, but the trustees' group was very good there. A lot of people were working with the Nav Nirman movement, Jayprakash Narayan's struggle in Gujarat, which had thrown the power-holders out, in seventy-four. But they did not have any fieldwork, so when I joined SETU, I started the fieldwork . . . So in two, three districts they worked . . . and it was a kind of training programme for the activists, working with the co-operative societies of the nomadic tribes, the dalits; the major group was dalits.
>
> (interview, June 2003)

Hence, much as in the case of the urban educated activists that started the process of mobilization of the adivasi communities of Alirajpur, Patkar's background was related to the flourishing of grassroots organizations in the late 1970s. In her particular case, she was involved with action research, which was an approach that gathered pace in the wake of the critique of development planning and the championing of bottom-up approaches to development.

Her first impression of the adivasi communities' conception of the SSP and its consequences was one of a lack of knowledge and concern: 'we realized that people didn't even know about the project . . . a bit of apathy, a bit of ignorance' (interview, June 2003). Elsewhere she has elaborated on these initial experiences as follows:

> In 1985, when I first visited the Narmada Valley and a few of its villages, the situation was that the project work on the Sardar Sarovar (SSP) was stalled . . . At the same time, in the field, the only message conveyed to the people was that the dam was going to be built and the people affected would have to be rehabilitated. To the Maharashtra people, it was said all the time in the meetings held (where only a few of the village headmen, patels, and Karbaris would attend after walking six to seven hours on hilly paths) that they would have to move out of their habitats and move to Gujarat.
>
> (Patkar 1995: 157)

What Patkar encountered was a manifestation of everyday tyranny: adivasis being kept in the dark about their imminent expropriation, and not even entertaining the thought that this was something that could be questioned and contested. However, upon probing deeper into the matter, she also found apprehension and uneasiness among the communities about the impacts of the dam:

> . . . when they used to apply their minds seriously during the meetings, they would raise questions that were very clear and very articulate. 'No one asked us as to whether we want to move out of here'. 'How can they decide to build the dam without taking our permission?' 'Have they really decided what would happen to us?' 'No one has told us where we would go and where we would be resettled.'
>
> (ibid.: 158).

The systematic failure of the responsible authorities to provide adequate information in turn prompted her to deploy her skills and networks to bring to light the extent of submergence and the nature of the plans for rehabilitation:

> So basically, when we moved through the villages, we realized that there was no information . . . it was possible for me, being in Gujarat, to dig out information . . . lots of documents I collected, the tribunal award and all the impact studies and all the correspondence with the World Bank and lots of things . . . It was enough to give the full picture.
>
> (interview, June 2003).

In this way, the process of discovery was deepened: having come across the problem of a lack of information in the villages, the activist probed deeper into the existent official sources on the project, and thus deepened her knowledge about the ramifications of the project for the dam-affected communities. 'The full picture' that emerged through this deepening of discovery also pointed in the direction of the necessity of organized mobilization; this was brought out to me in Medha's account of an initial difference between her and an erstwhile fellow-traveller, a lawyer who wanted to file a petition to the court on rehabilitation: 'I felt that no point in going to the court, the main thing is organization' (interview, June 2003). This is elaborated in the following passage:

> When it was discussed in three- and four-hour meetings in hamlet after hamlet, it was very clear that the issues were multiple and the people must get channels and access to the right places where they could raise these questions and get the answers.
>
> (Patkar 1995: 158)

I now turn to an investigation of how such channels were established through the construction of a multiscalar infrastructure of contention.

Building an infrastructure of contention

An *infrastructure of contention* can be defined as an organizational structure that joins together collective agents in ways that make it possible for aggrieved groups to articulate grievances and make claims and demands on and in relation to specific targets and opponents. In the case of the dam-affected communities in Nandurbar district, the creation of an infrastructure of contention was a necessary prerequisite for the politicization of issues that had previously not been contested. Crucially, the infrastructure that was constructed around the NDS was multi-scalar: at the local scale, it linked communities that were affected by the SSP, both within dam-affected communities in Nandurbar, and dam-affected communities in the riparian states; at the national scale, it linked the ongoing activism in the Narmada Valley to support-groups in urban centres as well as NGOs and activists working in the fields of environmental and human rights politics at the national level; at the transnational scale, it linked activism in the Narmada Valley to the activities of NGOs and activists in Europe and the USA, working on issues related to World Bank funding of infrastructure projects in the South. I will deal with developments at each scale from the local to the transnational.

Infrastructures in the valley

At the local level, the most immediate task was that of co-ordinating the dam-affected villages in the two *tehsils* of Akrani and Akkalkuva, so as to ensure representation of these communities vis-à-vis state authorities:

> So every month on the full moon day we would meet and take all the decisions . . . Immediately, actually, within six months, when we formed the block-level committees, after selecting representatives from each village, and there were representatives from each hamlet, then the village committee, then the Karbhari committee [A committee consisting of village leaders] of each *tehsil*, and then both the tehsils we covered, and then started representing with the delegation to the government, starting from the lowest level, reached the Collector, the Ministers.
>
> (interview, Medha Patkar, June 2003)

As this point, mobilization at the local scale revolved around demands for accurate information about the impact of the dam:

> Obviously, the first issue was that the planners, politicians, and other officials had not given us information. Come to the village and in our language give us information, show us maps, everything that you have, and thereafter discuss all the issues . . . On February 16, 1986, we had a meeting with representatives of all the villages of one tehsil and seventeen from another tehsil to form the Narmada Dharangrast Samiti. In that meeting, the decision was taken not to be moved out, not to accept anything from the government as part and parcel of displacement or work related to the dam till we got answers to all our questions.
>
> (Patkar 1995: 158, 160–1)

Following the February meeting, a memorandum was submitted to the Government of Maharashtra demanding the release of degraded forestland in Gujarat for R&R if revenue land was not available for such purposes. A couple of months later, there was a demonstration in Bombay, where the slogan 'first rehabilitation, then the dam' was fronted as a key demand of the dam-affected communities (Dwivedi 2006: 155).

Much like the reversal of the grammar of everyday tyranny in Alirajpur, the demand for information put forward by the NDS squarely challenged the prevalent workings of the state: where before the state's development interventions had been accepted as inevitable, and where it had been possible for the state and its representatives to ignore the right of the dam-affected communities to information about the project and its impacts, there was now an assertive demand that the construction of the SSP should not and would not move forward until proper information had been provided and the dam-affected communities had been convinced that they would receive proper rehabilitation and resettlement.

The demand for information to be released from state authorities was paralleled by the continued gathering of information about the dam-affected communities by the activists themselves (interview, Medha Patkar, June 2003). Moreover, the NDS also coupled its demands for and gathering of information with constructive activities that sought to address the systematic deprivation of the adivasi communities by seeing to it that dispensaries and ashram schools were sanctioned for the dam-affected adivasi communities (interview, Medha Patkar, June 2003; see also Parasuraman 1997: 41). Both the gathering of information about the dam-affected communities and the engagement in constructive activities foreshadowed key dynamics and strategies in the development of the Narmada Bachao Andolan (see Chapters 5 and 8).

Yet another crucial aspect of the construction of an infrastructure of contention at the local scale was the building of links to the other militant particularist struggles that had emerged in the dam-affected adivasi communities in Madhya Pradesh and Gujarat. I focus here on the evolution of links between the NDS and the KMCS.

Out of approximately 100 Alirajpur villages organized by the KMCS, 26 villages stood to be affected by the SSP reservoir. Much like across the river in Maharashtra, the communities knew little about the dams and regarded them with a sense of resignation, indifference and helplessness. Vaniya, an adivasi activist from the village of Jandana, explained that even though they had heard of the dam, they assumed that since the river had always been flowing, how can it be dammed? And anyway, if the government wanted to build the dam, then let them build the dam – they all knew it would not be possible to challenge the government (interview, March 4, 2003). Similarly, Luharia from Jalsindhi emphasized how their impression was that since the dam was coming up at Kevadia, a location at some distance from Jalsindhi, they would not be affected by it (interview, March 12, 2003). In the mid-1980s, Multiple Action Research Group had carried out a survey to ascertain what adivasi communities in the affected areas of Madhya Pradesh in fact knew about the impact of the SSP:

> The answer is: very little, and even less of this is clear information from official sources. This was especially but not exclusively so in the tribal areas. People had heard of the dam from the vaguest sources . . . Very few were sure of their own fate, should the dam come up. Would their land be submerged? The stone markers of the reservoir submergence level that were already in place did not always make sense to them. Sometimes they seemed to exclude low-lying areas from submergence and embrace the higher points.
>
> (Dhamgawar 1997: 93–4)

However, by the mid-1980s, activists of the KMCS had started to probe into the matter on the advice of the ARCH Vahini. Rahul Banerjee recounts this initial phase, and how it evolved through interaction with the NDS:

> I remember the first time Medha and I met, was when both of us were conducting preliminary surveys, we came to know that there was this other group working in Gujarat, ARCH Vahini, so we knew them, so they said 'look in your area also . . . we are working on this rehabilitation and all that, it's a big problem, and in your area also this problem will come up, so why don't you find out what's the level of awareness and all that'. So I had started doing that. I got some preliminary material from them, on what they are supposed to get on being ousted and all that. So I had started doing that. I got some preliminary material from them, on what they were supposed to get on being ousted and all that. And so Shankar and I, we went from village to village, and at that time those villages were not part of the submergence, the KMCS had not reached that area, we reached one or two, but most of them we hadn't reached. So we went there surveying the kind of thing. And that was the time when Medha also came there, surveying the whole area and holding meetings, and then we met at Hapeshwar and that's how the whole thing started. And then it went on in that way; surveys revealed that people don't know anything, and these are the things, so we must fight for this, because the MP or Maharashtra government is not doing anything, so that's how it started basically, with a demand for rehabilitation along the lines described by the Narmada Waters Dispute Tribunal.
>
> (interview, April 2003)

What was emerging was very much a similar process of discovery of problems of insufficient information about the ramifications of the dam project and a lack of adequate plans for rehabilitation as that which had taken place in Maharashtra.

When the Narmada issue started to crystallize into a cause of its own, the general sentiment seems to have been one of solidarity between villages inside and outside the submergence zone in Alirajpur, and between adivasi communities in MP and Maharashtra. Kemat reflected upon the relationship between the KMCS and the Narmada issue in the following way:

> Before the SSP emerged as an issue, all the villages in the area, including the villages in Alirajpur that were slated for submergence, right from Kakrana to

Jalsindhi, fought on their own issues, such as access to forests. Simultaneously, Medha was organizing in Maharashtra, and she talked to Rahul and others about the submergence of the Khedut villages. The KMCS then responded by saying that if adivasi villages are getting submerged, then they should also get involved and demand proper rehabilitation. The NDS and the KMCS both saw how tribals are always taken for granted in relation to development projects, and both organizations agreed that this should be brought to an end. Whereas the dam-campaign was issue-based, the KMCS activities had a wider scope, focusing on tribal life in general, and questioning the system that oppressed and exploited tribals. Also, the dam-issue touched upon several states, so the struggle had to be taken to many levels, and had to be focused on the dams. The KMCS was much more local, but they would still bring their banner to NBA programmes. Simultaneously, the people organizing around the dam would listen to the day-to-day problems of the Khedut villagers. Khedut decided to throw their lot in with the mobilizing around the dam issue in order to stand in solidarity with fellow tribal communities. For the KMCS activists, there was never really a hard and fast line between the mobilizing around the dam and the struggle of the KMCS.

(interview, March 2003)

The most crucial aspect of this dynamic of interaction between the NDS and the KMCS is of course that connections were made between militant particularisms: activists came to identify common problems and thus also increasingly the need for common strategies and, not least, solidarities. This process is important in that it constitutes the kernel of the dynamic through which a campaign may emerge, as it eventually did in the Narmada Valley.

Infrastructures beyond the valley

The building of an infrastructure of contention also extended outwards so as to link activism in the Narmada Valley to groups that operated on national and transnational scales.

A crucial aspect of the extension of the infrastructure of contention on a national scale was that of setting up support groups in cities throughout and beyond the states of Maharashtra, Gujarat and MP (interview, Medha Patkar, June 2003). These support groups have been of great importance for the Andolan throughout its existence in terms of lobbying authorities, providing support and eliciting media attention during actions and campaigns such as dharnas and marches, as well as in times of crises, for instance when severe police brutality has been unleashed upon the movement and its activists, or when mass arrests have been made in conjunction with protest actions.

Furthermore, links were built between the NDS and NGOs engaged in environmental and human rights politics at the national level in 1986–87. Dam-building on the Narmada had attracted the attention of various Delhi-based groups since the early 1980s: as early as 1983, the environmental group Kalpavriksh, in collaboration with the Hindu College Nature Club, carried out the first critical investigation of the project, and the granting of environmental clearance to the SSP in June 1987 'activated a chain reaction' in which '[e]nvironmentalists and NGOs outside the valley strongly protested the decision of the government to approve the projects when sufficient studies on their environmental and social impact had not been initiated, and those started had not yet been completed' (Dwivedi 2006: 157). In December 1987, a conference was organized in Delhi under the auspices of the World Wide Fund for Nature (India), in which the main organization working in the Valley as well as several significant NGOs participated, in order to 'facilitate the coordination of activities among the various nongovernmental groups and organizations contesting the Narmada Projects inside and outside the Valley' (Khagram 2004: 112). The conference yielded the Narmada Action Plan, a strategy document that sought to advance and organize further information-gathering activities, and which championed the demand that a full review and reappraisal of the SSP should be initiated (see Dwivedi 2006: 159).

Urban NGOs were also crucial in that they functioned as 'key links to the emerging environmental and human rights networks in India which, in turn, were becoming connected to similar networks in the South and the North' (Sen n.d.: 8–9). And this brings me to the extension of the infrastructure of contention at a transnational scale in the form of the construction of links between the NDS and US and European-based NGOs involved in the monitoring of World Bank funding of large-scale infrastructural projects in the South. The basis of the transnational extension of the infrastructure of contention lay in a very concrete experience of World Bank involvement with the SSP, as NDS activists first encountered the World Bank on their own turf, in the adivasi village of Manibeli, Maharashtra:

> Another parallel chapter in this struggle was our encounter with the World Bank. It seriously began when Bank consultant William Partridge, with a flock of officials from the World Bank office in Delhi – Abdus Salam, as well as many officials of the government, came to Manibeli for the first time in 1986. Government employees were translating what the villagers were saying to them, and we started exposing the false and distorted translations that these employees were making. I intervened, and they realized that we had lots of information. We shared whatever we had by that time about Manibeli village about how the land acquisition awards that were announced for only two villages in Maharashtra had been riddled with corruption. Rs. 200 were being extracted from each family by the land acquisition officer and one advocate, the local politicians with the patel of Manibeli village himself, and so on and so forth.
>
> (Patkar 1995: 173)

The encounter in Manibeli led to further meetings between NDS activists and Bank staff, in which NDS activists and World Bank representatives exchanged data and documents about the project. However, according to Patkar, activists' expectations that their views and criticisms of the project would be reflected in the

World Bank's appraisal 'never happened . . . there were many positive responses . . . but we never saw any commitments being seriously followed up or an acknowledgement of the logical conclusion that emerged from the ground reality' (ibid.: 173).

The NDS was not the only organization with an eye on the World Bank's involvement in funding the SSP. In the early 1980s Oxfam came to focus on the project and developed a working relationship with the ARCH Vahini (discussed later). Survival International (SI), a UK-based organization approached the World Bank in 1984–85 to demand that it enforce its own policies on ethnic minorities, and R & R in conjunction with its funding of the SSP. They took the matter before the International Labour Organization in 1985 and ultimately launched an international appeal to stop the World Bank's loan to the project. In the US, a campaign to monitor and prevent the funding of destructive infrastructural projects by multilateral development banks (MDBs) had been underway since the early 1980s. A network of environmental NGOs came to target the World Bank from 1983 onwards, through a strategy in which they sought to 'build pressure on member governments to move the Bank, through the executive directors, to institute environmental reforms' (Wade 1997: 659). The MDB campaign came to focus on the Polonoereste highway project in western Brazil, the transmigration projects in Indonesia, livestock projects in Botswana, and, crucially, the Narmada projects in India (Sen n.d.: 4).

The building of links to India and the Narmada struggle started in 1986, when Bruce Rich of the US-based Environmental Defense Fund, a central player in the MDB campaign, and Marcus Colchester of Survival International travelled to the Narmada Valley, where they met with Medha Patkar. This meeting occurred in a context of increased urgency as the Indian government gave the go-ahead to the SSP without clearance from MoEF. Two major outcomes resulted from the meeting between Rich and Colchester and the activists in the Valley. First, Medha Patkar was invited to Washington D.C. in 1987 to meet with Bank staff and US politicians in order to present the case against the SSP and 'to lobby the Bank to pressure the government of India and project authorities to adhere to environmental and resettlement norms' (Sen n.d.: 9). This was only the first of many trips that Narmada activists would make to the US to present their case in front of Bank representatives and politicians. Second, a decision was made to establish what would become the Narmada International Action Committee – described by Khagram (2004: 109) as 'a more formalized transnational coalition among international and domestic non-governmental organizations from around the world' to target the World Bank, donor governments and federal and state authorities in India. With these building-blocks in place, the basis was established for the international campaign against World Bank funding of the SSP – a campaign that has since become known as a prime example of successful activism through 'transnational advocacy networks' (Keck and Sikkink 1998). I engage further with this aspect of the campaign against the SSP in Chapter 6. Now, however, I turn to the trajectory of mobilization in the dam-affected adivasi communities in Gujarat.

The ARCH Vahini

Initial activities and confrontations

The ARCH Vahini (AV) commenced its work among dam-affected tribal communities in Gujarat in the wake of the Tribunal Award of 1979. Funded by Oxfam to conduct health work among adivasis in Gujarat, the AV gradually came to concentrate on the impacts of the SSP on the tribal communities. The scenario they encountered has been described by Anil Patel, a leading AV activist, as one of 'helpless-passive tribals':

> The tribals knew nothing about the project and their imminent displacement. The landowners were served land acquisition notices, but they knew little about their entitlements. They knew little about the place they were going to be resettled. The administrative setup for the resettlement and rehabilitation was in a pitiable condition. The administration was informed by a smug belief that, as in all major irrigation schemes in Gujarat and elsewhere in India, the project-affected people would just have to move, accepting whatever was offered to them . . . The elected representatives of the people were nowhere in sight. People dared not approach them with their woes. Everywhere in the submergence zone in Gujarat and the two other states, nobody thought it necessary to inform properly the people about the displacement, the reasons for it, and their entitlements. Almost always they came to know about the project and the future inundation of their land and houses through surveyors who were pitching the boundary stones of the reservoir.
>
> (ibid.: 182)

This is of course a scenario that resonates with the experience of activists in the tribal communities of MP and Maharashtra. Patel attributes the fact that the tribal communities were being kept in the dark about the impact of submergence to a widespread attitude among politicians and bureaucrats that adivasis were not to be reckoned with, as well as people's fear of approaching the authorities with worries and grievances – all central elements of the state-society relationship I have referred to as everyday tyranny.

The initial contacts between the AV activists and the tribal communities were made in July 1980. Patel highlights scepticism towards the outsiders as the first reaction of the communities, people were doubtful as to what young and inexperienced outsiders could achieve vis-à-vis seemingly almighty authorities. Patel also describes how they as activists were aware of their own limitations – in particular their 'inexperience and powerlessness' (Patel 1995: 183).

Eventually, however, the adivasis decided to give them a chance, and the activists decided to persevere. Their activities in the adivasis communities forced the government to respond:

> Local politicians descended on the scene and began both chiding and wooing people in the same breath: 'Who are these rootless, city-based young

> individuals? Don't you see that only the government can deliver anything substantial? And don't you know that we are the government? And who are they after all but non-tribals? We are your leaders and only we can get things done for you.'
>
> (Patel 1997: 71)

This attitude elicited an ambivalent response from the adivasis:

> People nodded their heads in wisdom. They even shared these feelings. But they also noted with ironic amusement that these very leaders had been totally absent when they, the people, had been voiceless. It was only because of the young people in question that the leaders were now there. The people's self-confidence grew, and so did our alliance with them.
>
> (1997: 71–2)

Events such as these, and their effects, resonate with significant processes in MP and Maharashtra, where confrontations with state authorities played a signal role in catalyzing processes of mobilization. The simple fact that incipient activities around issues of submergence and rehabilitation prompted the authorities to respond had a catalytic effect in that it constituted a small-scale subversion of the received wisdom of everyday tyranny where the plights of adivasis were non-issues and the state was unapproachable. Such tangible results in turn built confidence in the abilities and commitment of the activists, and thus bolstered the readiness of the communities to participate in mobilization.

By 1983, several villages had started to accept the official R&R package. This policy was perceived by the activists as being fundamentally inadequate as it failed to follow the guidelines for rehabilitation and resettlement stipulated by the Tribunal Award. In particular, the rights of encroachers were not recognized. Patel comments: 'The R&R policy was deeply regressive and it excluded a majority of the tribal families. We were reduced to monitoring the implementation of this bleak and unfair policy' (1997: 72).

However, the tables were turned when the government reneged on a written promise of rehabilitation. The AV took the matter to the Gujarat High Court, a move that turned out to be decisive in the trajectory of mobilization:

> This gesture was highly symbolic, and was made out of sheer desperation. But the Gujarat High Court almost upheld the tribals' complaint, and the government was forced to compromise. The effect was dramatic. Through their practical experience, the tribals now came to know that the government was not invincible after all, and that the law could be used to their advantage as well.
>
> (Patel 1997: 72)

Again we have a catalytic event through which received wisdoms are reversed, rendering possible further mobilization. Patel's focus on how the adivasis communities learned through practical experience that the state was not all-powerful indeed defines the essential dynamic of such events.

In 1983, the AV also made contact with the World Bank to draw their attention to the way encroachers and major sons and their entitlement to land-for-land compensation was not recognized. In response, the World Bank appointed Thayer Scudder to lead an inquiry into R&R policies for the SSP. The mission confirmed the issues that the AV had been campaigning around. This is significant in that it marks the first of several fruitful dialogues between the AV and the World Bank, through which the World Bank actually became a vehicle for the consolidation of the AV's case against the authorities (Patel 1995, 1997).

Land demands and mobilization

Following these events, the mobilization for encroachers' rights gathered momentum:

> The encroachers were a majority, and their voice became more and more emphatic. The label 'thieves' given to them by the officers, which they had at first meekly acknowledged and internalized, was slowly cast off as they understood the way the label was applied to them in the first place. The transition from being apologetic and defensive about encroachment to becoming assertive about their rights was slow and painful, but the trend was unmistakable.
>
> (Patel 1997: 74)

In March 1984, as a response to the increasing momentum of the mobilization process, the AV decided to organize a protest march of the tribal oustees of Gujarat and the adjoining villages of Maharashtra. This kind of mobilization was unparalleled in the recent history of the region (ibid.: 74). The march further strengthened the AV's links with NGOs – among them Survival International – working at the interface between development and environment, which in turn facilitated links with concerned officers in the World Bank.

By the end of 1984 there were intense negotiations between the World Bank and the three riparian states over the Loan Agreement for the SSP. There was a specific focus on R&R, and particular emphasis was put on the issue of the rights of encroachers to land-for-land compensation, which eventually were incorporated into the Loan Agreement (Patel 1997: 75). In Patel's view, the AV's activities left an imprint on the Loan Agreement in that it made explicit reference to 'landless oustees which is a broader term and includes encroachers' (ibid.: 75). This, to the AV, was a significant victory: 'The right to entitlement stubbornly denied to the [encroachers] by the states had at last been conceded' (ibid.: 75).

However, tangible manifestations of this victory – in the form of the implementation of an adequate policy for R&R – were not forthcoming. It gradually dawned on the activists that the state was not going to pay heed to the guidelines stipulated in the Loan Agreement. In response, the AV moved to secure a stay on displacement through the Gujarat High Court and then the Supreme Court, but these injunctions were 'violated with impunity' (Patel 1997: 76). The Government of Gujarat (GoG) was actively denying that encroachers had entitlements to R&R; they resorted to the designation of encroachers as thieves of government property, and referred to the Indian Forest Act to justify their actions. However, this strategy would eventually backfire as a 1987 Mission was instructed by the World Bank to investigate the AV's criticisms of the GoG (ibid.: 77). The head of the World Bank mission put the widespread suspense to an end by announcing that 'irrespective of what the government officers said to them in the village, the Gujarat government was legally bound to give a minimum of two hectares of land to each encroacher and to each major son' (ibid.: 77). This was a decisive triumph which facilitated the crafting of a satisfactory policy and strategy for R&R. Once again, then, the AV had been able to ally with the World Bank in putting pressure on the authorities to fashion and implement what was perceived to be an adequate policy and strategy of rehabilitation.

Through Patel's writings it is possible to catch a glimpse of a mobilization process that is in many respects similar to what we have seen in the case of the KMCS and the NDS. It is possible to identify an encounter with the contours of everyday tyranny, activists seems to have functioned as catalysts and the mobilization process seems to have gathered momentum through catalytic events, and the gist of the AV's activities have revolved around claiming the basic right to information for citizens that stand to be expropriated by the state. If there is a feature that makes the AV distinct from the other organizations at this stage of the movement process, it is the character of their interactions with the World Bank, and the ways in which this impacted upon mobilization in the adivasi communities in Gujarat. As I showed earlier, activists of the NDS also interacted closely with officials of the World Bank, but maintained that this yielded little or nothing in terms of actual commitments and practical measures to ensure the implementation of adequate R&R policies for dam-affected communities in MP and Maharashtra. As a rèsult of this, as I show in Chapter 6, there was a change in the character of the interaction with the World Bank which occurred in sync with the transition towards the anti-dam campaign: rather than seeking to use the World Bank as a vehicle through which to secure R&R, activist practice came to be directed at the cancellation of World Bank funding of the project altogether. However, for the AV the World Bank came to function precisely as a vehicle through which to exert pressure on state authorities to alter R&R policies in such a way as to incorporate their key demands for the inclusion of encroacher's rights. As I show in the next chapter, this was to have a decisive impact upon the relationship between the AV and the other organizations in Maharashtra and MP as the mobilization around the rights of dam-affected communities intensified in 1987–88.

The Narmada Ghati Navnirman Samiti

Memories of mobilization in the 1970s

The region of Nimad differs from the adivasi communities in the Narmada Valley not only in terms of their social, economic and political structures, but also in terms of the trajectory of resistance to the SSP. There have been three rounds of mobilization against the project; first in the late 1960s and early 1970s, second in the late 1970s and early 1980s, and third from the mid-1980s onwards. Secondary sources diverge somewhat in terms of the emergence of the first organization that contested the SSP – the Nimad Bachao, Narmada Bachao Samiti (Save Nimad, Save Narmada Committee, NBNBS). Sen (2000a) dates the emergence of the NBNBS to the late 1960s, whereas Sangvai (2000a) dates it to the Tribunal deliberations of the mid-1970s. The nature of the NBNBS campaign was related both to the inter-state rivalries over the distribution of water and to claims for the non-submergence of Nimad (Sangvai 2000a: 16). However, neither Sen nor Sangvai provides much information about the decline of this movement.

In the late 1970s, following the declaration of the Tribunal Award, yet another campaign – the Nimad Bachao Andolan – emerged to contest the height of the dam. The Congress Party and the Janata Party competed for control over the agitation as it would guarantee substantial political gains in the area, and more than 5,000 people demonstrated in Bhopal. The MP government – headed by the Janata Party – declared its opposition to the Award and resolved to have it amended (Sangvai 2000a: 20; see also Khagram 2004: 84–5). With the victory of the Congress Party in the state elections of 1980, Arjun Singh became Chief Minister of the State. Once an ardent opponent of the SSP, Singh quickly turned his coat and called off Congress support for the Nimad Bachao Andolan. Moreover, the leaders of the movement stalled its agitations as it believed that Congress would continue the struggle against the Award in the parliamentary realm. This failed to happen as Arjun Singh reached a compromise with the Congress CM of Gujarat that the construction of the dam should go ahead given that there would be inter-state discussions about rehabilitation of the dam-affected communities (Dwivedi 2006: 88–9; Khagram 2004: 85).

The narratives of the trajectory of the Nimad Bachao Andolan[1] offered by activists from the region are unequivocally stories of defeat and cooptation, of betrayal by politicians, and loss of faith in the fecundity of mobilization, and this experience of failure came to constitute a barrier that had to be overcome in the rejuvenation of protest in the 1980s. Consider the version of the story given by Jaganath Patidar, an elderly farmer of the village of Kundia:

> When the Tribunal Award was declared in 1979, there was a Janata government in Madhya Pradesh. The opposition leaders, such as Arjun Singh of Indore, and the ruling party joined hands in opposing the project. The sole purpose of this was to secure political support and votes in the area. The Congress leaders came to the villages to mobilize them; Shankar Patel of the Janata Party also went around the area for the same purposes, arguing that people should not run after the politicians and give them money, as they were only in it for the power politics. In Gujarat there was a huge ashram and the person in charge of the ashram had been instrumental in stopping the damming of the Kavat river. He also joined the mobilization in Nimad. Nimad Bachao Andolan lasted for about a year and a half. Its stand was not one of dam opposition, but of stopping

> the dam at 220 feet, which was the original design in the Nehru era. However, the movement fizzled out due to its being implicated in the power games of mainstream politics. People could see through the intrigues and lost faith in the campaign.
>
> (interview, April 2003)

Jaganath's account depicts a process of mobilization that was driven primarily by individuals who were embedded in party politics, and he also attributes the failure of the process to this fact: the exigencies of mainstream politics got in the way of truly popular mobilization. This was a perspective that permeated farmers' narratives throughout the area (field notes, April 2003). The withdrawal of local leaders also contributed to the collapse of the Nimad Bachao Andolan by creating a vacuum of political skill:

> In the 1970s, the Nimad Bachao Andolan emerged with the involvement of both the major parties – the Congress and the Janata Party. The problem was that no matter which party was in power, it would silence the local leaders in the area who criticized the Sardar Sarovar. When these local politicians failed to provide the needed guidance and leadership, the villagers gradually started to lose interest. People were frustrated when the Nimad Bachao Andolan fizzled out; there was no guidance, and they didn't really know what a movement was – they didn't have the skills of political mobilization. People were arguing that if big leaders couldn't fight the project, then who could? They thought that political struggles could only take place between states.
>
> (interview, Sitaram Patidar, April 2003)

On the one hand, then, we have a memory of defeat and cooptation due to mobilization being 'contaminated' by the exigencies of party politics, and, on the other hand, the frustration with the vacuum of political skill engendered by the withdrawal of local leaders from the mobilization process. In combination, the two had given rise to a local rationality of resignation and disillusionment that prevented the emergence of sustained and autonomous mobilization in opposition to the impacts of the SSP.

Whereas the absence of opposition and resistance was a common feature of the Nimadi communities and the adivasi communities in the three states, I think it is important to recognize that the fact that there had been some form of mobilization in the area testifies to a significant difference vis-à-vis the adivasi areas of Alirajpur and Nandurbar, where the dam and its impact had been accepted without many quibbles. This shows the extent to which the experience of everyday tyranny and the local rationality of acquiescence and deference was a feature that was specific to the adivasi communities. Whereas extraparliamentary political skills might have been in short supply at a local level in Nimad, and whereas the exigencies of electoral politics may have undermined the momentum of mobilization at this particular conjuncture, these areas were still courted by politicians vying for political support, which is of course radically different from the repression and neglect that characterized the presence of the state in the adivasi communities.

Efforts of mobilization in the 1980s

By the mid-1980s, a new organization had been formed in the dam-affected area of western Nimad – the Narmada Ghati Navnirman Samiti – at the initiative of veteran Gandhians and Sarvodayis. According to one of my interviewees, the NGNS primarily travelled around the villages to spread information about the SSP and negotiated with the government (interview, Mahesh Patel, April 2003). However, the general consensus throughout the area was that the NGNS was not a force to be reckoned with prior to the arrival of Medha Patkar of the NDS.

This is how Medha Patkar narrates the incursion into Nimad in the article 'The Struggle for Participation and Justice':

> In April 1987, when the clearance to the SSP was being continuously discussed by the center and the state, we went to Madhya Pradesh because we thought that the whole plains area to be affected must be brought in. So it was from April 1987 till May 1988 that we had mobilized a large number of villagers by holding public meetings in the highly politicized area of big middle-class farmers as well as small farmers and landless labourers. Compared to the tribal villages, these were the mixed communities with a heterogeneous population. They were thickly populated villages, with a chemical input-based agriculture and horticulture on prime agricultural land. The extremely different scenarios posed a major challenge from the point of view of using different strategies, skills, media, and idioms on the one hand, and bringing them together in a situation where the upper-caste landlords were using derogatory language when referring to the Adivasis. It was challenging keeping them together in the movement.
>
> (Patkar 1995: 162–3)

Here, the difference in scenario – in particular social stratification and the antagonism inherent in the structures of stratification – is highlighted as a possible obstacle to mobilization. Another potential obstacle to mobilization was the state of the NGNS at that point in time:

> . . . we had one contact in the Nimad, of the Narmada Ghati Navnirman Samiti; they were the old persons, actually, beyond 70, it was a group of five, seven person, and one of them the senior-most in Indore, Kashinath Trivedi. He had taken a walk in the villages, and they had held two, three conferences and invited some government officials also. There was one executive engineer, Anil Gupta . . . he was also against the project, so he had come and they had held one conference in Anjan, near Badwani. But when I got the contact in Dhar district where there were these ashrams, I went there and talked, and they said 'we are not able to go to the villages and mobilize, so now there is no work going on, but we have formed this committee'. So I went with them to few villages, just got the whole scale, scene; so there we started this whole process. I would go every ten or fifteen days, and some junior activists would accompany me sometimes, so that was one phase.
>
> (interview, June 2003)

What stands out here is the perception of the lack of an adequate infrastructure of contention in the sense that the extant organization was not properly grounded in an organizational structure of mobilized communities; it remained a free-floating body trying to disseminate information and negotiate with the authorities. The creation of an infrastructure of contention thus became the order of the day:

> I had to go every ten or fifteen days, and a small group of the Nimad farmers, we would take rounds in the jeep and hold meetings in village after village. And in every village representatives were selected and committees were formed. Earlier these Navnirman Samiti, these old persons were the only ones available most of the time, but they were not able to go from village to village, so we went throughout. Then again the tehsil level committee, whatever tehsils we covered, then the representation started.
>
> (interview, June 2003)

The organization evolved much as in the adivasi areas of Maharashtra, through the construction of committees at village, block and district levels in the areas affected by the SSP.

The narratives of villagers that were involved in this process mirror Medha's account in the sense that they bring out how the NGNS was revived and its infrastructure of contention was developed and extended. Consider, for instance, Sitaram Patidar's account of this process:

> When Medha came, she dug out who the persons were who had been involved with prior mobilizations. However, she found it difficult to mobilize people in the villages. She used to tell people 'I need one hour from you', and then she would talk to people about various issues related to the SSP. Some people would pick up the message, and slowly but surely meetings started to take place to as to facilitate the building of an organization in the area.
>
> (interview, April 2003)

Similar narratives were offered throughout the area. Mahesh Patel of Kundia emphasized that Medha's interaction with the NGNS focused on the functioning of their organization, and on touring the villages to spread information about the impact of the SSP and the possibilities for contesting it (interview, April 2003). This is also the gist of the narrative of Devrambhai, a committed activist and farmer from the village of Kaparkheda:

> When Medha arrived in the area people were totally disheartened by the failures of the previous rounds of mobilization. There was a general understanding in the area that the decision to build the Sardar Sarovar was a government decision, and who could fight the government? Medha, however, went around the area and told people about the Tribunal Award and how it entitled them for compensation – land for land, house for house – but that these entitlements had to be fought for. This was how the organizing was revived and strengthened.
>
> (interview, April 2003)

Similarly, Jaganath Patidar emphasized how Medha's intervention introduced a new awareness of the necessity and possibility of organized resistance:

> Before the NDS started its forays into Nimad, the Narmada Ghati Navnirman Samiti was in existence, but it was almost non-operational. Medha's arrival in the area and her interaction with the Gandhians and Sarvodayis in the Narmada Ghati committee entailed new rounds of going around the villages to spread information about the SSP and the need for organizing resistance. Intense organizing revitalized the NGNS. When Medha and her fellow-travellers had arguments with state officials over the SSP and its impacts, people saw that the officials had no answers, and they were also gradually convinced that mobilization was necessary. Their confidence in the potential of organized resistance grew.
>
> (interview, April 2003)

What stands out in villagers' narratives of the interaction between Medha and the NGNS is very much that which has been described as the transformation of local rationalities through catalytic work, albeit with some important differences from the adivasi areas. The spreading of an awareness of the impact of the dam and the actual rights of the dam-affected people is a familiar theme in this work. However, the difference here is that in the adivasi areas, the spreading of an awareness started at a more basic level, namely that of spreading an awareness of the rights inherent in citizenship. Moreover, the building of a sense of confidence in the utility of resistance is also familiar, but again this process seems to have been different in Nimad than in the adivasi areas. The main challenge and achievement in Nimad was not to overcome the received wisdoms of everyday tyranny so much as to overcome the disenchantment with resistance per se, a disenchantment rooted in the collective experience and memory of failure and cooptation. An aspect that should be noted in this respect is how the mobilization that was initiated with the interaction between NDS and NGNS represented a break with the past in that it constituted what can be called a 'non-party political process' (Kothari 1984). This is so in that whereas the previous rounds of mobilization had been initiated and driven through – and eventually lost their momentum because of – the interventions of representatives of the major political parties, the new organization was autonomous of mainstream politics. Whereas this was not stated explicitly by any of the interviewees, one might assume that the fact that the emergent organization was not 'contaminated' by the exigencies of electoral politics helped in overcoming the hurdle constituted by the collective memory of the perceived betrayal of mainstream politicians.

Concluding remarks

In the mid-1980s the Narmada Valley witnessed the emergence of militant particularisms struggling for R&R in all the communities that would be affected by the SSP. Essentially, what was achieved during this early stage of mobilization was the politicization of a development intervention which the state – through the concerted effort to keep local communities in the dark about the impacts of the dam and their rights to information and compensation – had tried to keep beyond the realm of political contestation. The notion of 'rightful resistance' used to conceptualize the politics of the KMCS in Chapter 3 is also an apt characterization of the militant particularist struggles for R&R: activists basically sought to hold the state accountable to constitutional principles and legislation relating to displacement in conjunction with development projects in a context where such principles and such legislation was *de facto* negated by the actual practices of the state. As I bring out in following chapters, the rationality of rightful resistance would continue to underpin popular mobilization in the Narmada Valley, and this was to have a profound impact on the trajectory of the movement process. Moreover, the processes through which these militant particularisms emerged to articulate a politics of rightful resistance share some basic similarities in that they were all predicated upon the transformation of local rationalities in which organized, collective resistance was conceived of as untenable, and in that these transformations were mediated by the intervention of external agents who came to function as catalysts of resistance. This was an achievement of profound importance as it generated the practical skills, cognitive resources and emotive dispositions necessary for adivasi participation in what would eventually be a pan-state anti-dam campaign.

In the case of the Narmada Dharangrasta Samiti, I showed how an integral dynamic of the workings of everyday tyranny was a severe dearth of information about the dam and its consequences for the adivasi communities, and how this was reflected in a local rationality in which people conceived of the SSP as unchallengeable. The arrival of an external agent triggered a series of catalytic events through which this local rationality was transformed. Following this, an infrastructure of contestation was constructed, unifying dam-affected communities in their efforts to secure R&R, and enabling the articulation of grievances and making of claims and demands on opponents across spatial scales.

In the case of the ARCH Vahini, mobilization was initiated in a similar context of lacking information and widespread fear of state officials. Again, urban educated activists who came to work in the area had to gain the acceptance and trust of the dam-affected communities through confrontations with the dam bureaucracy. This relationship of trust in turn came to constitute the basis for a struggle centred on forcing Gujarat state to develop and implement an adequate policy and strategy for R&R. A crucial feature of this struggle was that the World Bank functioned as an ally rather than an opponent, and this relationship, coupled with the successful outcome of the AV's demands for R&R had profound implications for the AV's relationship to the emergence of the anti-dam campaign.

The mobilization that took place in western Nimad was similarly predicated upon a transformation of local rationalities, but this transformation revolved around overcoming collective memories of defeat and cooptation in past processes of mobilization that had been closely intertwined with regional party politics rather than subverting practices of deference and submission rooted in fear. This transformation occurred through the resuscitation and redirection of the modus operandi of an already extant organization – the Narmada Ghati Navnirman Samiti – through the intervention of NDS activists. The resuscitation and redirection of the activities of the NGNS was centred on a move away from information-spreading and negotiations with state authorities towards the development of an infrastructure of contestation that would allow active mobilization of village communities around issues of information and rehabilitation outside the realm of regional party politics.

Importantly, at this phase in the movement process, activists that responded to situated and determinate experiences in specific communities also started communicating and building links between their respective struggles, as well as with national and transnational advocacy networks. Through this process, solidarities were crafted, common enemies were named, and a shared agenda started to crystallize – in other words, as activists started to join the dots, they also started to join hands. Albeit uneven and fractured, this dynamic would eventually give rise to the common strategies and the common identity that underpinned the Narmada Bachao Andolan as a pan-state anti-dam campaign. It is to this phase of the movement process in the Narmada Valley that I turn in the next chapter.

5 Towards opposition

The formation of the anti-dam campaign

> Now the time is over. After years of efforts, discussions and experiences we have concluded that this 13,500 crore Sardar Sarovar Project would not bring about development of the country; but it would mortgage this nation to the international moneyed agencies. This billion dollars project would not give any benefit to the poor, but would strengthen the consumerism and the urban areas through electricity and cash crops. It would destroy hundreds and thousands of us who are dependent on natural resources . . . This destruction is neither fully taken into consideration, nor is there any measure to stop it. In such a situation, the government is bent upon pushing this project ahead. However, we are also resolving that we will take on this challenge of Sardar Sarovar against our nation with all the strength.
>
> We will stop Sardar Sarovar! We will die, but will not move out; we will not leave Narmada Valley.[1]

So ended a statement issued on 18 August 1988 by the Narmada Dharangrasta Samiti, the Narmada Ghati Navnirman Samiti, and the Narmada Asargrasta Sangharsha Samiti.[2] Having come together in opposition to the dam, the organizations urged the Government of India to 'declare the decision to cancel Sardar Sarovar Project'.

In this chapter I unearth the major processes that led to the formation of the pan-state anti-dam campaign which came to be known as the Narmada Bachao Andolan, engage with the partly fractured nature of these processes, and discuss the relationship between the emergence of a politics of dam-opposition at a national scale in India and the mobilization of popular resistance to the Narmada dams.

The declaration of opposition to the Sardar Sarovar Project (SSP) was expressive of a qualitative shift in the mobilization process in the Narmada Valley, which revolved around (a) a radicalization of the central demands and claims levelled at central and state-level authorities, and (b) an abstraction of the politics of resistance from specific situations of dispossession to a generic situation of dispossession at a pan-state scale, and, concurrently, a generic challenge to dispossession at a pan-state scale. In the following, I argue that the radicalization and abstraction of popular resistance in the Narmada Valley must be understood in terms of how the movement became 'a learner and constructor of knowledge' (Kilgore 1999: 91) through its engagement with opponents in two basic ways. First, a process of confrontational learning took place in which the state's refusal to enter into a dialogue with the movement created an understanding among the activists that the responsible authorities were neither capable of nor willing to conduct proper resettlement and rehabilitation (R&R). Second, activists constructed a significant body of counter-expertise that revealed the flaws of official claims about the SSP, and abstracted from the specific local contexts in which demands for resettlement and rehabilitation had initially been voiced by formulating a critique of the SSP at a pan-state level and by embedding this critique in a generic opposition to dam-building as a development strategy.

I then turn to an analysis of how the abstraction from local situations of dispossession towards a pan-state anti-dam campaign was criss-crossed by processes of divergence and convergence at different spatial scales. The decision to move towards dam opposition on a pan-state basis was a fractured one: the ARCH Vahini, which had mobilized dam-affected communities in Gujarat, opted to collaborate with the Government of Gujarat in the implementation of resettlement and rehabilitation. I trace the rationale of this decision to the success of the ARCH Vahini in gaining a resettlement and rehabilitation policy which recognized the rights of project-affected households without formal title deeds to their land – so-called encroachers – and discuss how differentiations in local circumstances impacts upon processes of abstraction in movement processes. Following this, I move on to analyze how the emergence of the anti-dam campaign in the Narmada Valley converged with the formation of anti-dam networks on a national scale in the 1980s, and analyze how activist narratives systematically downplay the impact of this development on mobilization in the Narmada Valley.

The radicalization and abstraction of resistance

The dynamics of confrontational learning

In the previous chapter, I showed how activists created an infrastructure of contention that enabled the dam-affected communities to confront the state with demands for disclosure of information and to claim their right to resettlement and rehabilitation. However, when the organizations of the dam-affected communities confronted district- and state-level authorities with their questions about the impacts of the project and the capacity of the state to implement satisfactory schemes for rehabilitation and resettlement, the responses from the powers that be were not perceived to be passable. Whereas their statements on the matter were generally short, a common answer from activists in the dam-affected villages when I asked them how they had arrived at the decision to oppose to the dam was typically that 'the government could not answers our questions, so we were convinced that they could not resettle us' (field notes, March/April 2003).

The process they referred to unfolded from November 1987 to May 1988 in a context of increasing urgency. In April 1987, the Ministry of Environment and Forests (MoEF) recommended that the SSP should not be granted environmental clearance. As a response to this the Chief Ministers of Gujarat, Maharashtra and Madhya

Pradesh made it plain to Prime Minister Rajiv Gandhi that the Congress Party 'would lose the next election in these three states if he did not get the project approved' (Khagram 2004: 110). Gandhi had already suffered setbacks in several states in the mid-term elections and was highly cognizant of his dependence upon these three important states in central and western India. Hence he 'pushed the environmental clearance through in June of 1987, and a forest clearance was accorded in September of the same year' (ibid.: 110). The construction of the SSP could begin.

Mobilization of the dam-affected communities was taking place throughout the three riparian states by late 1987. Crucial to activist efforts was the politicization of the SSP through a critical questioning of its impact upon the communities of the Valley and the possibilities for rehabilitation. In November 1987, the NDS and the NGNS submitted a joint memorandum to the Narmada Control Authority (NCA), putting forward a list of demands concerning rehabilitation and information; it warned that unless answers were provided before 15 December, a large-scale movement would be inaugurated to put pressure on the NCA (Dwivedi 1997: 10). The activists held good on their warning when, on 30 January, 1988, following a series of smaller meetings in Maharashtra and Madhya Pradesh, a large public rally, attended by some 4,000 people that stood to be affected by the SSP, was staged in Kevadia, Gujarat to raise the issue of displacement and resettlement. Medha Patkar explains the rationale behind the rally as follows:

> The basic issue then became this: that those who have already been displaced should be resettled first. We said, 'Show us what you can do. The others will not move out till all the questions have been answered, not only regarding rehabilitation but also other crucial aspects'.
>
> (Patkar 1995: 161)

However, the authorities responded by stonewalling the movement: 'The government denied access to the main reports, and this was clearly mentioned in the Narmada Control Authority's reply to us, which also said that we could help them in implementation. This reply reached us in March 1988' (Patkar 1995: 161). The activists reached the conclusion that they would have to seek out the information themselves, and started examining project-related documents from the dam authorities and the World Bank. What emerged from this process was the knowledge that the SSP had not been through a satisfactory project appraisal. This meant that the costs of the project were likely to be severely underestimated and, conversely, that the benefits of the project were likely to be overestimated (ibid.: 161). This in turn prompted the involved organizations to call a meeting on 14 May 1988. Some 250 representatives of the affected communities of all three states attended to discuss the issue of the SSP and questions relating to displacement and resettlement, both among themselves and with representatives of the NCA and of the state and central governments. Medha Patkar sums up the result of the event:

> We then decided, after that six-hour marathon discussion in 1988, that we must give two months' time to the government and, then if we did not get the

> answers, oppose the dam. On the same day in the evening that we had the long discussion with the Narmada Control Authority and the three states and center's secretaries . . . After that meeting, we signed a common letter saying that we were giving the government two months' time, and if they did not answer all the questions in two months, we would oppose the project.
>
> (ibid.: 161–2)

The state responded to their ultimatum with silence. Consequently, on 18 August, 1988, mass rallies were held in six tehsils in the three states, including Dhule (Maharashtra), Badwani (Madhya Pradesh), and Kevadia (Gujarat), to signal the declaration of total opposition to the project.

The process that unfolded from late 1987 to August 1988 can be thought of as confrontational learning in which 'an increasingly adequate mode of organization and struggle . . . is generated in the conflict with a movement's opponents' (Cox 1998: 6). In terms of its dynamic, what we see at play is essentially 'the two-way learning process involved in *movement*' (Barker and Cox 2002: 38–9; italics in original). This two-way learning process revolved around, on the one hand, the knowledge that activists garnered through their encounters with their opponents – in this case, a 'shedding of illusions' and a 'confirmation of suspicions' about the willingness and capacity of state and project authorities to resettle and rehabilitate dam-affected communities – and, on the other hand, the knowledge garnered through intra-movement discussions and dialogues. The latter typically centres on strategic and tactical proposals, and the moral and ideological justification of a movement's activity related to these proposals. The central strategic and tactical proposal that emerged in the Narmada Valley was that of moving from demanding resettlement and rehabilitation to demanding the cancellation of the SSP on a pan-state scale, and the proposal was justified with reference to the evidence that suggested that adequate resettlement and rehabilitation was unlikely to take place.

The significance of this process in driving the radicalization of the movement process runs as a central theme throughout the NBA's own narrative of the emergence of the anti-dam campaign. The official declaration of opposition to the SSP emphasizes how the organizations had set out on their campaign for adequate information and resettlement in the hope that the authorities would enter into dialogue with them:

> The oustees from Madhya Pradesh, Maharashtra and Gujarat had expected the government to discuss with them the issues of official cost-benefit, the assurance of liberal resettlement policy, alternative land and the entire resettlement plan to be presented to the oustees. The oustees' organisations have put before the state and central government level their suggestions and demands for last some years on the basis of the resettlement provisions in the Narmada Water Disputes Tribunal (NWDT), the stipulations in the agreement with the World Bank, the information about government resolutions and the study and experience of the organisations in the project-affected area. It was hoped that the

> government would respond differently about the special project like the SSP, keeping in view the abysmal conditions of . . . those displaced hitherto. All have expected that government would implement in an integrated manner the common resettlement policy for all three states, with necessary government machinery and land and other resources with the co-operation of the oustees.
>
> (NBA 1988: 194)

The narrative emphasises how hope turned to frustration through encounters with an unresponsive state apparatus:

> Discussions were held with the officials from all concerned departments in states and central government for years. Definitely, some assurances were given, but there was no decisive answer on the demands. A mammoth rally of thousands of oustees on 30th January 1988, held near the damsite had once again called upon the Narmada Control Authority (NCA) to decide about the demands. As a result, detailed discussions were held with the high level officials of NCA and three state governments on May 14, 1988. The discussion once again made it clear that the state Governments have no policy or resources for the oustees. The issue of land availability is still unanswered.
>
> (ibid.: 194)

The message conveyed by the NBA, then, is that the failure of the responsible authorities to respond and to disclose information worked so as to galvanize an emergent awareness that, in all likelihood, the state had neither the capacity nor the required plans for resettlement and rehabilitation. This in turn provided the movement with rationale and justification for the dramatic move that they made: rightful claims had been pursued through established channels but to no avail; in light of this experience, there was no choice but to opt for a more radical stance of total opposition to the SSP.

Constructing counter-expertise

The other crucial dynamic of the process of collective learning that energized the radicalization of the campaign was the knowledge production that was spawned as a response to the non-disclosure of information by state and project authorities in March 1988:

> We discussed this situation and, in May, decided that we had to dig out the details ourselves. So we dug out the documents, studied those, compared various documents of the World Bank with those of the government, and identified interstate differences. We really went through everything. And finally, we came to the conclusion that there were very, very major gaps. The benefits also were not truly estimated.
>
> (Patkar 1995: 161)

The discovery of gaps and flaws in official documents is reflected in the declaration of opposition to the SSP, which singles out five areas of contention and criticism: first, in terms of resettlement and rehabilitation, it is pointed out that within and between the three riparian states there is neither sufficient land nor enough money to purchase the land necessary for the resettlement of those who are displaced; second, in terms of environmental impacts, it is pointed out that the responsible authorities have failed to carry out crucial impact assessments; third, in terms of the cost-benefit balance of the project, it is pointed out that costs have been escalating without concurrent reviews of the official cost-benefit ratio; fourth, it is pointed out that state and project authorities have failed to provide full information about the project and its impacts to the dam-affected communities; fifth, drawing in a larger frame of criticism, the project is criticized for its distributional bias towards prosperous regions and groups, its adverse impact on public finances, and – as a consequence of these shortcomings – its destructive, as opposed to developmental character (NBA 1988: 195–6).

Combining scrutiny of official documents with surveying of conditions on the ground in the dam-affected communities, the organizations that were active in the Narmada Valley eventually produced a body of knowledge which effectively contradicted the central claims about the project made by state and project authorities. I shall refer to this body of knowledge as counter-expertise. I draw the term from Skirbekk (1984: 84), who defines 'counter-expertise' as 'true insights about a particular matter . . . that part of the truth which is *left out* when *only* the established experts are granted the right to speak'(italics in original).[3] The production of counter-expertise combined with confrontational learning to radicalize the strategic choices made by activists in the Narmada Valley. Shripad Dharmidhikary, an urban, educated activist who joined the mobilizing efforts during this time commented upon the process as follows: 'more and more facts came to light, and the enormity of the environmental impacts became clear, as well as our realization that the very rationale of the project – the project benefits – was highly doubtful. All this led us to challenge the project itself' (cited in Fisher 1995: 23).

The production of counter-expertise of course entails the deployment of activist skills in multiple ways. In order to carry out surveys of the dam-affected communities, it is necessary to be in possession of some basic research skills, and so does the presentation of data and findings. Going through official documents requires language skills: one has to be able to read English, and indeed be able to penetrate dense technical and bureaucratic prose. Moreover, to conduct a critical reading of these documents one has to be familiar with official standards in terms of resettlement and rehabilitation, benefit-cost ratios, and environmental assessment so as to point out where the project authorities have failed to do their job. And in order to gain access to the necessary documents, one has to have the right contacts, either to sympathetic organizations that pass on the material or indeed to sympathetic employers in the dam bureaucracy who leak papers and information. The urban educated activists brought many of the skills that were necessary to perform these tasks to the movement. Recall that many of these activists were trained social workers, some had studied economics and held degrees in rural management, and others again had backgrounds in engineering. They knew what to look for and how to look for it, they read English and could penetrate official documents and research materials, they could contact the right organizations and knew the right people in the bureaucracy, and they could put together a presentation of this material which would satisfy standards of scientific rigour and so on. Moreover, the urban, educated activists have been crucial in transmitting this counter-expertise both externally and internally – in settings as diverse as congressional hearings in the USA and village meetings in the Narmada Valley. As such, the crafting of counter-expertise can be considered as the labour of what Eyerman and Jamison (1991: 95) call 'movement intellectuals' – a term which refers to 'those individuals who through their activities articulate the knowledge interests and cognitive identity of the movement' (ibid.: 97).

However, the production of critical knowledge about the SSP was not confined to the movement intellectuals of the NBA. Critical studies of the Narmada projects date as far back as 1983, when a study of the dams was published by the Delhi-based organization Kalpavriksh. This study was sent to Edward Goldsmith, editor of *The Ecologist*, who, along with Nicholas Hildyard, proceeded to publish an abridged version in the second volume of *The Social and Environmental Impacts of Large Dams* that appeared in 1984. Furthermore, the Kalpavriksh study contributed to the emergence of a wave of mobilization around the Narmada projects in the early 1980s as it was distributed to various NGOs in India and abroad, leading to the incorporation of environmental concerns in their lobbying efforts (Khagram 2004: 106). The study was also sent to India's Department of Environment, which took an interest in the study vis-à-vis their work on environmental clearance for the SSP and the upstream Narmada Sagar Project.

There were a host of other sources of counter-expertise as well. In 1986, Multiple Action Research Group published a report on the status of information about the SSP among the affected adivasi communities in Alirajpur. In 1988, Claude Alvares and Ramesh Billorey published their *Damming the Narmada* and in 1990, Vijay Paranjpye published *High Dams on the Narmada*. Research institutions such as the Tata Institute of Social Sciences have carried out studies on rehabilitation, so has the Indian People's Tribunal on Environment and Human Rights. International organizations such as International Rivers Network have also participated in this process of knowledge production, while at the same time being an important part of the International Narmada Campaign. The report of the World Bank's review team certainly also qualifies as part of this critical knowledge base, and has been used actively by the movement in its campaign. As Routledge (2003) has pointed out, the NBA has actively made use of such critical studies in their campaign against the SSP. Indeed, the production of counter-expertise has been characterized by an intense cross-fertilization between the knowledge production of activists, bureaucrats and academics at various scales from the local to the national, and to the transnational (see Khagram 2004: 113).

This being said, it should also be noted that counter-expertise and its use did not remain the exclusive domain of movement intellectuals. Rather, it has become a political vernacular in the villages mobilized by the NBA. A consistent feature in village activist narratives of their motivation for being involved with the NBA, or their views on various critiques of the anti-dam campaign, was the reference made to some aspect of the movement's counter-expertise – be it in broad sweep or great detail. For example, when I asked my informants what they thought about the allegations made by the movement's opponents that dam-opposition was a backward-looking agenda, a general feature of their responses would be to point to one or several of the claims made by the Andolan about the overestimation of benefits and underestimation of costs, and the uneven distribution of both. One activist, Gulabia, posed the following question: 'What sort of development are the dams supposed to create? If people are drowned, then it cannot be development. The dams are supposed to be built for electricity, but it's only for the rich; the dams are going to kill the adivasis' (interview, March 2003). Keshuvbhai, an adivasi activist from the village of Nimgavhan put it in a similar way: 'The government talks of development, but the villages that stand to be submerged by the dam are not developed at all – they have no infrastructure. So what is this development about? They should develop the villages first!' (interview, March 2003). Devrambhai, a Nimadi activist, emphasized the issue of costs and benefits: 'The government was only projecting the benefits and not the costs'. This, he argued, was a general feature of India's dams: 'All the dams built in India, have they been evaluated?' (interview, April 2003).

Admittedly, such references are centred more on the general theme of a skewed distribution of the costs and benefits of the project. However, leading village activists display knowledge of numbers and technicalities that have served them well in confrontation with the project authorities. For example, Keshuvbhai recounted an episode where the chief minister of Maharashtra had recognized the need for resettlement, and sent a demand to the central government that the Maharashtra oustees should be resettled on forest land, and that Taloda forest should be used for these purposes. Some 2,700 hectares were sanctioned for rehabilitation. The District Collector then called a meeting in Dhulia. The villagers asked how many people could be resettled in this area. The Collector's survey was faulty; he said that only 1,300 families in the 33 villages were going to be affected, and that they could be resettled in Taloda. They refused to accept these figures and argued that 5,000 families would be affected by submergence: 'How can they be resettled on 2,700 hectares?' Keshuvbhai asked. The Collector was at a loss for words in the face of Keshuvbhai's command of facts and figures (interview, Nimgavhan, 13 March 2003).

Counter-expertise as a discourse of resistance

Keshuvbhai's story of confrontation with state authorities brings me to the question of how counter-expertise has functioned as a discourse of resistance. In the following, I shall argue that counter-expertise has served two main functions within the NBA's anti-dam campaign as a discourse of resistance. First, it has articulated a challenge to the attempts of dominant groups to legitimate their hegemonic projects 'as being the motor force or a universal expansion, of a development of all the "national" energies' (Gramsci 1998: 182), both at the level of the SSP and more generally in terms of articulating a wider critique of the politics of development planning. Second, this discourse of resistance has been articulated in such a way as to enable activists to 'shift gears' and 'transcend particularities' (Harvey 2000: 241) by abstracting a common, shared threat of dispossession and a common, shared campaign of resistance at a pan-state scale, and, furthermore, embedding this campaign in a wider critique of dam-building as a development strategy. In the following, I investigate both aspects through a close reading of what is arguably the fullest written statement of the politics of the NBA, namely the manifesto *Towards Just and Sustainable Development* (TJSD), which was published in 1992.

In TJSD the critique of the SSP starts with the planning of the project. First of all, the decision-making process that has underpinned the SSP is criticized for its lack of adherence to stated rules concerning major development interventions and its lack of transparency, and this is in turn related to what is perceived to be a democratic deficit in the Indian polity. It is pointed out how, when clearance for the project was given in 1987, this was on the condition that a range of studies and impact assessments would be carried out by the end of 1989. These conditions have not been heeded:

> Today, as all these major studies are still incomplete, most of the conditions in the clearance stand violated, and MOEF had declared these clearances as lapsed and asked the dam authorities to apply afresh to get the sanction . . . The policy and pre-conditions set by the largest foreign donor, the World Bank, have also been violated. All this have serious repercussions for the justifiability of the dam that [is] being pushed ahead.
>
> (TJSD 1992: 6)

The issue of a democratic deficit is then raised:

> . . . [t]he decisions regarding the dam are but a reflection of the political culture and the structures that are dominating all of us. Right to know and right to participate meaningfully is constantly being denied to the project affected people, their organisations and the general public.
>
> (ibid: 6)

These are of course criticisms that resonate with the critique of centralized development planning that was at the heart of the politics of India's new social movements and grassroots organizations from the mid- and late seventies onwards (see Chapters 1 and 3).

The document moves on to criticize what it calls a 'Mirage of Benefits' that mars not only the SSP, but Indian dam projects in general:

> As in all the mega projects, in the name of development, in India, the human, environmental, financial and social-political costs of the SSP are grossly underestimated and undermined. The publicized benefits that are to justify the

> project, inflated by the lavish, state-sponsored advertisement campaign, are but a mirage if one sees through the government's own documents and pronouncements from time to time.
>
> (ibid.: 5)

A series of arguments is presented concerning the claimed benefits that the project will engender. In terms of irrigation, the argument centres on how the project authorities justify the dam by claiming that it will provide irrigation to the drought-prone regions of Kutch and Saurashtra, while it is more than likely that the brunt of irrigation will be diverted to the favoured lands of central Gujarat. Related to the issue of the distribution of benefits, the document questions the likelihood that the SSP will actually provide drinking water to such drought prone regions as Kutch and Saurashtra. The document then proceeds to interrogate the SSP's capacity for power generation: 'Power: How Much, At What Cost – To Whom?' is the guiding question. The argument first points out the overestimations put forward in official claims, and then goes on to argue that, even when official claims are taken at face value, the net gain of power will be substantially reduced by the fact that some 90 MW of the power generated will be used to lift water into Kutch and Saurashtra.

TJSD moves on from the 'Mirage of Benefits' to the 'Enormous Costs' of the project:

> SSP would cause the largest ever displacement in any project in India. The Government has been always underestimating the number of the oustees and does not recognize thousands of other affected families as oustees, Taking into account all sorts of displacement the number of those affected by the SSP comes to round 10 lakhs (1 million)
>
> (ibid.: 16)

The document claims that 'over 150,000 tribals-peasants from the 245 villages in the submergence zone spread in the three states' (ibid.: 16) will be displaced. The government's claim of 67,000 project-affected persons (PAPs) have been contradicted by the Water Resources Minister in a statement in Parliament in 1992 where he put the number of families to be affected at 30,000 (which, when calculated by five, which is the standard measure of family size, gives a total of 150,000 PAPs). Furthermore, the underestimation of the number of affected people in official estimates is attributed to the highly restricted definition of PAPs. The failure to resettle the six villages that were displaced by the establishment of Kevadia colony in 1961 and those under threat by displacement to ancillary projects adds to this list. The argument is concluded with a radically different estimate of the number of PAPs: 'Thus in all the number of those affected by the SSP alone touches the figure of one 10 lakhs [1 million]. However, there is no complete resettlement plan including all these affected people ready as yet' (ibid.: 17).

There are, in effect, two arguments being made here. First, the official estimates are criticized in *quantitative* terms for being inaccurate; hence the project appraisal does not live up to official standards of scientific rigour. Second, the official estimates are criticized in *qualitative* terms in the sense that the definition of a project-affected person is criticized for being too narrow, excluding a range of groups that will be dispossessed by the project. As such, the NBA's counter-expertise challenges the legitimacy of the administrative categories of the state. The critique of the underestimation of the number of displaced people in turn forms a prelude to a section dealing with the 'Impossibility of Resettlement': 'As there is no common policy among the three party states to resettle the people, till this date no comprehensive plan with the details of required land, infrastructure, time frame, allocations and the required political will is in the sight' (ibid.: 17). This contention is justified with reference to statements made by World Bank consultants and discussions held under the auspices of the Narmada Control Authority. Furthermore, the lack of proper surveying of the affected communities is pointed out. The argument proceeds:

> Even the Independent Review appointed by the World Bank (Morse Committee) has concluded that resettlement in present circumstances is impossible and it is impossible to resettle the oustees from MP and Maharashtra in Gujarat. It has indicted the M.P. the most as it does not know how many families would be shifting to Gujarat. There was no attempt to consult the people and get their consent, concludes the Commissioner for Scheduled Castes and Scheduled Tribes in his report. Accordingly, the displacement itself amounts to the violation of the Constitutional rights of the people, particularly the tribals. In fact, it is serious breach of Constitutional rights and just processes, when all the issues regarding the dam remain unanswered, the construction work is going on making the dam irreversible.
>
> (ibid.: 17–18)

In this passage the 'cross-fertilization' that has been intrinsic to the formation of counter-expertise about the Narmada Projects is evident in the references to the Independent Review of the World Bank and the reports of the Commissioner for Scheduled Castes and Scheduled Tribes. Also, the claim that the displacement constitutes a breach of constitutional rights adds a dimension to the critique in that the issue is no longer quantitative and technical in the sense of being based on criticisms of lacking procedures and surveys, but qualitative in the sense that it appeals to non-negotiable principles of citizenship.

The document proceeds to map out 'The Reality of Resettlement and the Impending Human Tragedy' (ibid.: 19). Citing 'the initial experiences' of the failure to resettle a small number of families in Gujarat, the claim is made that this presages the future of those communities for whom displacement is imminent. A moral question is posed and a familiar trajectory of change is invoked:

> The integrated, least monetised, natural resource based social, economic and cultural life of the tribal communities is the most difficult to be valuated and if lost or destroyed to be compensated . . . When the tribals have gods and goddesses that cannot be measured, who does have the moral right to snatch it

> away from them, evict their gods and cultural symbols and destroy those? . . . There is no doubt, seeing their plight today, that most if not all of them will land up into shanty-towns and slums in the cities, after losing their lands to the sugarcane growers or money lenders.
>
> (ibid.: 18)

The moral question of the right to erase the habitation, livelihood and cultural life-world of the adivasis adds to the qualitative, non-negotiable dimension of the critique. The trajectory of tribals shifting to city slums after having lost their land is of course the story of proletarianization in contemporary India in a nutshell.

The claims about the impossibility of resettlement are then justified with reference to survey reports by the NCA and other official surveying agencies such as Centre for Social Studies and Tata Institute of Social Sciences. Furthermore, several examples of failed resettlement are given: 'Not a single stipulation of the NWDT and that in the World Bank agreement has been fully implemented. The oustees from eight to ten villages in Gujarat have been disintegrated in 130 places. Not a single affected village is yet fully resettled, Many of them have not got the land, facilities or compensation as was assured. Many [were] cheated in the land deals or were given uncultivable, water logged lands' (ibid.: 18–19). A different but 'equally grave' scenario is put forward in the case of the farming communities of Nimad.

The predicted scenarios for tribal and farming communities can surely be considered as legitimate forecasts in light of both the experience of displacement generally in India and on the specific facts of the scale of displacement and the inadequacies of the official strategies for resettlement and rehabilitation in the case of the SSP. The various shortcomings that precipitate the impending failure of resettlement are then portrayed as more than 'administrative lacunae'; they are, it is claimed, 'a policy matter' and an outcome of 'the basic resource matrix of our country' – displacement is suffused by a social bias that is expressive of wider structural issues related to the power equations that permeate India's political economy (ibid.: 19).

Overall, the critique of the 'Mirage of Benefits' and the 'Enormous Costs' of the SSP is structured around three basic themes: first, the argument that the project does not stand up to scrutiny even by its own standards as the benefits that provide the justification for the project are overestimated and the costs in terms of displacement and resettlement are vastly underestimated; second, the distribution of the benefits of drinking water, irrigation, and electricity is skewed in the sense that they will accrue largely to already affluent regions and powerful social groups, and similarly, that the cost of displacement falls on backward regions and socially disadvantaged groups; third, particularly in terms of displacement, that the costs of the project are not merely a technical or quantitative affair, but rather a question of how unequal power relations engender development practices that lead to a profoundly immoral dispossession of people whose rights as citizens are violated. As will become clear, this is typical of the multilayered character of the NBA's discourse of resistance.

TJSD then presents a detailed criticism of the official benefit-cost (b-c) estimates that have been put forward by the project authorities. The claim is made that the official b-c ratio is adverse for the reason that that these estimates have been grossly underestimated as they have failed to take into account 'a number of incomplete studies and plans, with the new costs propping [sic] up, throwing the previous B-C ratio askew' (ibid.: 20). The Planning Commission has stipulated that a b-c ratio of 1.5:1 is required to pass a dam projected. The ratio for the SSP is stipulated to be far below this (ibid.: 20). At the time the document was put together, attempts have been made to speed up the project work so as to complete it by 1998 in order to generate a positive b-c ratio: 'However, and government never states openly, even under this new schedule the B-C ratio is less than 1.5:1 stipulated by the Planning Commission; it is only 1.12:1' (ibid.: 20). Moreover, it is claimed that it is impossible to mobilize the funds needed to finance this schedule (ibid.: 21). An 'inevitable' financial crunch is forecast for the dam project (ibid.: 21). The document maps several strategies deployed by the project authorities to raise the needed funds, none of which have been successful, and then moves on to question the morality of the use of public funds for the project:

> With the Sardar Sarovar, we seem to be set to rob whatever financial resources the already bankrupt state of Gujarat may have . . . When the nation is passing through serious financial crisis with foreign debts shooting upto [sic] Rs. 1,37,508 crores (TOI, 18th Dec 1991), can we afford to squander and seek loans from any nation right from Japan, Germany, Sweden, to the multilateral agencies like the World Bank?
>
> (ibid.: 23)

There are two significant elements in this passage that I want to highlight. First, the SSP is posited as a kind of 'daylight robbery' of public resources in a context of severe fiscal problems. This daylight robbery amounts to social banditry in reverse – stealing from the poor and giving to the rich – in that it is carried out so as to fund a project where the benefits are systematically distributed to affluent regions and powerful social groups, while more deprived regions and the kind of projects that they need are left behind. Second, by drawing in the context of the nation's financial crisis – the document dates back to the early 1990s, when India was facing a balance of payments crisis – and asking whether it makes sense to take up loans with foreign agencies, the NBA again links the SSP to issues and processes beyond the Narmada Valley.

Next, a strong criticism is put forward of the environmental impact of the dam and the cultural loss due to the submergence caused by the reservoir. In terms of environmental impacts, TJSD highlights a contradictory scenario:

> Sardar Sarovar would cause incalculable destruction of precious forests in the Narmada Valley, loss and in some cases extinction of flaura [sic] and fauna, and will cause problems of waterlogging and salinity in the command area. However, no full assessment of environmental loss has yet been made, nor is

> the loss properly valuated, let alone planning the measures to recompensate the loss or judging the feasibility of executing those.
>
> (ibid.: 23)

The criticism of the environmental impact derives its power from the fact that it displays severe shortcomings in terms of environmental impact assessment in a context where a project has in fact been given environmental clearance. Again, the Andolan's counter-expertise levels a critique of the project on its own terms, pointing out failings in the project according to national and international standards of project assessment.

In terms of the cultural heritage, traditions and practices linked to the Narmada river and the impact the SSP will have on this, TJSD focuses on how the submergence zones have not been fully researched, and final clearance was not given by the organizations trusted with the task of archaeological surveying. The example of the Shoolpaneshwar temple is given – 'one of the most revered temple [sic] on the banks of Narmada, visited by thousands of pilgrims in and outside the valley' (ibid.: 25) – as a site that will be erased by the SSP reservoir. This example is then contextualized:

> This is not an isolated issue of a temple. After Shoolpaneshwar, there are thousands of cultural centres, some religious, others more social-emotional, which stand doomed. Thus, the powerholders will be depriving the people of their life sustaining faith – a true organic faith and not generated through communal hysteria over a temple or mosque. And what of the faith of the tribals? No one is aware that their Gods and Demons are incarnated in hills, groves, rivulets, trees . . . And here the nation is adrift over the issue of one temple!!
>
> (ibid.: 25)

Again we have an argument that combines a critique of a specific loss – in this case, cultural loss – caused by the SSP with an argument that reaches beyond the specific locale of struggle. The contrasting of the 'organic faith' of the communities of the Narmada Valley with 'communal hysteria over a temple or mosque' and the unrecognized faith of the tribal communities with the nation that is 'adrift over the issue of one temple' is a direct reference to the demolition of the Babri Masjid in Ayodhya in 1992 and the carnage that followed. As such, the argument presents both a critique of an unquantifiable loss in the Valley and an appeal to secular forces and sensibilities in the nation at large.

Now, in Skirbekk's (1984) account, the function of counter-expertise is that of constituting a bulwark against the dominance of technocratic knowledge and serving as a resource for people to draw on in democratic deliberations. The NBA's counter-expertise serves this function as a discourse of resistance that challenges technocratic knowledge at two levels.[4] First, at the level of the specific campaign against the SSP, the rationale of the project is challenged on its own terms by the presentation of scientific knowledge that stands in contradiction to the official claims about the costs and benefits of the project. Beyond the 'factual' critique, in turn, there is a normative critique that points out how negligent and opaque planning procedures and the social bias in the distribution of costs and benefits violates the officially sanctioned rights and entitlements of the dam-affected communities. Second, and at a deeper level, the critique that is put forward in TJSD strikes at the very heart of the strategy through which ideological legitimacy has been sought for development planning in India, namely the positing of planning as an essentially apolitical 'technical evaluation of alternative policies and the determination of choices on scientific grounds' (Chatterjee 1993: 201) for the good of 'the nation' at large. Pointing out the shortcomings and flaws of the expert knowledge that provides the rationale of a development project such as the SSP and justifying this with reference to scientific standards amounts to a destabilization of the status of expert knowledge in terms of its quality. Pointing out the systematically skewed distribution of the costs and benefits of the project intensifies this destabilization by calling into question the claimed objectivity of development planning and the extent to which it is genuinely dedicated to a generic 'greater common good'. The sum effect is to reveal how planning has served as 'a modality of power outside of the immediate political process itself' (ibid.: 202). Interestingly, at both levels of critique it is possible to discern the logic of rightful resistance in that what has been articulated in this discourse of resistance is a challenge to 'power holders who compromise the ideals that justify their rule' (O'Brien and Li 2006: 24) which proceeds via an appropriation of those ideals – in this case ideals related to scientific objectivity and universal progress.

Furthermore, as a discourse of resistance the NBA's counter-expertise has also had an internal function in relation to the building of a pan-state anti-dam campaign. The building of a campaign essentially revolves around bringing together a range of groups involved in specific conflicts 'through a process of abstraction from particular instances and circumstances' (Harvey 2000: 241–2). This is done at two levels in the NBA's counter-expertise. First, the critique that is put forward in TJSD is formulated at pan-state level, drawing together the situations and experiences of dam-affected communities in the riparian states and abstracting a generic situation and a generic challenge from those specific contexts:

> The oustees in Madhya Pradesh and Maharashtra are well-organized and are *challenging their displacement itself... They have termed the impending displacement as unjust, unjustifiable* and have questioned the very Public Purpose for which they are being forced out of the valley. Next they have asserted their right over their own resources, like land, forest and waters and have been opposed to taking away these resources, the source of livelihood and right to life, from them and without their consent. This has marked an advance in the struggle against displacement all over India.
>
> (ibid.: 19)

Second, as indicated in the last sentence of the passage just cited, the abstraction from specific contexts extends beyond the Narmada Valley. Indeed, this is done very explicitly at the outset of TJSD, where the SSP is posited as being symptomatic of wider problems in the political economy of India's development:

> The issues raised by the Andolan are interrelated, interwoven . . . The projects like SSP are justified and pushed ahead in a suspicious haste only on the ground of the 'Development' which the political elites in India had adopted after the Independence, and the foreign assistance resulting in a vicious debt cycle.
>
> (ibid.: 1)

This is followed up throughout the critique of the SSP, as evidenced by the argument that the socially and environmentally harmful impacts of the SSP are typical of 'all the mega projects', that opaque planning is 'but a reflection of the political culture' in India, that the social bias of the allocation of costs and benefits is expressive of 'the basic resource matrix of our country', that the financial ramifications of the SSP are morally unacceptable in a time when 'the nation is passing through severe financial crisis', and in the contrasting of the pluralistic religious heritage of the Narmada Valley with the communal fury which plagued India at the time TJSD was penned. As a discourse of resistance, then, the Andolan's criticism of the SSP goes well beyond a 'not in my backyard' stance where dams as such would be accepted but 'not this particular dam', towards the articulation of a generic challenge to dam-building and the wider developmental regime of which they are a part. In doing so, it points towards the movement project of alternative development that I subject to analysis in Chapter 8.

By the middle of 1988, then, a pan-state anti-dam campaign centred on a multi-faceted critique of the SSP, which in turn was embedded in a generic critique of dams as a development strategy, was a fact. This represented a significant achievement in terms of the labour of translation between and abstraction from the specific contexts in which militant particularist opposition first emerged. However, to portray it as a permanent and unanimous achievement would be a misrepresentation; the campaign has been riddled with intersecting processes of convergence and divergence at different scales, and it is to this aspect of the formation of the anti-dam campaign that I turn now.

Divergence and convergence in the formation of the anti-dam campaign

Divergence: The trajectory of the ARCH Vahini

The ARCH Vahini (AV) did not follow the groups in Maharashtra and Madhya Pradesh on the path towards total opposition to the SSP. This divergence has to be understood in relation to the trajectory of the Vahini's struggle for R&R in the dam-affected communities of Gujarat in 1987–88. The decisive moment in this process was the announcement made in December 1987 by the Government of Gujarat that it would implement a policy that recognized the rights of so-called encroachers to R&R (see Chapter 4). This generated a scenario where communities in the three riparian states faced highly differentiated circumstances relating to R&R:

> The new Gujarat resettlement and rehabilitation policy appeared to provide the opportunities for which groups like ARCH-Vahini had lobbied, though it represented a significant step forward only for those project-affected people willing to resettle in the state of Gujarat. Unfortunately, the Gujarati policy was not matched by similar policies in Madhya Pradesh and Maharashtra where the Narmada Ghati Nav Nirman Samiti and the Narmada Dharangrast Samiti respectively, had their constituencies.
>
> (Fisher 1995: 23)

In light of this change in policy, the ARCH Vahini opted for concentrating its activities on monitoring the resettlement and rehabilitation of displaced communities in Gujarat, rather than joining hands with the other organizations in opposing the SSP.

This strategic divergence has in turn become the object of an intense representational struggle over legitimacy between Anil Patel, the leader of the ARCH Vahini, and Medha Patkar of the NBA. Patel (1995: 189) stresses how, prior to 1987, the scenario in terms of R&R in the tribal communities of Maharashtra and Madhya Pradesh were very similar to that found in Gujarat, with encroachers being denied land-for-land resettlement, and villagers generally wanting 'good quality agricultural land after being displaced'. This, in turn, was 'reflected in the memoranda that these organizations were submitting to their state authorities' (ibid.: 189). Much like the AV, he argues, the mobilizations in these areas also 'invoked the World Bank Loan Agreement to demand denuded forest land identified by [the communities]' for resettlement (ibid.: 189). What follows in his account is a story of his surprise at what he perceives to be an about-face on behalf of the Maharashtra and Madhya Pradesh organizations:

> Soon after the December 1987 resettlement and rehabilitation policy of Gujarat state was hailed as a revolutionary policy by all concerned, the organizations working in Maharashtra and Madhya Pradesh stopped looking for the ways to achieve similar policies in their states and started raising doubts about the policy of Gujarat, stating it was destined to be merely a piece of paper. There wasn't going to be enough land available, they concluded. Before long, city-based intellectuals in Bombay, Delhi, and so on, jumped into the arena, arguing vigorously that this was a charade and the tribals were bound to be cheated and they must not trust the government. A United States based environmental organization, Environment Defense Fund, which until this time had lobbied with the World Bank in concert with Oxfam (UK) and had supported resettlement and rehabilitation demands of the tribals suddenly changed course.
>
> (ibid.: 190)

The EDF, Patel claims, submitted a memorandum to a US Senate subcommittee in June 1988, arguing that tribals were opposed to the SSP. This was 'surprising', he argues, as the organizations of Madhya Pradesh and Maharashtra had still not announced their opposition to the project. However, when they did so, in August 1988, 'their opposition was as sudden as it was total' (ibid.: 190).

What stands out in Patel's representation of the decision to move towards a stance of total opposition towards the dam is the emphasis on suddenness and rupture. First of all, the claim that adequate resettlement was not likely to happen followed, according to Patel, from the fact that the organizations in Maharashtra and Madhya Pradesh 'stopped looking' for ways in which to achieve arrangements similar to those offered to the oustees in Gujarat. Gone are such factors as the underestimation of the extent of submergence and hence also the underestimation of the number of displaced people and the lack of available land of sufficient quality that compelled the decision to oppose the SSP. Also, his reference to 'city-based intellectuals' and the actions of the EDF more than hints at external interference being a factor in the process of articulating a stance of opposition to the dam. Moreover, the shift to opposition was 'sudden' – i.e. it was not, in Patel's view, based on experience, learning processes, and knowledge production that intertwined to generate a reasonable strategic conclusion. Rather, it was a spurious decision based on a lack of constructive attitudes, informed by outside forces, and representing a sudden break with an established approach of seeking proper rehabilitation and resettlement.

It is striking how this account differs from Medha Patkar's account of the events of 1988. According to her account of the meeting in May of that year, where the organizations of the dam-affected submitted a letter to the authorities demanding answers to their queries about R&R, the ARCH Vahini was part of this process:

> On the same day in the evening that we had the long discussion with the Narmada Control Authority and the three states and center's secretaries, I vividly remember that the Gujarat organizations, especially Arch-Vahini, had also come . . . After that meeting we signed a common letter saying that we were giving the government two months' time, and if they did not answer all the questions in two months, we would oppose the project. This was handed over by the Vahini activists to the secretaries from the center sitting in the circuit house on the 14th or 15th of May 1988.
>
> (1995: 161–2)

The AV's participation in the questioning of the government, however, is not even mentioned in Patel's account. Patkar goes on to argue that it was only after this event that the AV decided that they wanted no part in an anti-dam campaign:

> The Vahini took a different stand. They felt that it was not necessary because in June some Government resolutions were issued by the Gujarat government, and in December a few more came so they decided not to join us in unitedly opposing the dam. We felt that the few resolutions by one government did not mean much since the issues were much broader. For instance, even on rehabilitation, the issues of all three states should be looked at together. Since that time, the Vahini and we have had different paths to follow.
>
> (ibid.: 162)

Of course, what is striking about Patkar's narrative is the way in which she downplays the significance of the AV's achievements in Gujarat. What was viewed as a potential watershed in R&R policy by Patel and his fellow activists, is referred to by Patkar as 'some Government resolutions' that were unlikely to have any real impact on the ground. As such, the decision of the AV to assist in the implementation of R&R is represented as a case of co-optation where radical agency is given up in exchange for insignificant concessions.

Returning to Patel's narrative, he moves on to claim that the move towards total opposition of the dam effectively constituted a betrayal to genuine adivasi interests:

> We knew the tribals in Gujarat, although apprehensive and suspicious about the government's true intentions, were rearing to get the new policy implemented, that the tribals did not want to join the battle against the dam announced from Bombay. This was natural. We were almost certain that the tribals in Maharashtra and Madhya Pradesh would not want to abandon their quest and struggle for resettlement and rehabilitation policy similar to that of Gujarat. And yet the battle against the Sardar Sarovar Project was joined in the name of the tribals of the valley. Bewildered and anxious, we asked the organizations if they had informed the tribals, who relied on them about the revolutionary contents of the Gujarat policy, and if they then had asked for their informed consent. We also raised doubts about the strength of the antidam case they had advanced, given the fact that only a few months ago these very organizations had acknowledged that the case against the Sardar Sarovar Project had to be developed and decided to develop such a critique of the Sardar Sarovar Project for the sake of record even when it was too late to stop its construction. In the context of this, we asked, 'Was it a responsible activism to keep the tribals in front of the fight against the Project?'
>
> (ibid.: 189–90)

Again, we find that Patel's account diverges from that of NBA activists. What to them was a process of decision-making based on deliberations between urban educated activists and villagers in the light of situated experience and emergent facts, is to Patel more akin to an act of imposition of a political programme tailored to the whims of urban intellectuals than a logical step in the development of political activism that truly resonated with the wishes of the adivasis of Maharashtra and Madhya Pradesh.

The strategic divergence between the groups in Maharashtra and Madhya Pradesh and the AV in Gujarat testifies to how the immediate parameters set by differing local exigencies impacts on the processes of translation between and abstraction from militant particularist struggles and the ability to construct a generic challenge to a generic problem. This is not a smooth-running process of unification, but rather a complex process of negotiation of specific exigencies and the way in which they influence activist preferences and choices. For some activists, the question of 'what is to be done' is answered with reference to the possibility of gaining tangible concessions on specific issues in the here and now; for others, opting for such concessions entails 'winning ha'pennies and losing pounds' and is thus ruled out in favour of a redefinition of the stakes involved in a conflict.

This is in turn reflected in the representational struggle over the strategic divergence. When Patel argues that 'the tribals in Gujarat . . . were rearing to get the new policy implemented' he seeks legitimacy for making a strategic choice that responds to the immediate exigencies of a militant particularist struggle – i.e. a strategic choice that is informed by the perceived success of a specific challenge to a specific situation. Conversely, Patkar's stress on the necessity of viewing 'the issues of all three states' in relation to each other reflects a desire to legitimate the choice to construct a generic challenge that abstracts from local specificities and immediate exigencies. Now, the fact that the latter strategy failed does not warrant a black-and-white judgement on the merits of the respective strategic choices. In June 1995, the AV withdrew from the Gujarat Government Committee on Resettlement. Anil Patel justified the decision as follows: 'The policy promises made to us by the Gujarat government have not been kept. We accept that it was a failure on our part not to have managed to keep up the pressure' (cited in Dwivedi 2006: 177). Whereas Patel maintained that the ARCH Vahini had not changed its 'fundamental position' in that the organization 'said no to dam without proper rehabilitation then, we say it now' (ibid.: 177), their disappointment with the implementation of the Gujarati R&R policy does lend some credence to Patkar's remark that a 'few resolutions by one government did not mean much since the issues were much broader'.

Convergence: Dam-opposition at the national scale

In 1988, as the pan-state anti-dam campaign was in the process of crystallizing in the Narmada Valley, significant developments were also taking place at the national scale as activists from across India came together to articulate and co-ordinate their opposition to large dams. The NBA and its struggle against the SSP were to play a central role in this process.

The emergence of an oppositional politics around large dams at a significant scale in India can be traced to the 1970s, with the successful campaigns against the Silent Valley project in Southern Kerala and against several dams planned on the Godavari and Indravati rivers. Important campaigns were also conducted against the Subarnarekha Project in Bihar and the Tehri dam in Uttar Pradesh. Crucially, all of these campaigns were linked to transnational lobbying efforts (see Khagram 2004: chapter 2). In the late 1980s, dam-opposition once again came to the fore at the national scale through what has come to be known as the Anandwan Declaration. The Anandwan Declaration was closely related to the activities of the veteran Gandhian social worker Baba Amte who, during the 1980s, increasingly turned the focus of his attention and efforts towards the emergent resistance to dam-building.[5] In June 1988, he spearheaded the organization of a conference of environmentalists and other activists in Anandwan, Maharashtra to discuss the politics of resistance to big dams. From this conference emerged a resolution formally entitled 'Assertion of Collective Will Against Big Dams' – also known as the

Anandwan Declaration – which was signed by more than 90 representatives of various strands of Indian civil society. The resolution called for a halt to the building of large dams:

> All projects on which construction has not begun should be scrapped. All work should be suspended on projects where it has already started, and a fresh holistic approach should be made by an independent body with representatives of people's organizations.
>
> (cited in Sen n.d.: 11)

What is more, the resolution declared that the focus of the efforts to achieve such a moratorium should be centred on one particular dam-project which would constitute 'the foundation of a national movement against dams' (cited in Sen n.d.: 11). Towards the end of 1988, as Sen (ibid.: 11) notes, 'it was evident that Sardar Sarovar was to be the dam site where the people's collective will would be asserted'.

The emergence of organized opposition to large dams at a national scale of course constitutes an achievement similar to that of the construction of a pan-state anti-dam campaign in the Narmada Valley in that it is the outcome of translation between and abstraction from the specific contexts of specific struggles and efforts to, through such translation and abstraction, construct empowering connections between subaltern groups in and around opposition to a generic threat of displacement. Now, given that Medha Patkar participated actively in this process and that the campaign against the SSP would be the focal point of the efforts to advance the politics of opposition to large dams at a national scale, it would arguably be natural to assume that this process would be recognized as constituting a political space in which synergies and solidarities between activists made a positive contribution towards galvanizing the strategy of opposing the SSP. However, when I discussed this with leading NBA activists they argued – more or less strongly – that this had not been the case. The decision to move towards a pan-state anti-dam campaign, it was argued, stemmed from endogenous exigencies, common to the dam-affected communities in the Narmada Valley.

For example, when I asked Medha Patkar about the significance of the emergence of opposition to big dams nationally and whether her participation in the Anandwan meeting was important in prompting the shift towards dam opposition she responded as follows:

> . . . there are many misunderstandings about that also, but you have picked up the right thing. See, some people say that because of that, we started opposing the dam. Not at all. Position since beginning was that the questions should be raised, and depending on the dialogue we were taking a position. 31 July 1988 was the meeting in Anandwan, ok? And on 3 August 1988 we were to take a decision; coincidentally, 3 August 1988 was the meeting in Rajghat, on the bank of Narmada, near Badwani, to take a decision. And on 31 July, we had almost decided, but because that meeting was to be held, I could not say there that we had decided, so I said 'we've almost decided'. Presented the whole

> story, I presented on Sardar Sarovar and Ramesh Billorey presented on Narmada Sagar and, actually that time I appealed to Baba to come to Sardar Sarovar area, but Baba said very crudely, you know, that, 'Sardar Sarovar, what is there in Sardar Sarovar? It's already done, finished. Now everyone should concentrate on Narmada Sagar'. So I wept in front of him and I said 'How can you say that, so much organization is there . . .'. Anyway, it remained at that level. But within a year, like once we started opposing . . . the issue raised . . . the forum, national and . . . then Baba realized that there is . . . and he felt . . . I mean his heart was always in opposing dams, big dams . . . .
>
> (interview, June 2003)

First, her answer to my question starts with an outright denunciation of claims to the effect that it was the Anandwan Declaration that led to the declaration of opposition to the SSP. Second, she emphasises that the temporal conjunction of the two processes was purely coincidental. Third, she points out that given that the organizations of the dam-affected communities were to declare their stance after the meeting in Anandwan, she did not attend the meeting as an opponent of the SSP per se. Fourth, Baba Amte is portrayed as not realizing the importance of the SSP struggle, and indeed, as being uninterested in it. According to Patkar, it was only after the mobilization around opposition to the SSP started to take place that he took interest in it as a focal point for a national campaigns against dams. The message is clear: the Anandwan meeting and the declaration that came out of it did not affect the choice to oppose the SSP; the move from claiming information and rehabilitation to dam opposition was an autonomous choice based on realities and experiences endogenous to the Valley.

Discussing the events that led up to the declaration opposition to the SSP, leading NBA activist Chittaroopa Palit took a similar position, stressing how the urban milieus from which many of the radical critiques of large dams emerged in fact criticized the organizations in the Narmada Valley for not opposing the SSP:

> . . . there was a lot of discussion in many forums, and in fact when I was coming there was a lot of criticism of this movement . . . and friends in Delhi told me 'don't you know they're working for rehabilitation, they don't have any real conception of the opposition to dams' and so on. So I didn't say anything because, you know, even if somebody is opposing the dam . . . that is less important to me than someone who is working with those people and who is formulating differing and varying strands, depending on what people is thinking.
>
> (interview, May 2003)

However, later on in the interview, when I asked her if there were any connections between the NBA and the wider environmental movement and its questioning of and opposition to dams, her answer was more ambivalent:

> Well, I actually don't know . . . Some of the groups, like Kalpavriksh, which was one of the students' groups that brought this issue to the fore, and they also

> looked at the dams, you know [inaudible] through its environmental impacts, both [inaudible] and forest, wildlife, fauna, societies and so on. So there were a number of voices; I mean there were voices like Claude Alvares and Ramesh Billorey who were looking at the benefit-cost issues of the dams, and how destructive they would be, or Vijay Paranpaye who was looking at the economics of these dams. In fact, I think it was in eighty-six or eighty-seven when Baba Amte also called the consortium to express the will against large dams. So it was at that time also when the opposition to large dams was being crystallized, and that impacted the work within the formations that later came to be known as the NBA.
>
> (interview, May 2003)

So far, the emergence of an anti-dam milieu is recognized as having impacted on the politics of the emergent NBA. However, Palit went on to refer to a meeting in Indore in 1988 where, because the organizations had not yet taken an overt stand against the SSP, Patkar was criticized for failing to develop an adequate political programme:

> . . . basically there were a lot of people who were feeling that the movement was running into some sort of sandstorm by not looking at the larger impacts . . . But I think movements take a long time to absorb, take decisions, and also because with a mass movement where the primary concerns are survival concerns . . . then you have to go by the pace of the survival concerns coming to a conclusion about whether people want to ask for land, or whether they want to oppose the dam and so on.
>
> (interview, May 2003)

So we return back to the situation where on the one hand, there were urban groups who were critical of an apparent hesitance to adopt a stance of dam opposition, and, on the other hand, there was a movement which grounded its decision-making processes in the realities and experiences of the communities directly affected by the SSP. Again, the emphasis is on the autonomy of political and strategic choices.

The reasons for the emphasis put on the turn to dam opposition as an autonomous decision based on endogenous experience, and the relative downplaying of the importance of political spaces, can be many. On the one hand, it can be a genuine expression of the autonomous and endogenous character of the dynamic that led to the stance of dam opposition. On the other hand, it could be a 'defence mechanism' against allegations that the decision to oppose the dams was misguided, and imposed by external forces.[6] Most likely, there is an aspect of cross-fertilization between the two.

However, in terms of the importance of the emergence of co-ordinated dam-opposition at a national scale, I think it is defensible to argue the following: the NBA crystallized as an anti-dam campaign at a time when there was an emergent opposition to dams both in India and internationally. As I show in the next chapter, this was highly significant for the successful conduct of the international campaign against World Bank funding of the SSP between 1990 and 1992. Moreover, the NBA itself became a fulcrum point for the further development of the international anti-dam movement, the clearest indication of which is the Manibeli declaration of 1994 – named after an adivasi village in Maharashtra that was an epicentre of the struggle against the SSP for many years – in which more than 2,000 NGOs from 43 countries called for an end to World Bank funding of large dams.[7] As such, the embeddedness of the Narmada anti-dam campaign in a multiscalar political space testifies to how such spaces enable the imaginaries, rationalities, and skills that activists engender in situated struggles to travel, and how this underpins the defining trait of campaigns in movement processes, namely the construction of general challenges to general situations.

Concluding remarks

Campaigns emerge when a range of local and specific responses to local and specific situations are organized so as to construct a challenge to such situations in generic terms. This process typically revolve around the abstraction of the practices, skills, forms of consciousness, and imaginaries that define a given local rationality or militant particularism in the sense that these 'are taken out of their immediate, taken-for-granted lifeworld context and "put to work" in building practical and communicative bridges to *other* lifeworlds' (Cox 1999a: 114; italics in original).

In this chapter I have shown how, from 1987 to 1988, the movement process in the Narmada Valley entered into a phase of radicalization and abstraction the outcome of which was the constitution of the NBA as a pan-state anti-dam campaign.

Radicalization and abstraction were energized by the ways in which activists acquired and constructed knowledge about the situation that they were engaging with. One aspect of this was the confrontational learning that flowed from activists' interaction with state authorities around their claims for access to information and the instalment of satisfactory plans for R&R. The refusal on the part of the authorities to enter into a dialogue was of two-fold significance in this process: on the one hand, it led to a 'shedding of illusions' and 'confirmation about suspicions' about the will and capacity of state and project authorities to implement R&R; on the other hand, it fed into deliberations over strategic and tactical proposals among the activists – deliberations that ultimately resulted in radicalization and abstraction as the stance of dam-opposition was adopted by the majority of the organizations that were involved in the process.

Closely related to this was the construction of a dense body of counter-expertise about the SSP and its impacts. The NBA's counter-expertise consistently and effectively demonstrated the flaws and shortcomings of the central claims that state and project authorities made about the costs and benefits of the project. As a discourse of resistance, counter-expertise has been used to articulate a challenge to the attempts of dominant groups to legitimate their hegemonic projects as serving the universal interest of 'the nation' as a non-conflictual unity, both in relation to the determinate context of the SSP and more generally in terms of postcolonial development planning. Moreover, at this level it has been instrumental in abstracting a common, shared threat of dispossession from specific circumstances so as to underpin a common, shared campaign of resistance at a pan-state scale and embed this campaign in a wider critique of dam-building as a development strategy.

Abstracting from and translating between a range of local and specific responses to local and specific situations is unlikely to be a smooth process; rationalities that privilege local and specific exigencies are liable to enter into conflict with rationalities that seek to 'meet the exigencies of . . . greater diversity and [a] more challenging ontological situation' (Cox 1999a: 115). Such a conflict emerged in the Narmada Valley when the ARCH Vahini decided to assist the Government of Gujarat in the implementation of a R&R policy that was considered to meet the key demands that had been made as part of the militant particularist struggle for R&R. For the AV, opposing the dam was a betrayal of genuine adivasi interests and reflected the 'external' agendas of urban elite environmentalists. For the NBA, the stance of assisting the implementation of resettlement and rehabilitation amounted to an act of co-optation in which minor concessions were prioritized over a political initiative that took the pan-state situation into consideration.

Divergence at the local scale contrasted with convergence around the politics of dam-opposition at the national scale. At the same time as the pan-state anti-dam campaign was crystallizing in the Narmada Valley, activists from across India converged on the Anandwan Declaration which called for the abandonment of large dams. This represented a substantial achievement in terms of activist efforts to connect 'different local situations practically and theoretically into movements' and to facilitate 'coordination and communication between different movements towards a shared movement project' (Cox 1999a: 115). However, activists tended to downplay the significance of developments at the national scale and emphasize that the decision to oppose the dam was made on the basis of local circumstances. This was most likely a defensive rhetorical strategy reflecting how the NBA has had to fend of allegations that the anti-dam campaign was a project imposed by external agents.

Looking at the decision to oppose the SSP with the benefit of hindsight, it would be easy to conclude that it was a misguided move – it did, after all, end in failure. However, such a conclusion is in itself misguided. The fact that the ARCH Vahini ended up withdrawing from the Government of Gujarat's Committee on Resettlement of course indicates that Patkar's misgivings about the limited value of the rehabilitation policy were indeed correct. Moreover, the current scenario in which '[t]he evidence is overwhelmingly of completely inadequate rehabilitation, in contravention of previous promises, declared procedures and court strictures' (Ghosh 2006b: 1), goes a long way to confirming the compulsions that brought about the turn to a stance of wholesale opposition to the SSP. Thus, if we are to understand the defeat of the NBA's campaign to stop the SSP we need to investigate the strategy through which this goal was pursued; I turn to this task in the next chapter.

6 Cycles of struggle

The trajectory of the anti-dam campaign, 1990–2000

In this chapter I map and analyze the trajectory of the Narmada Bachao Andolan's campaign against the Sardar Sarovar Project from 1990 to 2000. The dates that demarcate the scope of the analysis are chosen with good reason. In 1990, the NBA launched its central method for stopping the construction of the SSP in the following decade: in terms of strategy, the demand for a state-led review of the project and its social and environmental impacts became the chief means through which the NBA sought to achieve the ends of stopping the dam, and various forms of non-violent direct action and symbolic protest methods became the major vehicle for bringing this demand to bear on state and central authorities. In 2000, the Indian Supreme Court effectively put a stop to the anti-dam campaign, when its ruling on the public interest litigation submitted by the NBA six years earlier ordered the completion of the SSP according to project designs.

Drawing on Vester's (1978) argument that cycles of struggle are simultaneously cycles of learning, the analysis seeks to bring out how the shifting cycles of the anti-dam campaign were animated by a dynamic in which activists developed strategies and repertoires of contention on the basis of certain assumptions about their opponents as well as about the internal dynamics of the movement itself, in which these assumptions were changed through practical experiences garnered through conflictual encounters with opponents, as well as changes and debates internal to the movement, and in which this eventually resulted in the development and implementation of new strategies and new repertoires of contention.

These cycles of struggle also provide the basic structure of the chapter. The first part of the chapter focuses on the cycle of struggle that unfolded from 1990 to 1991, when the NBA for the first time launched its strategic demand that the state should implement a full review of the SSP and lobbying gave way to non-violent direct action as the movement's defining 'repertoire of contention' (Tilly 1978). I show how the strategy of demanding a review of the project – essentially a strategy of 'jury politics' (Dwivedi 1997) – was grounded in the rich body of counter-expertise that the NBA had generated at this point in time, and discuss the ethical and tactical dimensions of non-violent direct action.

I then move on to engage with the second cycle of struggle, which was inaugurated in 1991 and stretched to the mid-1990s. It was marked by the substitution of non-violent direct action for a repertoire of contention centred on the dam-affected adivasi villages in Maharashtra and Madhya Pradesh, in which non-cooperation with state and project authorities and the introduction of monsoon *satyagrahas* – protest actions in the adivasi villages – were central elements. I analyze the village-based repertoire of contention as a symbolic-communicative practice of resistance which drew on the collective memories of the Indian freedom struggle, and discuss its ambiguous relationship to the mobilizational dynamics of the movement process.

The third cycle of struggle revolved around the international campaign against World Bank funding of the SSP, and overlaps partly with the former cycles. In this part of the chapter, I show how the World Bank's 1991 decision to implement an independent review of the SSP was the result of intensified transnational advocacy from 1988 onwards, and then trace how the report of the Morse Commission resulted in World Bank withdrawal from the SSP.[1]

The fourth part of the chapter analyzes the final cycle of struggle, which started in 1993, when, in the wake of the World Bank's withdrawal from the SSP, the demand for review again came to the forefront of the NBA's activities. This revival was initially a successful one, resulting in the central government's appointment of a Five Member Group (FMG) to review the project, and, following the submission of public interest litigation to the Supreme Court, stoppage of construction on the SSP. However, the FMG's report proved to be inconsequential and the Supreme Court eventually brought out a judgement in favour of the completion of the SSP.

In the fifth and final part of the chapter I discuss the reasons for the eventual failure of the NBA's campaign against the SSP. Comparing the abortive outcome of the anti-dam campaign with the successful outcome of the KMCS's engagement with the state, I argue that the failure to stop the SSP is ultimately rooted in the character of the campaign as such: opposition to the SSP in fact entailed opposition to basal structures of proprietary power and the ways in which the Indian state has functioned as a modality in the reproduction of those power structures. The intended ends of the campaign were too radical relative to the means through which they were pursued. Thus, the political economy of state power seriously constrains the strategic viability of jury politics, and this in turn warrants an important qualification of the argument that social movements from below in contemporary India can and/or should pursue their oppositional projects in and through the state.

Jury politics and direct action

The demand for review as jury politics

In a departure from its initial, ineffectual strategy of lobbying government experts and intellectuals through petitions, the NBA in 1990 put forth the demand that the Government of India should implement an extensive review of the SSP, assessing its technical feasibility, cost-benefit equations, and its social and environmental impacts; during the course of the review, construction on the dam should be halted. If the review proved the project to be technically and economically unfeasible and inappropriate in terms of social and environmental impacts, it should be abandoned. This marked the onset of the first significant cycle of struggle in the NBA's anti-dam campaign.

Jai Sen (n.d.: 18) has argued that the demand for review amounted to the adoption of 'a more moderate position and strategy' compared to all-out opposition to the dam. This move was 'a tactical one, probably made for two main reasons: to restore the movement's declining credibility and manoeuvring room because of its adamant 'no-dam' position, and also to give the [World] Bank more room to manoeuvre (ibid.: 18).[2] In my view, however, there were other factors at play animating the move from wholesale opposition to the demand for review.

In explaining why the movement shifted from demanding the direct cancellation of the SSP to demanding that the project be reviewed, Medha Patkar points to 'the overall reality' that the Andolan had uncovered: the adverse cost-benefit ratio, the underestimation of the total number of oustees in the master plan for rehabilitation and resettlement, the underestimation of environmental impacts, the exaggerated hydrological data on the water available in the river, and the skewed social and regional distribution of the benefits the dam would yield. This was the backdrop for demanding a review of the project:

> Therefore, in the context of this overall reality, we decided that sticking to the land, water, and forests was the only way to challenge the government, not in a negative sense but through a democratic process, believing that when people raised focused issues and declared their commitment, a representative democratic government (and a 'socialist' one at that) would really respond across the table, possibly via neutral moderators as we were proposing or any other mutually agreed-upon process. That is why in March 1990 we had decided not to go on saying, 'No dam, no dam' but to propose a definite review process as a way out.
>
> (Patkar 1995: 170)

The basic rationale for demanding a review was thus rooted in the rich body of counter-expertise that the movement had generated (see Chapter 5). It was clear to the Andolan that the weight of the evidence flatly contradicted official claims that justified the SSP. Furthermore, the evidence established that the project violated a wide array of domestic and international norms, rules, and procedures related to dam building. This in turn suggested that a review of the project would in fact lead to its abandonment. The important point here is of course that the demand for review did not amount to the abandonment of the politics of dam opposition as such. The review was not an end in itself, but a means by which to achieve an end, and the end remained that of stopping the SSP

In strategic terms, the demand for review constitutes a case of what Dwivedi (1997: 28) calls 'jury politics'. Jury politics basically revolve around the presentation of a body of evidence about an object of contestation – in this case, a large dam – to a committee of experts and specialists that assess this evidence and then in turn function as a jury in that they pass judgement on the claims that have been made about the object of contestation based on the assessment of the evidence that has been presented. Now, this choice of strategy reveals an expectation or assumption that the state would function as a jury capable of assessing and evaluating in an independent and unbiased way bodies of evidence against or in favour of a 'defendant' – in this case the SSP – and to pass judgement on this 'defendant' solely on the basis of this evidence; as Patkar argued in the previous passage, the activists expected 'a representative, democratic government' to 'respond across the table'. There is, then, a clear continuity between the rationality of rightful resistance that characterized the militant particularist struggles for R&R and the rationality that underpinned the anti-dam campaign, in that both sought to hold the state accountable to what Abrams (1988: 76) has called the 'state idea' – that is, the idea of the state as 'an integrated expression of common interest cleanly dissociated from all sectional interests and the structures . . . associated with them'. However, this expectation failed to hold true for the NBA's anti-dam campaign, and this in turn brings back the question first broached in Chapter 3, namely the question of the limits that might exist to forms of movement strategies that are predicated on making use of the official principles and procedures of the liberal-democratic state. This question is discussed in detail towards the end of the chapter.

Non-violent direct action as a repertoire of contention

Dwivedi (1997: 28–9) emphasizes that jury politics privileges the role of experts and specialists over mass mobilization. In the case of the Andolan, however, mass mobilization and jury politics co-existed, with mass mobilization serving as a vehicle for the movement to pressure the state to implement a review of the project. Here I focus on the ethical and tactical rationales for choosing non-violent direct action as a repertoire of contention.

Leading NBA activist, Chittaroopa Palit answers the question of why the NBA opted for non-violent direct action as follows:

> The main forms of mass struggle in the Valley have been non-violent direct action – marches, *satyagraha* and civil disobedience . . . If we fight for the inalienable right to life, and insist that such concerns should form the basis for assessing any development paradigm, how can we resort to violence? There have been a few unplanned incidents involving self-defence that cannot count as non-violent; situations where people have been pushed beyond the edge. But as a strategy, how could physical violence on our part ever match the armed might of the Indian state, or of imperialist globalization? Most importantly, only a non-violent struggle can provide the silence in which the questions we are asking can be heard. A strategy of violence results in a very different kind of political discourse.
>
> (2003: 96–7)

Palit's explanation of the rationale for adopting a strategy of non-violence contains both ethical and tactical dimensions.

The former dimension is related to an evaluation of the ethics of ends – 'the inalienable right to life' – and means of struggle that resonate with the reasoning that underpinned Gandhi's notion of non-violence, denoted by the term *ahimsa* – a concept of non-violence which revolves around 'qualities of respect and sympathy for the opponent, freedom from anger, and a desire for peace' (Hardiman 2003: 58). Gandhi believed that 'as no one knew the absolute truth, nobody had a right to commit violence on others lest they be in the wrong' and thus an individual's truth should be asserted 'not by infliction of suffering on the opponents but on oneself' (ibid.: 59). For the NBA, then, the end of asserting the inalienable right to life would be defeated by the means if violence had been the chosen strategy.

The tactical element can be found in the assessment of the balance of forces – 'how could physical violence on our part ever match the armed might of the Indian state, or of imperialist globalization?' – between the movement and its opponents. Medha Patkar argues in a similar way about non-violence when commenting on the climax of the *Sangharsh Yatra*:

> We said, 'Okay, if the waters rise, we will still face it and you will have to face this non-violent action at a very different moral plane', because it was only this that we knew it was beyond the government's capacity to respond. Otherwise they had guns and lathis, they had bombs – (whatever they wanted) – they had the military at their disposal, and they also had money if they wanted to purchase some of the activists and try and break the movement and the agitation.
>
> (1995: 171)

Thus, as Baviskar (1995: 224) has noted, non-violence is also 'a strategy which seems to be deliberately chosen by the activists to ward off police action that could completely crush the movement'.[3]

Non-violence, however, should by no means be considered a risk-free venture. Rather, much like resistance to everyday tyranny, non-violent direct action is an enterprise that entails building the courage to put one's body in harm's way. For example, going on a march or a demonstration entails braving police lathi-charges and imprisonment, and going on a hunger strike is an action that could possibly entail death. Activists reflected in various ways about the nature of these risks:

> Sitaram Patidar is a veteran activist from the village of Kadmal in submergence zone of the SSP in Nimad. As he was telling me how the movement developed after they had decided to oppose the dam, he explained that fasting turned out to be one of their most efficient weapons. He attributes his own willingness to go on fast as being moored in the desire to help others. Providing a vivid metaphor, he pointed out how one cob of corn contains around four hundred corn-seeds, but in order to create that one cob of corn, you have to sacrifice one seed to use for sowing. The strength you need to go on fast comes from knowing that an individual sacrifice will contribute to the lives of thousands of others. The prospect of tens of thousands of people being deprived has fuelled his will to resist the dam.
>
> (interview, April 2003)

Activists also expressed that they drew confidence from a perception of strength in numbers. Rukshmeni Patidar, one of the leading female activists from Nimad, expressed how the practical experience of participating in numerous large rallies and demonstrations had caused her to lose her fear of the police and the violent repression they might unleash. Others again would remark how arrests and beatings had become an almost routine affair, and how they had simply stopped being afraid of repression (field notes, April 2003).

Finally, the fact that non-violent direct action constituted the fulcrum of mass resistance to colonial subjugation also makes it a strategy ripe with symbolic reverberations in that it appeals to the collective memory of the national freedom struggle. As Hardiman (2003: 64) observes, Gandhian notions and techniques of non-violent, civil resistance has 'continued to be a central element within the Indian polity since Independence in 1947, again deployed by all sorts of groups and political parties'.[4] Whereas I shall discuss the political use of collective memories at greater length later, what can be established here is that adopting Gandhian tactics entails situating one's struggle in the lineage of national liberation, which makes for an effective and emotive appeal to the sensibilities of the nation at large.

The trajectory of the demand for review, 1990–91

The first significant action in what was to become an intense struggle for review of the SSP was a blockade of the Bombay-Agra highway in Madhya Pradesh on 6 March, 1990, where 10,000 activists of the NBA blocked traffic for 28 hours. The BJP state government of Sunderlal Patwa heeded the activists' demands and declared that not only would it push ahead with review at state level, it would also put forward the demand for review to the central government. A substantial dialogue, however, failed to materialize, as the Patwa government was internally divided on the issue of the SSP (Patkar 1995: 170; Jayal 2000: 171). The actions to put pressure on the MP state authorities were followed by a dharna in Mumbai to put pressure on the Maharashtra government from 28 March. Several activists went on fast from 29 March until 5 April, when the Congress Chief Minister of Maharashtra, Sharad Pawar, issued a letter assuring the protesters that there would be no submergence until alternative lands were made available for resettlement. However, much as in the case of Patwa's promises, such assurances failed to have any practical consequences (Patkar 1995: 164–5).

The Andolan's effort and attention then turned to Delhi and the central government. In 1990, the central government was in the hands of the National Front/Janata Dal government of V. P. Singh. During the campaign for the Lok Sabha elections Singh had promised a full review of the projects if his party was voted to power, and more generally Singh's premiership was very much based on 'a mandate of change and . . . social movement backing' (Omvedt 1993: 274).[5] Consequently, there was an expectation among leading activists in the movement 'that they would get a more sympathetic response from him and his administration' (Khagram 2004: 122)

Demonstrations were conducted outside the offices of the Ministry of Labour and a three-day rally was held at the Delhi Boat Club in April (Patkar 1995: 165).

The efforts, however, were of little consequence, eliciting only 'contradictory and confusing' ministerial statements (Jayal 2000: 171). Then, from 14 May to 18 May, a sit-in demonstration was staged outside V. P. Singh's residence in Delhi. After four days, the activists were invited in to the Prime Minister's residence to make their case. Singh then agreed to initiate a review of the SSP (Khagram 2004: 122). This was a potential watershed for the Andolan, but it was quickly stymied by the intervention of the Chief Minister of Gujarat, Chimanbhai Patel, and the massive support and propaganda machinery that had been built up around the SSP in Gujarat (Jayal 2000: 172). This display of popular support for the SSP in Gujarat and its potential ramifications in relation to the fortunes of electoral politics rattled V. P. Singh, who quickly reneged on the promises of review (Khagram 2004: 122; see also Patkar 1995: 165).

At this point, the construction of the SSP was proceeding without impediments, and the Andolan was involved in 'a race against time' where it had to stage 'ever-larger, increasingly dramatic protests' (Baviskar 1995: 207). This was the context for one of the NBA's most noted protest actions, the *Jan Vikas Sangharsh Yatra* (March of Struggle for People's Development), generally referred to as the *Sangharsh Yatra* or the Long March, which aimed 'to physically stop the work on the dam, by offering peaceful *satyagraha* at the dam site and thereby pressure the government to comprehensively review the SSP' (NBA newsletter, cited in Dwivedi 1997: 14).

On 25 December 1990, some 6,000 men and women from the dam-affected communities set out from Rajghat, just outside Badwani (MP), towards the dam site. After six days, on 31 December, having covered approximately 200 kilometres, the *Yatra* reached the village of Ferkuwa on the border between Gujarat and Madhya Pradesh, where the police and a substantial gathering of dam-supporters from Gujarat stopped the activists. Attempts by the activists to cross the border were met with beatings and arrests. Ferkuwa then became the site of an intense confrontation between the movement and the authorities (Sangvai 2000a: 57).

On 7 January 1991, as a response to the failure of the authorities to respond to the demand for review, six leading NBA activists went on indefinite fast. Several other activists joined them in the following days (Patkar 1995: 167). Officials tried to intervene by offering to look into questions of resettlement and rehabilitation as long as the construction work was not stalled, but the activists declined. There was increasing pressure on the state governments by the Centre and the World Bank to enter into negotiations with the protesters. Gradually, the situation got increasingly dramatic, with both the World Bank and Central Government failing to announce reviews. The police swooped down in raids, beating and arresting protesters (Khagram 2004: 123–4). The central government could not commit to a review of the Project as Chandra Sekhar, who had become Prime Minister after V. P. Singh's government fell in November 1990, and his minority government was dependent on support from Gujarat. The Centre's efforts were thus reduced to minimizing the degree of violent confrontation. On 28 January, the fast was called off and the activists withdrew from Ferkuwa. The first cycle in the struggle for a review of the SSP had come to an end.

So what were the results of this initial cycle of struggle for a review of the SSP? The outcome of the *Yatra* in terms of the attempt to elicit a commitment from the state to implement a review of the SSP is aptly summarized by Baviskar (1991: 479), who argues that '[t]he *Yatra* seemed to end in an impasse' in that it 'failed in its objectives of stopping work on the dam while a review was carried out' (1991: 478). Similarly, Jayal (2000: 174) argues that '[t]here is little doubt that the Gujarat government won this skirmish easily, even if at an estimated cost of Rs. 3 crores raised by organizations like the Gujarat Chamber of Commerce and Industry'. However, she also adds that 'there is even less doubt that this was . . . a dramatic event that not only generated widespread sympathy for the movement, but also brought it to the notice of the nation, and placed it at the very centre of the debate on development and environment in India' (ibid.: 174). Her assessment is shared by NBA activist Chittaroopa Palit, who argues that:

> The Ferkuwa Programme was quite significant because it was a very large programme, it involved a very large mobilisation, not only from the Valley [inaudible] but also, you know, from a lot of other places, and, you know, because it was for a whole month, it created, at least on the border and so on, it was able to create a lot of ripples.
>
> (interview, May 2003)

In terms of tangible outcomes, though, her assessment was more ambiguous: on the one hand 'the political establishment chose not to respond in any of the states', but on the other hand, due to the international attention that the *Yatra* attracted and the increased intensity of transnational advocacy on the Narmada issue (discussed later), the announcement by the World Bank that there would be an independent review was a significant achievement (interview, May 2003; see also Khagram 2004: 124).

'Hamare Gaon, Mein Hamare Raj'

Gaon Bandi and Satyagraha

Medha Patkar commented on the immediate changes that occurred in the aftermath of the *Sangharsh Yatra*: '. . . when we returned from Ferkuwa, the *Sangharsh Yatra*, we declared *"hamare gaon, hamare raj"* – our village, our rule . . . because a new phase had to begin, you know, with the government not responding' (interview June 2003). Village non-cooperation – *gaon bandi* – was developed as a 'symbolic strategy' to 'outlaw an unresponsive government' (Jayal 2000: 180), and it basically entailed 'non-cooperation with anything and anyone who was working related to the dam. Only archaeologists we allowed. And everyone else we stopped' (interview, Medha Patkar, June 2003).

This resulted in actions such as barring state and project officials of all kinds from entering the village. For instance, during the monsoon of 1992, the Chief Engineers of Gujarat and Maharashtra were sent by the Bombay High Court to inspect the effects of the backwaters from the SSP on Manibeli. The activists took them around the village, while M. S. Gill, the Additional Collector, was prohibited from entering the village. Again, during the monsoon of 1993, a signboard was put up on the outskirts of Manibeli refusing entry for all government officials, allowing only health personnel and teachers to enter the village. The order was signed 'By Order of the People' (Jayal 2000: 179–80, 185). Also, the stone markers that the government put up to mark out the submergence area of the SSP were dismantled and brought back to the project headquarters. Moreover, the villagers refused to participate in any survey work related to the dam. Censuses were boycotted, and, in 1991, the Andolan encouraged a boycott of the Lok Sabha elections, leading to 33 villages in the Akrani-Dhadgaon parliamentary constituencies of Maharashtra opting out of the elections (ibid.: 175–6).

Accompanying the adoption of *gaon bandi* was the inauguration of annual protest actions, carried out during the monsoon months, and referred to as *satyagrahas*. Basically, what the *satyagraha* revolved around was a braving of the rising of the waters of the Narmada which set in with the monsoon rains and the closing of the floodgates of the SSP. The *satyagrahas* were centred on villages in the tribal areas of Maharashtra and Madhya Pradesh, where the resident families, Andolan activists, and domestic and international supporters of the movement would stand their ground as the waters of the Narmada started to rise.[6] The braving of the waters thus signalled a defiance of the displacement wrought by the project and constituted an emotive image of the opposition to the SSP as such, contrasting, as one activist put it, 'the violence of the development project with the determination of those who stand in its path' (Palit 2003: 97).

The monsoon *satyagraha* was first organized in the village of Manibeli (Maharashtra) in July 1991 as a reaction to the project authorities giving notice to the villagers of Gadher (Maharashtra) and Vadgam (Gujarat) that they were to vacate their homes within five days as the villages were slated to be submerged with the coming monsoon. Following this, the monsoon *satyagraha* became an annual event; sometimes they assumed hugely dramatic proportions, with rising waters, intense political negotiations, severe repression by the state, and national and international attention; at other times they were more muted affairs, characterized by non-submergence, low participation both from within the Valley and from outside supporters, and less political drama. The ultimate manifestation of this will to brave the waters was the *Jal Samparan* – Sacrifice in Water – where the *Samparit Dal* – a sacrificial squad of activists – vowed to immerse itself in the rising waters and drown if necessary, to express the ultimate commitment to the struggle against submergence. The *Samparit Dal* would usually stay in the *Narmadyi*, a special hut built near the banks of the river so that it would be the first dwelling to be submerged as the waters rose, with their hands tied in order to express their commitment to non-violence (Dwivedi 1997; Jayal 2000; Sangvai 2000a).

Collective memories and symbolic-communicative practice of resistance

Whereas the *satyagraha*, the threat of *Jal Samparan*, and non-cooperation have at times been important in the instrumental sense of forcing state authorities into dialogue with the movement, they are also deeply *symbolic-communicative practices*. I use this term to denote practices that are *symbolic* in the sense that they represent and express the identity of the movement and the nature of the political project which it seeks to advance, and *communicative* in that they seek to convey this identity to various recipients, spanning the general public, other social movements, opponents of the movement, and indeed the movement's participants and activists.

Non-cooperation as the NBA has practised it can neither be equated with the establishment of autonomous zones by guerrilla movements, nor with 'dual power' situations that may emerge in revolutionary situations. In contrast to this kind of strategy, the NBA implemented non-cooperation selectively in the areas of its mass base, and maintained close relations with the state through negotiations for review. Moreover, the frequent repressive police crackdowns that occurred during this period of the struggle also testify to the lack of an ability to ward off large-scale state coercion. What the adoption of a strategy of non-cooperation did do, though, was to express a rejection of state legitimacy. In order to properly grasp the significance of non-cooperation as the NBA practised it, I propose that we think of it as *a symbolic reclaiming of eminent domain.*

'Eminent domain' is the legal principle by which the state claims ownership over and stewardship of the nation's natural resources, or, as Sen (2000b: 6) puts it, 'an artifice which is premised on the proposition that the state always, by definition, acts in the public interest and that it therefore can claim eminent domain over all social entities; and conversely, that people so-called 'citizens' must equally by definition submit to it'. When the Andolan inaugurated the practice of *gaon bandi* it efficiently communicated to the general public, its opponents, its participants, and its supporters 'that the sovereignty of the peoples of the valley has been grossly trampled upon, curbed, and violated'. In doing so, 'the institutions of state which have taken it upon themselves to promote and undertake such projects . . . have arrogated to themselves and exercised huge powers, powers which are far beyond the powers that any system of natural justice would allow' thus delegitmizing itself and depriving itself 'of the authority by which alone it can function' (ibid.: 4). When the movement then opted for a strategy at the heart of which was the refusal to interact with a state that had delegitmized itself through its own actions, it symbolically reclaimed eminent domain in the name of the people it represented. The people of the Valley were posited as the rightful stewards and guardians of its resources and as the defenders of 'the right and freedom of people to have and to here, to retain – a place to live with dignity' (ibid.: 7).

Satyagraha can be thought of as a performance or enactment of sacrifice and resolve directed at multiple audiences. The very process through which village communities were submerged while the resident population refused to leave constitutes a powerful image of the sacrifice that these communities are asked to make in the name of the national interest, and their refusal to leave simultaneously testifies to their resolve to the struggle against the dam, and their attachment to the Narmada Valley as a place. These were messages intended to reach and appeal to several audiences. First, the messages were directed at the movement's opponents (state and central governments, dam supporters), combining 'moral argument' – 'does your conscience really allow us to drown?' – and 'non-violent coercion' (Hardiman 2003: 54) – 'if you do not respond to our demands, you will have the blood of martyrs on your hands!' – in an effort to force the opponent into dialogue. Second, it was a message intended to reach the national and international public at large in order to garner support for the movement. The vulgar display of power by the state in the form of submergence and police repression contrasts with the earnest resolve of non-violent protesters to stand their ground and in effect poses the question to the public: 'Can you be a silent bystander to such an injustice, will you really let this happen to us?' Rituals are of course central in the reproduction of social cohesion within communities, and here we reach the third of the *satyagraha*'s audiences. The *satyagraha* also communicated a message to the movement's participants in that it affirmed the movement's resolve to stop the dam and to the slogan coined in conjunction with this resolve: 'Koi Nahin Hatega, Bandh Nahin Banega' – 'No One Will Move, the Dam Will Not Be Built'. Simultaneously, by bringing together activists from different states and regions in spectacular acts of defiance of an overpowering opponent, the *satyagraha* reconfirmed the erasure of differences within the movement expressed in the slogan 'Hum Sub Ek Hai' – 'We Are All One'.

When a contemporary movement like the NBA deploys such strategies as *satyagraha* and non-cooperation, it effectively appropriates the collective memories of the social movements of yesteryear for today's purposes;[7] this calls for some further reflection. As Middleton and Edwards (1990) point out, the process of collective remembering can be thought of as a creative process, in which a certain image of past events, objects or persons is invented as a cultural idiom. The organization of rhetorical skills involved in the process of collective remembering is carried out 'in relation to broader ideological considerations that place people in a contradictory relationship with what they would report or make of the past in the present' (ibid.: 9). In conflictual situations, the main focus becomes how 'the struggle for possession and interpretation of memory is rooted among the conflict and interplay of social, political, and cultural interests and values in the present' (Thelen cited in Middleton and Edwards 1990: 3).

Now, the repertoire of contention that evolved with the NBA's turn to the villages is deeply imbued with collective memories of India's struggle for national liberation, and particularly with the heritage of Gandhian modes of resistance. *Satyagraha* was part of the 'new language of protest' created by Mahatma Gandhi as he developed the technique and philosophy of non-violent resistance. *Satyagraha*, Hardiman (2003: 52) explains, 'is an amalgamation of two Gujarati words, *satya* (truth) and *agraha* (taking, seizing, holding), the implication being that one seizes hold of the truth'. Seizing the truth, in turn, involved 'a complex dialogue in which reasoned argument had often to be reinforced with emotional and political pressure . . . for people tend to be swayed as much by emotion as by rational argument' (ibid.: 52). *Satyagraha*, then, was an integral and defining element in Gandhi's strategy of 'dialogic resistance' where there were no enemies as such, but rather opponents whose reason, morality and compassion had to be appealed to through a combination of 'moral argument and non-violent coercion' (ibid.: 54). The notion of *satyagraha* and the practices of resistance associated with it has lingered with great vibrancy among social movements in India after Gandhi's death (ibid.: 64–5). Like *satyagraha*, non-cooperation also alludes to Gandhi's efforts during the freedom struggle. First formulated in 1919 as a suggestion of boycotting British textiles, non-cooperation, as Fischer (1983) puts it, 'became the name of an epoch in the life of India and of Gandhi' in the wake of widespread frustration within the Congress with the Montagu-Chelmsford governance reforms. From August 1920, the Mahatma criss-crossed the nation to rally the masses to the new strategy, promising self-rule as its inevitable and imminent outcome. Non-cooperation was a key strategy of the freedom movement until 1924.

Crucially, the adoption of such a strategy as *satyagraha* becomes more than merely a strategy or a technique chosen on the grounds of, say, instrumental rationality or moral compulsion. The adoption of a Gandhian repertoire of contention becomes an act of collective remembering in the sense that the movement places itself in a long and proud lineage of resistance towards oppression and exploitation. This resistance was once directed against colonial domination, but it now comes to be directed against national and foreign elite interests and their corruption of the ideals that defined and fuelled the energies of the freedom struggle. It is in this sense that the deployment of such techniques of resistance constitutes a symbolic-communicative practice: the choice of 'weapons' with which to face the opponent gives the movement itself a symbolic form and conveys a message about the movement and its politics to its participants, supporters, opponents, and other movements.

To participants, drawing on the collective memories of freedom struggle provides inspiration and moral legitimacy. Appealing to the memories of Gandhian politics also resonates well in urban, intellectual milieus in India, and the movement thus conveys a message that it is worthy of their support. To opponents, the message conveyed can be understood as a reframing of the narrative of public history. This is so in that the movement chooses to fight the institutions that claim to represent the national interests with the methods that were deployed in order to create those institutions in the first place. In doing this, the Andolan in effect contested the state's claim to being the supreme trustee of the national interest. This is of course also an important message to the public at large. With respect to other movements engaged in oppositional politics, the use of Gandhian philosophies and strategies of resistance can be considered as an act of positioning. For example, a clear signal is sent out that the NBA is different from the mainstream, parliamentary left. Simultaneously, the Andolan also distances itself from the Naxalite elements of the new left that have opted for revolutionary violence. All in all, then, the repertoire of contention that was developed by the Andolan after the showdown at Ferkuwa was one that was densely symbolic, which effectively wove together the idioms and strategies of past and present struggles, and in doing so effectively conveyed multiple messages to multiple audiences about the Andolan and its politics.

The adoption of a village-based repertoire of contention in the wake of the *Sangharsh Yatra* can readily be interpreted as a shift emanating from a determinate experience that had 'demonstrated to the people of the Valley the futility of expecting any satisfactory response from the government . . . if they continue[d] to couch protest in the idiom of "appeal"' (Baviskar 1991: 478). Indeed, it can be viewed as a shrewd strategic move, in which appeals to the state is substituted for a strategy which seeks to consolidate a movement's identity and project, both inwards in relation to its own participants, and outwards, in relation to the general public, opponents, and other movements. Moreover, the Andolan's new and symbolically saturated repertoire of resistance – and the ability to sustain it under conditions of severe repression – can be interpreted as testifying to a movement of considerable strength, capable of creative reinvention of itself in the face of strategic dead-ends.

Yet, the adoption of such a repertoire of contention also conveys a more implicit, and deeply ambiguous, message about the dynamics of the movement process. Critical voices have claimed that during this phase of the struggle, symbolic-communicative practices in fact came to substitute for actual political striking power. Rahul Banerjee, for instance, asserts that the *Sangharsh Yatra* and the events of Ferkuwa became a negative turning point for the NBA:

> This was the turning point for the NBA. Many of the indigenous oustees of Maharashtra and Madhya Pradesh perceived this to be a crushing defeat and decided that the dam could not be stopped. So they thought it more prudent to opt for rehabilitation. Within a month of the *Yatra*, more than 50 per cent of the oustees of Maharashtra decided to take the land being offered to them in Akkalkuva taluka by the Maharashtra government . . . Thus the whole bottom fell out of the Maharashtra component of the NBA. A similar process started in Madhya Pradesh though in a less dramatic manner . . . Most of the backward caste farmer oustees of Madhya Pradesh have not opted for rehabilitation yet, but their active participation in the NBA has waned . . . The subsequent journey of the NBA has been one in which lobbying and advocacy has played a greater role than mass actions. With a drastically reduced mass base mass actions have had to be of a symbolic type like *Jal Samparan*. This has resulted in the total dominance of middle-class activists as indigenous and backward caste oustees just do not have the kind of expertise required to lobby with national and international decision-makers, the press and the urban elite.
>
> (2000: 37, 38)

While the urban, educated activists of the Andolan fiercely deny Banerjee's claims (see Sangvai 2000b), certain aspects of the phase of the anti-dam campaign that unfolded from 1994–2000 do indicate that his contentions are not completely unwarranted. Crucial to this phase was the adoption of judicial activism as the NBA turned to the Supreme Court, and some observers have interpreted this as a move that was made to circumvent emergent constraints on the Andolan's capacity for mass mobilization. I will explore these developments further later in the chapter. Now, however, I turn to a brief mapping and analysis of the international Narmada campaign and the independent review that led to the withdrawal of World Bank funding of the project.

The international Narmada campaign and the independent review

The international campaign against the World Bank: 1988–93

From 1988, when opposition to the SSP was declared in the Narmada Valley, the reach of this transnational infrastructure of contention established in 1986–87 widened and deepened, the intensity and scale of its operations increased considerably, and the aim became that of forcing the withdrawal of World Bank funding from the SSP. The announcement by the Bank, made towards the end of the stand-off at Ferkuwa, that it would implement an independent review of the SSP was in large part an outcome of this process.

The intensification of transnational advocacy can be explained in terms of how the various groups that were active in the early days of transnational activism around the Narmada issue discovered that their engagements with the Bank's Operations staff yielded few results, and concurrently decided to set their aim at the higher echelons of the Bank: 'Gradually the Narmada campaign moved to more systematic lobbying of the executive directors' (Udall 1995: 206). As Udall points out, the Bank's Board of Executive Directors stand responsible for the general operations of the Bank. Executive Directors in turn take their voting instructions from the finance ministries they represent. Still, with the exception of highly contentious projects, 'formal votes are quite rare' (ibid.: 204). Decisions as to whether actual projects are to be suspended or cancelled lie with the Operations Department. This amounted to a loaded dice as 'Bank staff who make the decisions about continuing a project despite loans violations are the same people with a vested interest in the project, and since careers are rewarded inside the Bank for pushing projects forward and not for project quality, the continuation of a project is usually guaranteed' (ibid.: 204).

What was evident in the case of the SSP was that the staff of the India Operations Department had not reported the discontent with and controversy around the project to the Executive Directors. Executive Directors requesting information on the SSP would receive either 'an oral briefing from staff or a specially prepared, sanitized document that frequently did not present a candid or accurate view of the ground reality' (Udall 1995: 206). When activists turned to lobbying the Board of Executive Directors, they sought to use counter-expertise to break the veil of incomplete information that the SSP had been shrouded in by Operations staff, and, in doing this, to put pressure on the Bank to stand accountable to its own policies and codes of conduct.

In May 1988, against the backdrop of increasing mobilization in the Narmada Valley, NBA activist Smitu Kothari testified at a US Congressional hearing on the SSP. The Narmada campaign was perceived as significant and was increasingly addressed by all major shareholders in the Bank. However, activists based in Washington D.C. sensed that Bank management and staff were not seriously committing themselves to considering the SSP anew and hence addressed the Board of Directors and the Bank's Senior Vice President for Operations, Mooen Qureshi, directly. In response, Qureshi proceeded to send a Bank resettlement mission to

India to investigate the projects. Qureshi himself participated in the mission, and met with project authorities, politicians and activists in India. The visit left him with an impression of a project that was running seriously askew, and upon his return to Washington D.C. he penned a letter to Chief Minister Arjun Singh in Madhya Pradesh threatening to suspend Bank funding of the SSP unless a new plan for resettlement and rehabilitation was crafted.

The next significant event occurred in April 1989, when another Bank mission travelled to India to follow up on the conditions Qureshi had stipulated. Thayer Scudder, an anthropologist who had carried out preappraisal work of the SSP in 1983/84, was part of the mission. The mission found no improvements in the plans for rehabilitation and resettlement, but rather identified tendencies towards deterioration since 1984. Following these findings, it recommended permanent or temporary termination of World Bank disbursements. However, the Bank ignored these recommendations (Udall 1995; Khagram 2004).

Then, in October 1989, the United States House of Representatives Subcommittee on Natural Resources, Agricultural Research and Environment, and its chairman James Scheuer, organized an oversight hearing on the World Bank financial support of the SSP. At this hearing, testimonies were presented by Medha Patkar, Girish Patel, a human rights lawyer from Gujarat, and Vijay Paranjpye, an economist who had carried out an independent cost-benefit analysis of the Narmada projects. Frank Vukmanic, the head of the office of Multilateral Development Banks in the US Treasury, and Peter Miller and Lori Udall of the Environmental Defense Fund also testified at the hearings. The Bank's representatives, however, were absent: 'While the World Bank as an international organization was not legally bound to appear before the legislature of any country, even Scheuer's offer to the Bank to testify off the record was refused' (Khagram 2004: 119).

The hearings engendered a flurry of letter writing as Members of Congress sought to pressure Barbar Connable, the president of the World Bank, to suspend funding of the SSP. James Scheuer took up the issue through Global Legislators for a Balanced Environment (GLOBE) and held informal discussions with Japanese and European authorities. Moreover, the Dutch executive director to the World Bank, Paul Arlman, who had followed the controversy around the project for some time, arranged a meeting between Medha Patkar and the Executive Directors of the World Bank. Lori Udall recounts the impact of the meeting: 'After the meeting ended, an executive director said, "When I hear what NGOs say about this project and then what the Operations staff say, it sounds as if they are talking about two different projects"' (1995: 206).

The congressional hearings and the events that followed in their wake led to increased interest in the controversy around the project in Europe and Japan. In Japan, environmentalist groups started to put pressure on the authorities to cancel their funding of the SSP. In April 1990, Friends of the Earth Japan and other NGOs organized the first International Narmada Symposium, a conference which constituted a meeting place for activists from across the world, lawyers, academics and journalists. The Japanese campaigners were eventually successful in their efforts when the Japanese Ministry of Foreign Affairs announced the cessation of funding

7 Enablements and constraints

The making of the Maheshwar anti-dam campaign

Resistance in the Narmada Valley is often equated with the Narmada Bachao Andolan's campaign against the Sardar Sarovar Project. However, just as the Narmada Valley Development Project is more than the SSP, the NBA is also more than the struggle against the SSP. On 11 January 1998, 25,000 villagers from the submergence zone of the Maheshwar Hydroelectric Project (MHP) in eastern Nimad (MP) stormed and captured the dam-site, and six activists launched an indefinite fast until the demand for a comprehensive review of the project was acceded to. This was the first major NBA action against the MHP, signalling the coming of an intense process of mobilization that was ultimately successful in forcing the withdrawal of several transnational corporations (TNCs) and financial institutions, which resulted in the temporary halting of the project in 2001 (see Chapter 1).

At first glance, the success of the campaign in effecting the withdrawal of several TNCs from the project, and in lodging spanners in the wheels of the early attempts to fund the project via liberalized financial institutions, points towards an interesting comparative analysis of the different challenges and opportunities that confront activists when they campaign against a public project (the SSP) and a private project (the MHP) respectively. Indeed, an immediate, and perhaps somewhat counter-intuitive, inference would be that the outcome of the campaign against the MHP indicates that contending with TNCs, which albeit unaccountable to democratic norms are conscious of the opportunity costs of going ahead with investments in a highly controversial project, is actually more likely to succeed than contention aimed at state authorities whose democratic accountability is curtailed by the ways in which state power is congealed from regional and national class structures. However, the recent undermining of the NBA's initial victory by the interventions of the Government of Madhya Pradesh to facilitate funding for the MHP (see Chapter 2), and the concurrent re-ignition of struggle in the dam-affected communities in eastern Nimad prevents such easy comparisons; indeed, as a parallel to my argument about the relative insignificance of the World Bank's withdrawal from the SSP, the current scenario suggests that the workings of the domestic state-system, both in facilitating the operations of regional capital and in terms of mediating transnational financial flows, may be more crucial factors in some cases than the direct presence of the corporate juggernauts of transnational capitalism. In any case, it is still too early to pass judgement on these questions, and I choose instead to focus on the making of the campaign against the MHP and the ways in which it has been criss-crossed by factors of enablement and constraint.

What is perhaps most striking about this campaign is the swiftness with which it came into being: rather than passing through years of gradual mobilization around demands for resettlement and rehabilitation (R&R) and consequent radicalization as in the case of the campaign against the SSP, the campaign against the MHP was constituted within a year, with a strong anti-dam stance and with significant mobilizational capacity in the dam-affected communities. The following analysis focuses on the presence of extant skills and experiences both among the NBA activists that took on the task of mobilizing in the area, and among the representatives of the Nimadi peasantry which came to form the bridgehead between the NBA activists and the dam-affected communities, as the most crucial factors of enablement in the making of the campaign against the MHP.

Next, I focus on the role of women in the campaign. I present a critical discussion of claims that women's active participation in the campaign can be attributed to a traditional, non-commodified link between women and the natural environment, arguing that women's participation must instead be understood in the light of socially constituted material interests. I also focus on how women's participation brought a partial/temporary reversal of patriarchal power in the communities, and discuss how this brings out how movement processes are not exclusively directed 'outwards', against an 'external' opponent, but that they can also trigger change in the internal workings of the insurgent communities.

I then turn to an analysis of factors of constraint that may impede the future development of the campaign, and in particular the development of a movement project beyond the politics of dam opposition. I locate these factors of constraint in the social structures of caste and class that prevail in the Nimadi communities. In contrast to the active mobilization of women and the challenge that has been levelled at gender relations in the dam-affected communities, dalits and landless labourers have not been the direct target of mobilization, and issues related to caste discrimination and exploitative class relations have not been subjected to a direct challenge by the Andolan. This, I argue, constitutes a limit to the extent to which a wider social movement project centred on a politics of social justice might emerge from the struggle against the MHP.

Factors of enablement in the Maheshwar campaign

Extant skills and experience 1: NBA activists

The making of the campaign against the MHP drew heavily on *exogenous extant skills and experiences* – that is, the experience, skills and confidence of activists that had been involved in the campaign against the SSP in the late 1980s and 1990s. These skills and experiences were translated into a generic knowledge about mobilization, and then applied very effectively in the specific context of mobilization against the MHP. The centrality of such skills and experience is brought out in the following statement by one of the leading NBA activists in the Maheshwar area:

> So whatever it was, I must also say that the leadership from the NBA that came into Maheshwar, which included people like Alok, Vegambhai, Devrambhai, Remat, me, Jaganath Kaka, Rukmeni Kaki, were also far more confident at that time then we had been in Sardar Sarovar, because we'd stopped Sardar Sarovar, and from ninety-four, ninety-five to 2000, Sardar Sarovar remained stopped. And that was also a major source of confidence for the people of Maheshwar: we'd stopped the dam there through all these struggles. So actually the process, although we did travel blind here too, but somehow one feels that one had travelled far more blind in the Sardar Sarovar struggle than in Maheshwar.
>
> (interview, Chittaroopa Palit, May 2003)

What does this passage tell us about the importance of the experiences and skills of the NBA activists? First, the experience of having been successful in stopping the SSP[1] made the activists confident that resistance could in fact yield results, even when faced with an overwhelming opponent like the Indian state. Second, the fact that the NBA had been successful in halting the SSP also served as an example to the MHP-affected communities that resistance was a possible and fruitful path to pursue. Third, the remark that the activists felt that they were travelling less blindly when mobilizing against the MHP as compared to when they mobilized against the SSP points to how they had garnered lessons about movement processes through their involvement in the SSP campaign that could be generalized and applied elsewhere.

As an example of how this abstraction and re-application of such experiential skills and knowledge, Palit offered an instance of crisis management which occurred in 1998: dam builders were increasingly aware that violence and repression would not deter resistance in the area. Instead they attempted to undermine the momentum of mobilization by offering cash compensation to the dam-affected communities. Initially, the tactic seemed to have an impact, as village leaders grew demoralized at the sight of the dwindling of the mass base:

> So we were in Delhi because of the Supreme Court case for three months or two months and we came back and this was happening and everybody was completely demoralized, the village leaders, and they said 'the game is up' . . . But the same thing had happened in Sardar Sarovar, when Akadia and Jalsindhi, half of them had chosen to leave, it was far more difficult then for us to cope. But this time around, although it was a tortured situation, we said 'it doesn't matter, because we've learnt that even if some people go, if people choose to stay and fight we will be able to win' . . . So within two or three months, when we were able to keep that confidence in the village leaders, there was a turnaround, and we were able to cope with the situation . . . So there was the experience of the Sardar Sarovar beforehand which also gave us a lot of confidence.
>
> (interview, May 2003)

What this example shows is how the specific experience of downtimes and how they were handled in the campaign against the SSP had become a kind of generic knowledge of downtimes and how to tackle them, which was then applied to the specific circumstances of the MHP-campaign, enabling the activists to tackle the challenge of tendencies towards disintegration in the mass base.

More generally, the way in which NBA activists applied the skills and experiences they had garnered through the struggle against the SSP is an example of how the skills and experience garnered in movement processes 'travel' through abstraction from specific contexts and re-application in other specific contexts. Processes of abstraction and re-application in turn provide momentum to mobilization in the sense that activists do not have to re-invent the wheel when they set out to mobilize in new contexts, which in turn makes it possible to more immediately build momentum and mobilizational capacity. However, in order to truly understand the factors that enabled rapid mobilization against the MHP, we have to take into account how activist skills and experiences were coupled with the extant skills and experiences of local political leaders, most of whom were representatives of Nimad's class of rich farmers.

Extant skills and experience 2: Nimadi farmers

Mobilization against the MHP got underway in 1997, when the NBA was approached by a delegation from the dam-affected villages in eastern Nimad who sought assistance and advice as construction work had started and village land had been forcibly appropriated by the dam-builders. The delegation was made up of what Ramchandr, an activist from the village of Pathrad, called 'influential people', meaning men with experience as local political leaders and who wielded substantial clout in the area due to their political power and economic affluence. One of them had served unopposed as the *sarpanch*[2] of the village *panchayat* in Pathrad for the past 40 years, and had earned widespread respect as the 'architect' of the relocation and reconstruction of the village to avoid the impact of repeated floods. Similarly, the representative from the neighbouring village of Mardana was a sarpanch of great standing and respect (interview, May 2003).

As Chittaroopa Palit pointed out, these men and their skills, experience, influence, and clout would prove to be a valuable resource in the mobilization process:

> So you have these communities, and . . . and there's a lot of access to the media . . . lot of access to education and so on . . . so therefore you had already a self-confident middle class, a rural middle class, a middle class that could, you know, that were exposed to and that could articulate the concerns. And this middle class also was highly politicized and they had a lot of political power, power beyond the sort of power that adivasis in the communities in Alirajpur or Maharashtra could wield.
>
> (interview, May 2003)

The local leaders seem to have been influential in two senses, or, more precisely, the salience of their participation in the campaign seems to have had both 'internal' and 'external' aspects. Internally, in the dam-affected communities, they enjoyed substantial respect which in turn earned them the right to speak to and on behalf of the communities, meaning that they could rally support around the campaign against the MHP and simultaneously represent the communities both in the movement and in encounters with the dam-builders and the GoMP. Externally, their regular dealings and familiarity with the state bureaucracy and its personnel and their general political clout meant that their interactions with the NBA, and not least their support of and participation in protests against the MHP attracted the attention of state officials, state politicians, and members of parliament from the area.

As an example of how these local leaders commanded respect beyond their communities, Palit recounted how, during protest actions and mass arrests, members of the state legislative assembly and even members of parliament would arrive at the scene to try and negotiate the situation; this is of course a radically different scenario compared to the way in which bureaucrats and politicians more or less completely neglected the politically marginalized adivasi communities of Alirajpur and Nandurbar, and testifies to the significant role of the rich farmers as local leaders of the campaign (interview, May 2003).

However, this degree of politicization was not solely a resource to be tapped; to NBA activists, it was also a potential barrier to mobilization outside the parameters of party politics: 'the negative features were also very clear, that because of the politicization, people are divided, villages are divided into BJP and Congress and so on' (interview, Chittaroopa Palit, May 2003). Much as in the process through which the Narmada Ghati Navnirman Samiti (NGNS) was rejuvenated in the late 1980s, a crucial aspect of mobilization was to facilitate the transgression of the entrenched fault lines of parliamentary politics in the communities and draw people into the realm of the 'non-party political process'. Ramchandr, who is simultaneously a vice-sarpanch and an NBA activist, did not regard it as a problem at all. Whereas the panchayats are part of mainstream politics, he argued that his own interest was not party politics as such. He was primarily interested in the panchayat because it enables him to influence the development of the village. The government provides funds for village development, and his chief ambition, he asserted, was to make sure that these funds were used to further the development of Pathrad. Whenever he participated in NBA activities, he would simply 'stop' being vice-sarpanch (interview, Pathrad, 3 May, 2003).

Conclusive evidence as to the success of the process of entrenching a non-party political process would of course necessitate an investigation of voting records for the area, or an in-depth survey of changing patterns in people's participation in and perception of party politics before and after the MHP campaign got underway, all of which is beyond the parameters of this study. However, the militant resolve that characterized people's participation in mass protests and the contempt with which people in the villages speak of the political establishment goes some way towards suggesting at least a partial and temporary success in this respect.

The role of women in the Maheshwar campaign

The feminine principle or gendered vulnerabilities?

NBA activists would often refer to women's participation as a crucial factor in explaining the strength and momentum of the campaign. For some, women's participation had been crucial in remedying a certain moral deficit in the mass base, which stemmed from the farming communities' integration into the market economy:

> . . . because of the market economy, the moral basis of the struggle of the adivasis, non-negotiable nature of the struggle, that was not there to start with. Because to start with there was this male, politicized leadership which basically came together to save their skin or to get a better deal. And so there was this whole process of needing to convert the struggle, and to seek and mine those moral resources from other parts of that economy.
>
> (interview, Chittaroopa Palit, May 2003)

The moral conversion of the struggle, according to Palit, occurred through women's participation, which brought certain uncorrupted sensibilities into the movement, such as a 'relationship to the land and the river' and a 'sense of being part of that larger landscape, and identity', which 'was completely different from the men' as it derived from 'the feminine principle'. This endowed women with an ability 'to cope with the struggle' and its strains which 'wouldn't be the same for men' (interview, May 2003).

What is notable in Palit's account is its strong ecofeminist slant; the reference to 'the feminine principle' for instance, derives directly from the key principle of ecofeminism, namely 'the idea that women are especially sympathetic and responsible managers of the rural environment' (Sinha, Gururani and Greenberg 1997: 76). Many of these features are discernible in Palit's narrative, where women's relationship to the river, the land and the natural environment in general is described as uncorrupted by markets and politics, which in turn makes for a profoundly moral motivation for participating in the struggle against the MHP.

There is, however, a burgeoning body of research that points out the weaknesses in the claims and reasoning of ecofeminism.[3] Sinha, Gururani and Greenberg (1997: 79), for example, draw on research from the Himalayan region to demonstrate that women's decisions in terms of use of the natural environment are first and foremost based on local environmental constraints and social conditions, rather than an essential female proximity to nature, and that women's ways of using the natural environment often conflict which 'ecofeminist idealizations'. Moreover, they argue that the notion of a shared womanhood centred on a harmonious relationship to nature fails to take cognizance of how caste divisions, age, marital status, position in the household, and geographical location fracture women's actual perception of responsibilities for environmental degradation (ibid.: 80).

Whereas my own research in eastern Nimad did not look into women's motivations for participating in the struggle against the MHP,[4] the more general critiques of ecofeminist reasoning seem equally applicable to this region; in particular, it seems problematic to maintain that there was a uniform source of motivation for women's participation in the campaign given the ways in which gender is criss-crossed by caste and class structures in the Nimadi communities. A more likely explanation can perhaps be found in the more tangible fact that women's risks of livelihood loss in the event of displacement are more severe than those of men. This is brought out in Lyla Mehta's (2002) research on how gender differentiates the impact of displacement in the Narmada Valley. Dominant patriarchal relations, she argues, exacerbate the impact of displacement on women in a dynamic which is referred to as 'the double bind': on the one hand, 'the wide-spread nature of male biases in Indian society help perpetuate gender inequality in terms of unequal resource allocation and distribution and also legitimise the silencing of women's interests' in the displacement process, and, on the other hand, 'biases within state institutions, structures and policies help perpetuate these societal inequalities' at the point of compensation (ibid.: 4–5).

Challenging patriarchy

Now, the above argument should neither be read as downplaying of the importance of women's participation in the Maheshwar struggle, nor as ignoring the challenges involved in mobilizing women as such. Indeed, I observed women's role in the forefront of the struggle very vividly during a five-day march through the villages in the MHP submergence zone in August 2000, where women were the most numerous and active participants, and in rallies in villages and towns where powerful female speakers commanded the attention and respect of huge crowds.

Mobilizing women in the dam-affected communities was a many-faceted process. First of all, it entailed challenging and negotiating the existent patriarchal structures of the village communities and insisting on the vital importance of women's participation, and generating an awareness that conventional divides between men and women's roles in the public and private spheres had to be suspended in the interest of creating a viable process of mobilization:

> And that was a difficult process of getting women to be a part of the decision-making process because, you know how it is, the men would come and say 'oh should we get them too' . . . So there was a lot of, a long process of challenging that and asserting that the women came for the meetings.
>
> (interview, Chittaroopa Palit, May 2003)

In the attempts to create an awareness of the necessity and possibility of women's participation in the mobilization process, the knowledge generated from the experience of bringing women into the campaign against the SSP played an important role. An important role in this process was played by Rukmeni Kaki, an elderly woman from the village of Chota Bardha in the SSP submergence zone who became an active participant in the NBA when Medha Patkar rejuvenated the NGNS. This is how she narrated the story of how she came to be involved with the NBA and how she came to work with women's mobilization in eastern Nimad:

> Rukmeni Kaki had been involved with the Andolan for some 15 years. Prior to her involvement with the NBA, she had no concept of what a movement was. The Nimad Bachao Andolan was active in the village for a short period, but it was only the men of the village who participated in this initiative. When Medha arrived in the village and held meetings, she spoke to Rukmeni, and explained to her what consequences the dam would have, what a movement was, and why it was necessary to mobilize. She insisted that women should be a part of this process. They got an organization started in the village, and she travelled with Medha to the adjacent areas to mobilize. Slowly but surely women started to get involved; at one point more than 10,000 women participated in a mass action in Badwani. When the mobilization started in the Maheshwar area she was asked to go there and organize the women of the area. She stayed there for two years. Her work centred on explaining the necessity of women coming out of their homes and attending the meetings to men and women alike. Gradually the women started to participate, for instance when they occupied the dam-site
>
> (interview, April 2003)

Finally, women's actual participation in mass protests were instrumental in consolidating their active position in the campaign:

> I think basically the [roadblock] process in which every single member had to be a part, you know, this week, or the next week, or the week after that, and women were at the forefront and their new-found ability to be militant and to get away with it, which is what they wanted to be, all that also added and contributed to this process.
>
> (interview, Chittaroopa Palit, May 2003)

Indeed, this illustrates the importance of demonstrating the necessity and possibility of women participating in the movement in practice. Such actions, involving braving police repression and facing beatings and arrests, can be understood as contributing to undermining patriarchal common sense concerning women's 'proper place' in the private sphere, thus clearing the way for women's active involvement with the movement. In fact, women's participation in protest actions can be thought of as catalytic events (see Chapter 3) which in effect subverted the grammar of patriarchal relations of domination and subjugation internally in the insurgent communities. The question that then arises is the extent to which this subversion has been a permanent or temporary achievement.

Participation in the campaign against the MHP has clearly been an experience of empowerment and learning for women in the villages. When I first visited the Maheshwar area in 2000, I spoke to Urmila Patidar, one of the leading female activists from the area about her involvement. Urmila was involved in politics prior to the Andolan's coming to the area, as she was elected to the village panchayat of Pathrad in 1994–95. As far back as the late 1980s, state authorities had illegally acquired land in the area, but people were unsure about why this had happened. When the NBA started mobilizing some ten years later, carrying out studies of the dam and its consequences and questioning the authorities, the truth of the matter finally crystallized, and she joined the movement:

> Urmila went on to talk about how her involvement with the movement has enabled her to see beyond the confines of the locality, and to understand the schemes of national and international capital. The Maheshwar project is all about dispossession and has to be stopped, she argued. The Andolan had been raising larger issues, issues beyond that of the Maheshwar project, like the role of women in society and the whole issue of what development is or should be. Before she joined the movement, her life was monotonous. Through her involvement she has become capable of asking questions like 'what is development?', 'what is the essence of democracy?', or 'what is the essence of relations between human beings?' Generally, Urmila maintained the NBA has brought a change in women's lives in the area. Prior to the coming of the NBA, their lives were largely confined to the four walls of the house, whereas now they have the confidence and courage to question powerful authorities.
>
> (interview, August 2000)

However, there is substantial reason to question whether the reversals of patriarchy and the empowerment that this has entailed are permanent phenomena. When I returned to the Maheshwar area in 2003, Urmila had married and moved from Pathrad to her husband's village; she was expecting her first child and her activity with the Andolan was considerably reduced. There is of course nothing new about the observation that activist involvement is characterized by phases and cycles where people are more or less involved and that family-life and child-rearing are significant vectors in determining such phases and cycles. My point here is merely that Urmila's example constitutes an intimation of how the extant structuration of family life has remained intact in spite of the ways in which women's participation in the campaign against the MHP had ruptured patriarchal common sense, and that the structuration of these practices override activism in terms of laying down the parameters for people's life-course.

Tendencies towards a backlash against women's newly-acquired presence in the public realm following the stalling of the MHP also testify to the resilience of patriarchal structures. While denying that there had been a reversal of the achievements of women's mobilization, Chittaroopa Palit nevertheless pointed out how, when the construction of the MHP was brought to a standstill, men – and in some cases also women – in the villages claimed that there was no need for women's further participation in the campaign:

> . . . so I think also women have, at different phases, been able to see that backlash when men find it no longer so important and imperative to have women at

the helm of the struggle, because, you know, the danger is less, so that's important and that's something that has to be defended – the right of women to be part of the leadership of struggles.

(interview, May 2003)

A dual insight emerges from these aspects of women's mobilization in the struggle against the MHP. On the one hand, the fact that women have been able to participate and that their participation itself was crucial in generating an acceptance of women's entry into the public realm is expressive of how collective learning in a social movement is not restricted to the relationship between the movement as a collective actor and its opponent. The dynamic of mobilization can also engender tendencies towards changes in the way social relations are constituted and thought about within insurgent communities; through mobilization, people learn that extant social relations and practices, and the justification of these relations and practices, are neither immutable nor unassailable, and can be subject to change and contestation. On the other hand, the fact that women's entry into marriage and family-life significantly constricts their ability to participate in activism, and even more so the fact that men try to usher women back to the confines of the private sphere as soon as the immediate goals of mobilization have been achieved testifies to the temporary and negotiated character of such changes. Thus, while the fact that mobilization can trigger learning processes that generate pressures towards the subversion of oppressive relations within the communities that engage in resistance is of considerable interest and importance, it is crucial to be aware of the fact that the reversal of patriarchy and empowerment of women in the Maheshwar struggle is an incomplete process, rather than an achieved state of affairs.

Factors of constraint in the Maheshwar campaign

Caste domination and class divisions in the Maheshwar campaign

When I first visited the Maheshwar area in 2000, I was immediately struck by the cross-class and cross-caste alliance that seemed to characterize the campaign against the MHP. When I asked leading NBA activists whether issues of caste and class was or had been a problem, the usual answer was that whereas it had been a problem in the beginning – with such practices as untouchability imposing a strict barrier on interactions in the communities – domination, discrimination and segregation on the basis of caste had been reduced in the area. The exigencies and necessities of struggle – the common interest in stopping the dam, co-operating in mass actions, travelling together to state capitals – had ameliorated caste domination. Examples were given of high caste villagers who would now eat in the houses of dalits, and who would express a new-found understanding of togetherness and equality that defied caste distinctions (field notes, August 2000).

However, the fact that this was only part of the picture became evident to me as I accompanied the activists on a five-day protest march through the villages of the MHP submergence zone. On the evening of the first day of the march, in one of the affected villages, the activists called a meeting in the dalit *mohalla*[5] to discuss the present state of the campaign against the dam. After a short while, a heated discussion broke out, with members of the dalit community calling attention to the paradox of how the villages were supposed to be united in the struggle against the MHP, while everyday life in the villages was still characterized by the domination of the higher castes. A young man stood out in particular, arguing that he had strong doubts whether the Andolan would ever be able to address the concerns of the dalit community. Later on, the activists told me that the young man, Narayan, had been active with the movement for some time, and was also a member of a dalit organization. However, he was also just about to finish his education, and wanted to get a job in the public sector. Against the advice of the activists, he was inclined to seek an individual escape route from caste oppression (field notes, August 2000).

Wanting to talk to Narayan about the issues he had raised in the meeting, I sought him out after the march was over to interview him. The interview took place in the village of Gogawa, in the front-yard of a house belonging to a high-caste trader who supported the NBA. When I asked Narayan about the role of dalits in the campaign against the MHP, he started by explaining to me that dalits stood to lose their livelihood as labourers due to the dam, hence their stakes in the struggle were high. The authorities were not serious about rehabilitating the dalit community, so it was natural for them to join the struggle. However, dalits did face problems within the movement: they lacked the necessary confidence to participate fully, and sometimes it was difficult to stand shoulder by shoulder with other groups. Narayan went on to assert that there would be problems within the alliance unless caste discrimination came to an end. Still, he asserted, the NBA is conscious of the problem, and if the issue was dealt with and resolved the alliance could survive. It would be necessary to get to the root of the problem and create affection between the communities, he argued (interview, August 2000).

At this point, a fierce discussion broke out between Narayan and the trader whose house we were sitting in front of. Having sat quietly listening to the interview, he was now clearly agitated and wanted to speak his mind. He rose up and embarked on something of a tirade, denying that there were any problems with caste discrimination in the villages, and arguing that the higher castes had always contributed to the uplift of the dalit community. Narayan followed suit and argued angrily that caste discrimination was a fact of life for dalits in the area. Two NBA activists who were present at the scene intervened and tried to cool things down. While they supported Narayan's arguments that caste discrimination was a problem in the area, they argued that a long-term perspective and a movement with a wider mandate were required for a transformation of oppressive relations in the villages (field notes, August 2000).

Events such as the discussion in the dalit *mohalla* and the quarrel between Narayan and the high-caste trader made it clear to me that in spite of activist claims that discrimination had been ameliorated in the villages, discontent and antagonisms clearly simmered below the surface. This was even clearer when I returned to the area in 2003 to find that Narayan had moved to an urban centre to work in a bank. The individual escape route had clearly seemed a better option than to remain in the area and in the movement. Furthermore, Narayan's assertions about the lack of confidence among dalits which prevented them from participating fully in the movement, and his claim that it was problematic to stand shoulder by shoulder with other caste groups were confirmed by other dalits and landless labourers that I spoke to when I returned to the area in April and May 2003 (field notes, February 2003).

Speaking to a group of dalits that was hanging around one of Pathrad's teashops, it became clear to me that although they perceived the struggle against the dam as important, their participation in the movement was limited. For them, participating in the movement meant going to rallies and demonstrations; one of the younger men in the group proudly told me that he had been arrested four times in connection with NBA actions. However, they had not been a part of the decision-making processes or been consulted about the Andolan's strategies. Whenever there is a mass action where their participation is required, an announcement would be made from the temple, and work would be stopped for the day. They had never interacted directly with the NBA leadership; only the local activists would sometime come to their houses. They all categorically rejected that relationships between the caste groups had improved in the wake of mobilization. They deplored this, and felt that some kind of action was necessary to bring an end to discrimination and segregation, for instance court action, but they felt powerless for a variety of reasons: they did not have the money required to go to court, and the people they were pitted against were simultaneously their employers, hence they feared that any action on their part could cost them their jobs (field notes, April 2003). Similarly, a landless labourer that I interviewed told me that participating in the movement for his part was restricted to having attended two mass actions, one in Mumbai and one in Mandleshwar. When I asked him why he participated, he replied, 'The farmers call me'. I went on to ask him if he would have attended the actions if the farmers had not called him, and he replied, 'We don't know anything, how can we be expected to go on our own initiative?' (interview, April 2003).

In contrast to the relative success of the NBA activists in terms of mobilizing women and integrating them into the decision-making processes of the movement and thus temporarily subverting patriarchal relations, caste domination and class divisions seem to have subsisted to a greater extent and clearly create a local core-periphery structure in the campaign, with the rich farmers located at the core and the dalits and landless labourers at the periphery. Furthermore, the mobilization process as such seems to have focused less on challenging caste domination and class divisions than on challenging patriarchal relations and drawing women to the helm of the struggle. Certainly, the movement has encouraged solidarity and affection across the fault lines of caste and class, but whereas the explicit focus on gender eventually led to the establishment of the Narmada Shakti Dal as an organization that would explicitly address women's concerns, no similar organization exists for dalits and landless labourers. Now, if the temporary subversion of patriarchal arrangements testifies to how mobilization has the potential to trigger learning processes that lead to changes internally in insurgent communities, and this in turn constitutes an intimation of how movements contribute to the transformation of local rationalities that is needed for the creation of a social movement project capable of advancing an agenda of radical social change, the failure to achieve a similar kind of subversion in relation to caste and class is expressive of the limits of this potential. As I go on to show in the next section, the core-periphery structure has also impacted upon the appropriation of the counter-expertise that the NBA had produced about the MHP in that it came to be filtered through the local rationality of the rich farmers in the dam-affected communities, which meant that issues of oppression and exploitation internally in the insurgent communities were occluded and erased.

Counter-expertise and kisan consciousness

The processes of collective learning and abstraction through which activists have sought to transcend the single issue of opposing the MHP has focused on understanding how the particular conflict over the dam is ultimately rooted in the complex gamut of privatization and liberalization that has defined the parameters of the political economy of development in India since the early 1990s. Talking about the characteristics of the mobilization process in the Maheshwar area, Chittaroopa Palit commented on how this process was one of learning 'from the generic' and using this knowledge 'in specific situations':

> So . . . it was also being able to focus on the whole privatization issue, which is to widen it, but also to focus it, because here you're not dealing with the government, you're dealing with a private party, a private [corporation] . . . in a given moment, historical moment . . . basically it meant looking at what was happening to, let's say, independent power projects all over India, all over the world, and from that . . . and the links, you know, between global capitalism and this private, corporate . . . So to learn from the generic and to use it in specific situations . . . in Maheshwar, the whole model was about globalization and privatization. And that's how it was articulated, whether it was through public speeches, or whether it was village meetings, or whether it was pamphlets – there was a huge number of pamphlets – or whatever. So there was never any discussion of the dam without this context. . . . and also if you're fighting an enemy which is private, or whatever, privatization, or corporate globalization, you jolly well learn who your enemy is. You don't have to be only given a pamphlet for that; you have to learn because you're going to attack them. . . .
>
> (interview, May 2003)

Joining the dots between the generic and the specific took the form of building up a solid body of counter-expertise that detailed the workings of privatization and liberalization so as to reveal how 'the financial institutions have now [become] conduits for international financial institutions, to continue with their agenda, without being frontally responsible for that', to 'discover those connections and the conduits and to expose them, and to hold those institutions to task' and to use 'that understanding and that debate to make connections in Maheshwar' (interview, May 2003) – indeed, the use of that understanding was made tangible when the NBA made Indian financial institutions the target of their campaign in 2000–01.

Hence, in the campaign against the MHP, counter-expertise revolved around the complex, emerging relationships between domestic and transnational institutions that define the epochal shift towards global capitalism, and how these relationships work themselves out on the ground in a particular locale such as the Maheshwar area. As was the case with the building of counter-expertise to bolster the campaign against the SSP, the NBA has made good use of experts outside the movement. For example, through the NBA's collaboration with the German NGO Urgewald, a detailed report on the liberalization of India's financial sector and how it feeds into the privatization of the electricity sector and the construction of projects such as the MHP has emerged.

In locating the specific conflict around the MHP within a wider context of neoliberal restructuring, the movement also effectively broadened its appeal and sought to reach out to a wider audience. Just as the NBA's campaign against the SSP was posited within a politics of opposition to dams and other destructive development interventions more generally, the campaign against the MHP effectively identified common ground between the villages in the submergence zone and rural communities in MP more generally and potentially also throughout the nation as it raised questions about how public funds are utilized, and the extent to which the utilization of public money for funding private hydroelectric projects is actually accountable:

> I think it's very important strategically and it continues to be important . . . it's not an issue that has mass appeal only in the Valley, it has wider mass appeal, you know, all over India, because the question of public money . . . And so it makes the struggle stronger because, you see, when you raise the question of public finance, it's no longer a question of those poor farmers, or those poor tribals, and it's an alignment, in a sense of, of self-interest in larger sections and constituencies, and then they say 'Oh God, so is Maheshwar going to become another Enron, so is my power going to be expensive?' . . . So therefore the whole social issue has been conjoined with the larger issue.
>
> (interview, May 2003)

The ways in which activists in the Maheshwar area sought to understand how the conflict in which they were involved was embedded in global processes of restructuring of the political economy of capitalist accumulation are essentially processes of abstraction, where the local and particular is situated within the wider parameters of the global and universal. In doing so, the movement not only created a comprehensive map of the terrain of resistance for itself, it also carved out and cleared the ground for the establishment of bonds of solidarity beyond the locale of resistance itself. Finally, much like in the case of the anti-SSP campaign, the building and dissemination of counter-expertise have provided activists with a political vernacular to deploy in mobilization and confrontation.

The use of counter-expertise as a political vernacular is evident both in contexts of mobilization, i.e. when activists try to convince people that they should join the movement, justification, i.e. when activists explain to outsiders why they are resisting and why it is right for them to do so, and confrontation, i.e. in encounters with opponents characterized by patterns of challenge-and-riposte. This was evident to an observer such as myself when I participated in NBA rallies, where counter-expertise is deployed in speeches that seek to simultaneously rally popular support for the movement, justify its activities, and indict the movements opponents. Moreover, it was evident in my encounters with local activists, most of whom had an impressive command of the body of counter-expertise and who readily explained the intricacies of the impacts of the dam and the networks of collusion between international financial institutions, domestic capitalists and central and state governments. For example, in cases where representatives of the TNCs that invested in the MHP visited the project area at times when the leading, urban educated activists were not present, they would be confronted by village activists who beforehand had agreed a division of labour as to who would question these representatives on various aspects of the project and the role that their funding played in it (interview, Chittaroopa Palit, May 2003).

However, the use of counter-expertise among the village activists revolves around much more than the acquisition of knowledge about global processes and the utilization of this knowledge in confrontation with external actors. As evident in the excerpts from farmers' narratives presented later, leading village activists have in fact appropriated this body of counter-expertise and framed it within certain horizons of meaning that resonate with a local rationality that is typical of the segment of the farming community which they represent. I shall refer to this outlook as *kisan*[6] *consciousness*. The term refers to an ideology that has been articulated by leading political representatives of India's middle and rich farmers, and by the so-called new farmers' movements that represent these interests (see e.g. Brass 1995). The ideology typically revolves around a juxtaposition of the communities of rural India – typically referred to as 'Bharat' – on the one hand, and a coalition of urban industrialists, politicians, bureaucrats, and global capital on the other. In this juxtaposition, the rural communities are typically represented as socially harmonious and as the home of an undifferentiated peasantry which is the victim of exploitation through unequal terms of trade and policies that favour the interests of urban industrialists and foreign capital.

> Bavani Ram is one of the core activists in the village of Pathrad. Taking time out from wheat-harvesting to talk to me, he explained at length how and why Indian farmers are struggling with a reproduction squeeze. Input prices have risen considerably, and one of the major reasons for this is that many of the inputs – pesticides, hybrid seeds and fertilizers – are monopolized by multinational corporations, and through the Green Revolution they have managed to trap the farmers, who depend on these inputs. Being in a monopoly situation, they can increase the prices just as they please. The multinational corporations also have a grip on the state and its politics; the government is dancing to their

tune. This is why the state government has been increasing the prices of electricity, and why they have put the remunerative prices at such low levels. Simultaneously, labour costs have increased. The state, according to Bavani Ram is squarely on the side of the industrialists. This is due to the reason that the farmers are scattered all over the country, and the villages are divided along party lines, while the industrialists are concentrated in the big cities and are highly organized. During elections, industrialists make generous donations to the political parties and hence secure policies that cater to their interests.

(interview, April 2003)

Jagdishbhai is one of the key activists from the Maheshwar area. In his view, the dam conflict is played out between the state and the capitalists on one side, and the village communities on the other. This is also an issue of development and development policies. The development policies pursued by the state, he argued, are basically anti-people. The Bretton Woods institutions and the WTO pursue development policies such as dams and Green Revolution technologies, and through these policies the big corporations get access to national markets. Your country goes into debt, and structural adjustment are imposed by international institutions; this is what has happened in Madhya Pradesh with the Asian Development Bank giving loans to the state on the condition that they privatize the power sector.

(interview, April 2003)

Kalu Singh Mandloi is a key activist from the village of Mardana; he was one of the representatives of the delegation that contacted the NBA in 1997, and has also served as sarpanch of the village for several years. In his view, the main reason why India's farmers are facing a crisis is the international conspiracy which started with the distribution of hybrid seeds. When the farmers got used to these hybrid seeds, the local seeds were almost rendered extinct, and people came to depend on the international seed market. In addition to this, farmers are suffering because the WTO forces the Indian government to cut subsidies to farmers, while Western agriculture remains heavily subsidized. The same goes for what is happening to electricity, which is an important input in Nimadi agriculture. The state government has taken major loans from the Asian Development Bank, and in return it imposes rigid conditions that lead to price hikes. This basically destroys farming. Kalu argued that 'the political class' is to blame for the present situation. The politicians and bureaucrats implement these policies out of their own self-interest, and in the process they mortgage the country. It is not strictly a conflict between the city and the countryside because the WTO policies will be ruinous for both; the small industries will find it hard to survive in the future. The major contradiction, according to him, is between North and South, in that countries like the USA are seeking to capture the natural resources of the Third World. As he sees it, there are also groups within India that gain from this process: the big industrialists and the politicians have opened the door for these policies, and the Indian capitalists are joining forces with foreign partners.

(interview, May 2003)

Throughout these three narratives of the underlying contradictions and fault lines that animate the conflict over the MHP the loci of consciousness formation that characterize what I have called *kisan consciousness* loom large. A major schism – the defining conflict of interest – runs between the rural communities and the urban industrialists and their cohorts in the politico-bureaucratic apparatus. The industrialists, politicians and bureaucrats are in turn regarded as having sold out to the interests of foreign capital, international financial institutions and powerful Northern countries by willingly opening the nation's doors to these marauders of global capitalism. Domestic elites line their own pockets while the majority of the population is left impoverished. The present situation is also viewed as having antecedents in the Green Revolution; indeed, the Green Revolution comes to constitute something akin to a fall from grace or a Faustian bargain in these narratives, where farmers exchanged their independent status as producers using local seeds and traditional farming methods for the promise of riches held out by new technology, chemical inputs and high-yielding seeds. The bargain has gone sour; the farmers are now dependent on the corporations that monopolize technology, inputs and seeds, and are thus victimized by their predatory search for profits.

Now, let us turn to consider how these same activists represent the Nimadi communities.

> The village communities are harmonious, Bavani Ram claims. There is no exploitation – the farmers give whatever wages the workers demand. In fact, the lives of the labourers are far more pleasant and care-free than those of the farmers. As long as the farmers are poor, the workers will also be poor. The condition of the farmers and the workers are interlinked. If the wages increase, he argues, the farmer will opt for a crop which requires a minimum input of labour. If the labour input goes down, unemployment will rise, and the wages will decrease again. If the farmers get good prices for good crops, then the workers will earn more. So the wages are determined by the external markets for agricultural produce, not by the farmers. There is also a cultural reason why there is no exploitation in the villages. When workers from the countryside go to work in the urban factories, the industrialists have no sympathy with the workers, because he doesn't know them; that's why the industrialist offers low wages to the workers. In a village, things are different; people know each other from birth, and the farmer is therefore more sympathetic towards his workers. For this reason, the farmer will also pay the workers decently.
>
> (interview, April 2003)

When asked about social relations in the village, Kalu maintained that these had changed substantially. The abolition of the *jagirdari* system[7] has undermined the economic rationale of traditional hierarchies of domination and subordination. However, even after 56 years of Independence, the feudal mentality or ideology is still there, and those who are influenced by it still use it so as to maintain a position of power and privilege within the village community. Still, there have been substantial changes in the relationships between

> castes; for example, when he was a kid, if he ever ventured into the Dalit mohalla, the elders would sprinkle water on them before they could come back into the house. Such notions of untouchability, he claimed, do not exist anymore.
>
> (interview, April 2003)

> Jagdishbhai acknowledged that social relations in the villages are unequal and exploitative, and he maintained that it would be necessary to do a lot of work to change the farmers' consciousness as well; only then will it be possible to gradually start talking about social change through land reforms and a general democratization of the social relations in the village.
>
> (interview, April 2003)

The Nimadi communities, then, are by and large portrayed as harmonious social entities. This is most clear in Bavani Ram's narrative, where farmers and landless labourers are posited as groups with common interests and shared destinies. It is not for reasons of greed that the farmer pays low wages; it is for reasons beyond his reach – market downturns that are rooted in the wrongdoings of the industrialists, politicians, transnational corporations, and global institutions of governance. The villages are characterized by a culture of affection that effectively wards off oppressive or exploitative tendencies. Kalu acknowledged that there are still remnants of feudal attitudes in the village, but simultaneously insisted that these had been decisively undermined by the impact of land reforms and the processes of social change that followed in its wake; the most rampant forms of untouchability, according to him, were no longer in existence. Similarly, Jagdishbhai acknowledged that domination and subjugation was a part of village life, but insisted that changing this would be a long-term process where the farmer's mindset had to be changed before it would be possible to work towards changes in the material underpinnings of these relations.

Now, while these narratives are expressive of a high level of political consciousness and testify to the significant processes of collective learning that activists have been involved in, they also contain intimations of the possible limits of the movement process in the Maheshwar area. The representation of the village communities as bound together by bonds of affection and commonalities of interest – or as unequal in some respects but susceptible only to a long-term and piecemeal process of change – in these narratives is arguably expressive of the vested interests that stems from the positionality of the rich farmers in the communities as landowners and fairly high-ranking groups in the caste hierarchy. These vested interests are in turn anathema to the formulation and implementation of a political agenda of radical social change centred on redistribution and recognition internally in the village communities. And to the extent that these representations and the groups that wield them are the main vectors in giving direction and form to mobilization at the local level, it is indeed hard to imagine the evolution of a movement project that takes aim at 'the transformation of productive inequalities' and 'the dismantling of disenfranchising social hierarchies' (Moore 2003: 203) out of the Maheshwar campaign.

In this sense, then, what was initially a factor of enablement in the making of the campaign against the MHP might become a factor of constraint that breaks potential development beyond the politics of dam opposition. This duality is not lost on the urban educated activists in the area:

> . . . you see, it's difficult because, in Maheshwar, because of this middle class there are vary valuable resources, you know, I mean the bourgeoisie . . . it has the ability to see . . . the whole structure of society and so on. And therefore they have, you know, strategic vantage points so that they're able to give leadership. And I'm talking about the rural bourgeoisie here. But the other thing is this, the whole character of the bourgeoisie . . . is the whole question of whether this will actually, you know, in the long term, whether they will stay with the kevats, kahars and dalits, whether they will be progressive and move forwards in terms of progressive movements, or whether they will stay where they are, and that question still remains.
>
> (interview, Chittaroopa Palit, May 2003)

Reflecting to the situation in 2003, at a time when the construction of the MHP had been brought to a halt, this was seen as a particularly urgent issue:

> . . . the question that rises, that is rising in the movement right now, when we are at this point between a movement that has been fighting against the dam, for physical survival, and which has come to a point where, you know, you have had the dam stopped . . . and a broadening of the movement to larger questions of fighting the reform process . . . who's going to do that? . . . I mean, how deep will be that process, to carry that continuity in terms of leadership and so on? . . . The other thing is about social change, and, you know, of single-issue struggles, especially in communities like this, which are so divided, with cleavages on the basis of so many divisions is . . . the whole larger struggle for equality and dignity for all . . . Of course, several village leaders . . . their understanding and consciousness have been transformed, but is that enough? Is the pace enough? Is the extent enough? . . . So are those people willing to be fairly radical . . . the activists? For fighting sort of freedom struggles rather than survival struggles?
>
> (interview, Chittaroopa Palit, May 2003)

Experiences so far indicate that the transition from 'survival struggles' to 'freedom struggles' which combine opposition to neoliberalism with struggles for equality and dignity at community level will be a difficult one. In 2002, with the MHP stalled, the NBA's organization in the Maheshwar area went through a transmutation as a parallel organization emerged in the form of the Nimad Malwa Kisan Mazdoor Sangathan (Nimad Malwa Farmers' and Workers' Organization (NMKMS)). The immediate reason for the formation of the NMKMS was the hikes in electricity prices that followed when the GoMP embarked on a programme of privatization of the state's electricity sector; the devastating impact of the price hikes on communities in the region in turn constituted a potentially fecund basis for linking local experiences to a politics of opposition to neoliberalism. As price hikes hit villages both within and beyond the MHP submergence zone, the ambition was to build farmer-worker unity around opposition to neoliberal reforms on an extended basis in the Nimad and Malwa regions. However, a leading activist wryly remarked in a discussion about the NMKMS in 2003 that it was characterized by 'more kisan and less mazdoor' – more farmers and less workers – in terms of representation and interest (field notes, January 2003). This was confirmed by dalits and landless labourers in the villages: they would say that they had heard about the NMKMS, and some had come along to mass meetings, but they had only a vague idea about its politics and did not participate in the decision-making processes (field notes, April 2003). In other words, the core-periphery structure that has characterized the campaign against the MHP was reproduced within the NMKMS. For the past three years, the NMKMS seems to have been hibernating as the construction of, and thus also resistance against, the MHP has been resumed. There seems to be good reasons to doubt whether it will wake from its slumber to become the progressive 'anti-reform, anti-globalization struggle' (interview, Chittaroopa Palit, May 2003) it was envisioned to be by its founders.

Concluding remarks

This chapter has subjected the NBA's campaign against the MHP to analysis, focusing on factors of enablement that allowed for swift and effective mobilization, and factors of constraint that may constitute long-term obstacles to the development of a social movement project against neoliberal restructuring.

A principal factor of enablement was the NBA's ability to use and develop extant skills – both exogenous and endogenous. Exogenous extant skills were important in the sense that it provided these activists and the communities in the MHP submergence zone with the confidence that resistance was fertile, even in the face of substantial opponents. Perhaps more fundamentally, participation in the SSP-campaign had yielded lessons – for instance about how to handle downturns and defeats – that could be generalized and applied elsewhere. Endogenous extant skill had an external aspect in that their regular dealings and familiarity with the state and their general political clout meant that their interaction with the NBA commanded the attention of state politicians, and an internal aspect in that they commanded the respect required to earn them the right to speak to and behalf of the dam-affected communities.

The mobilization of women was a significant aspect of the MHP-campaign. In the narratives of urban, educated activists women's participation tends to be portrayed as providing a moral fabric to the campaign due to an intrinsic link between women and the natural environment and landscape of the region. However, I argued that a more likely explanation for women's active participation can be found in social and material factors, such as the increased risks of impoverishment that women face in processes of displacement. As it militated against patriarchal structures of domination, the mobilization of women in the area entailed an intense process of negotiation and the utilization of activist experiences from the SSP-area. Women's actual participation in mass protests consolidated this process. Significantly, participation in NBA activities was an empowering experience for female activists as it reversed patriarchal common sense. This reversal of patriarchy demonstrates how movement processes are not exclusively directed against external opponents, but can also trigger changes in the internal workings of insurgent communities. However, the trajectory of women activists and attempts to roll back women's participation when the immediate goals of the campaign had been reached, suggests that this reversal of patriarchy is partial and temporary rather than complete and permanent.

The chief factor of constraint in the MHP-campaign has been that of caste domination and class divisions. Through an examination of observations of interactions between high-caste and dalit activists and conversations with landless labourers I pointed out how caste domination and class divisions have survived to a great extent, and constitute the basis for a core-periphery structure in the campaign, with rich farmers located at the core and dalits and landless labourers at the periphery. This may constitute a constraint on the capacity to develop something akin to a social movement project against neoliberal restructuring out of the campaign against the MHP. The campaign against the MHP has been integrated in a critique of neoliberal reform in India and global neoliberalism more generally. Now, in their deployment of this critique as a political language, leading activists have framed it within the general outlook of *kisan* consciousness, in which the major conflict of interest runs between the rural communities on one side and the urban industrialists, their cohorts in the political and bureaucratic apparatus, and foreign capital on the other side. The rural communities are by and large represented as harmonious social entities. This framing is in turn expressive of the vested interests that stem from the positionality of leading local activists within the social matrix of power as major landowners and representatives of dominant caste groups. As is evident from the reproduction of a core-periphery structure in the NMKMS, these vested interests may militate against the articulation and implementation of a broader agenda for social justice that also encompasses redistribution and recognition internally in the village communities. I will explore these issues related to the sidelining and relative erasure of community-based forms of exploitation and oppression in the next chapter, which engages with the NBA's movement project for alternative development.

8 Development, not destruction

Alternative development as a social movement project

'The struggle over the Sardar Sarovar has to be a larger struggle for the alternate model of development' (NBA 1992: 29). As this statement makes clear, the Narmada Bachao Andolan (NBA) has consistently sough to embed its campaign against dam building on the Narmada River in a social movement project for alternative development. A significant manifestation of these attempts to broaden the parameters of the struggle occurred on 28 September, 1989 when activists in their tens of thousands, representing a wide array of social movements and grassroots organizations from across India, gathered in the town of Harsud in Madhya Pradesh to attend the National Rally against Destructive Development. The rally brought together '[p]eople struggling against past or proposed displacement by massive irrigation and power projects' to articulate '[a] defiant message to the politicians and planners . . . that people are no longer prepared to watch in mute desperation as project after destructive project is heaped on them in the name of development and progress (NBA, cited in Dwivedi 1997: 13). Joining together activists around the slogan 'Vikas Chahiye, Vinash Nahin' (We Want Development, Not Destruction), the rally culminated in the formation of an alliance of the attending groups under the moniker of Jan Vikas Andolan (JVA, People's Development Movement), with a political platform that explicitly set out to challenge India's postcolonial development project.

Indeed, the rally at Harsud constituted a watershed in the trajectory of new social movements in India generally: never before, as Omvedt (1993: 269–70) points out, had new social movements in India managed to stage an event of such proportions, and never before had there been a nationwide alliance formed to champion their issues. The Harsud rally was an intimation of the emergence and crystallization of a politics that went beyond campaigns against destructive development strategies and interventions such as large dams, and articulated the connections between such strategies and interventions and the direction and meaning of development in postcolonial India. What is more, the rally at Harsud embodies the two constitutive features of a social movement project: first, the articulation of a challenge to the social totality – in this case, the postcolonial development project – and, second, the building of a capacity for hegemony – i.e. the construction of alliances between social movements from below – that would enable the realization of the challenge to the totality through the establishment of control over the self-production of society. In this chapter, I present a detailed analysis of these two aspects of the movement process in the Narmada Valley.

The first part of the chapter presents an analysis how the NBA has articulated a challenge to the dominant direction and meaning of development in postcolonial India. Through an investigation of protest events, political manifestoes and the NBA's programme of constructive activities in the adivasi communities – known as *Nav Nirman* – I decipher a set of discourses and practices that, contrary to current intellectual fashion, is best understood as an immanent challenge to the postcolonial development project – that is, a challenge that originates from the contradictions of this project, and appropriates rather than rejects its idioms of legitimacy. Finally, the challenge to postcolonial development is articulated in a populist mode in which its key agent – the agent that will take the challenge forward – is designated as 'the people' (of the Valley and of the nation) and its key opponent – the beneficiaries of the postcolonial development project – is designated as 'the elite' (both national and global). This part of the chapter concludes with a discussion of problems related to the politics of representation related to the NBA's movement project for alternative development.

The second part of the chapter turns to analyze the NBA's attempts to build a capacity for hegemony to underpin the project of alternative development through the construction of alliances between social movements at a national scale. I reconstruct the dynamic that has characterized the efforts to construct alliances from the mid-1980s until the present and focus on how alliance-building originated from the perceived need to build a support network for and between social movements across India and then transmuted from a functional adjunct to single-issue campaigns to an institution that articulated a political agenda that embedded these single-issue struggles in a broader politics of alternative development. I also bring out how this process has been fractured according to different approaches to the scope of the mass base and the modus operandi of the various formations that have emerged. Finally, I turn to a critical discussion of the extent to which the construction of such alliances have actually resulted in the generation of a capacity for coordinated and sustained mobilization of social movements from below around the project of alternative development.

Challenging the postcolonial development project

Alternative development as a discourse of resistance

The monsoon satyagraha of 2000 was based in the villages of Domkhedi and Nimgavhan (Maharashtra) and Jalsindhi (Madhya Pradesh) with Domkhedi being the focal point. At the riverbank in Domkhedi stood the Tree of Resolve, the trunk of which was peppered with little plates carrying the names of villagers and activists who had resolved to not leave in spite of the impending submergence. Next to the Tree of Resolve stood the Narmadyi hut; at this point it housed a motley crew of activists, filmmakers, and supporters and researchers from within and beyond India; if and when the waters rose, the hut was to be used for *Jal Samparan*.[1]

This was the backdrop for a celebration of Independence Day laden with political symbolism.

On the morning of 15 August we boarded one of the movement's motorboats to cross the river from Jalsindhi (MP), where there had been a meeting the previous evening, to Nimgavhan (Maharashtra) where the celebrations were to begin. First, setting the scene for what was to follow, two flags were hoisted by a veteran Gandhian, Siddharaj Dhadda and a senior adivasi activist of the NBA: the Indian flag and the NBA's banner were flown side by side, signalling the notion of village self-rule not as a rejection of the Indian nation as such, but rather as an alternative path towards the 'tryst with destiny' entailed in the freedom struggle.[2] The flag hoisting was followed by fiery speeches by Medha Patkar and Siddharaj Dhadda, before an illuminating confrontational event erupted.

Two teachers were present at the ceremony. These teachers were supposedly employed at local state-run schools, but the fact of the matter was that their teaching was as absent as the schools they were supposed to be running; indeed, it is a dismal truth about education in the adivasi areas that state-run schools exist only on paper.[3] Agitated villagers confronted the teachers and claimed that their vocation amounted to little more than picking up their paycheques. The teachers made a rather pathetic attempt to defend themselves by arguing that the hilly areas were too inaccessible and that the adivasi children showed little interest schooling. Siddharaj Dhadda dryly retorted that if an old man like himself managed to climb the hills, so should young men like them. Geetanjali, a young female NBA activist, made a passionate argument that the lack of interest in schooling merely reflected the curriculum's lack of relevance to adivasi realities. This dismal state of affairs was then thrown into sharp relief with the following point on the programme: the honouring of young adivasis who had fared well in official schools after first having completed basic schooling in the Andolan's *Jeevan Shalas*. On Independence Day, their achievements were recognized with diplomas, small gifts and announcements. The utter failure of the state to deliver on its promise of development was revealed, and this failure was made even more evident when compared to the vibrant achievements of a social movement and village communities with limited resources. An NBA press release commented on the event as follows:

> Amidst the slogans of '*Hammare Gaon me Hamara Raj*' (our rule in our village) respected Sarvodayi and freedom fighter Siddharaj Dhadda unfurled the national flag in the presence of over 700 representatives from the valley, on the 54th Independence Day of India, in Nimgavhan. The Narmada Bachao Andolan flag was raised beside the Indian flag along by the senior activist, Ranya Padvi. This notion of tribal self-rule as the pathway to true independence was a theme throughout the day in meetings . . . Independence Day is so often a celebration of a country's victory over oppression, but in Nimgavhan, it had an additional meaning of the people's continued resistance against the injustice and exploitation within a nation. The people of the Narmada reshaped the vision of independence on a day, in a country where the archaic dam

technology is still held forth as a symbol of progress and modernity, where teachers collect money for teaching students who exist on paper only, and where the loss of land and livelihood is termed development.

(NBA 2000b)

What is notable here is the reference to adivasi self-rule as a means by which to achieve *'true independence'*, the assertion of continuity between the freedom struggle and 'the people's *continued resistance* against the injustice and exploitation within a nation', and not least of how 'the people of the Narmada *reshaped the vision of independence*' through these celebrations. This was a theme that was to run as a guiding thread through the day.

After the Nimgavhan ceremonies, we proceeded to cross the river once more, back to Domkhedi, where another significant event was to take place. With support from the People's School of Energy, a Kerala-based group committed to the promotion of sustainable technologies at a grassroots level, a small stream adjacent to the village had been harnessed through the construction of a small check-dam, which, when combined with a pedal-powered generator, provided electricity to the village for the first time ever. The micro-hydel project constituted yet another contrast to the failure of the postcolonial development project: whereas the SSP threatened to displace the villagers from their lands and produce costly electricity that would only be available to affluent and predominantly urban consumers, here was a project controlled and executed at village level that actually had the potential of delivering a tangible improvement in people's lives, as opposed to the havoc that the SSP threaten to wreak upon these communities. This is how the NBA represented the inauguration of the micro-hydel project:

On Independence Day (August 15th) the first micro-hydel project was launched in Domkhedi. The project has an installed capacity of 300 watts and will provide light in each of the eight houses in Khutavari-pada (hamlet) . . . Along with generating electricity, the project brings drinking water from a spring to the houses. Water is usually carried long distances, and this feature of the project will significantly reduce workloads, especially for women in the village, around water collection. Under globalization, foreign investment funds are flowing into the power sector, making power generation and control over these services that much more removed from the people who use them. With a power generation capacity of 90,000 mw 60% of rural households do not have electricity in this country. Decentralization of the power sector and tapping into hybrid sources of energy, examining alternatives such as solar, wind and bio-mass are the only viable solutions to disparities in access to power. The project in Domkhedi is a step towards utilising the alternative potentials in the Narmada Valley, as was the pedal power generator that was installed earlier during this Satyagraha. Projects such as these give the people control over the benefits generated, a stark contrast to mega projects such as Sardar Sarovar.

(NBA 2000b)

In this passage, the micro-hydel project, based in the sharing of skills, knowledge and labour in and through movement networks, is highlighted as an intervention that brings benefits to a section of the populace that has generally been excluded from – or exploited in the name of – state initiatives for development. Importantly, a stark contrast emerges between the democratic and socially just aspects such a community-controlled project and the severe inequalities that follow from an electricity strategy that is increasingly based on corporate, and hence undemocratic, control.

Much like the strategy of non-cooperation and the satyagraha, the NBA's celebration of Independence Day can be understood as a symbolic-communicative practice of resistance saturated with the collective memories of India's Freedom Struggle. In such practices of commemoration, persons and events become 'the object of intentional commemoration and is ascribed some historical significance' (Middleton and Edwards 1990: 8). This in turn engenders a 'commemoration narrative' – that is, 'a story about a particular past that accounts for this ritualized remembrance and provides a moral message for the group members' (Zerubavel, cited in Gongaware 2003: 490). In the present context, Independence Day as a social practice of commemoration was appropriated by a social movement for insurgent purposes and transformed into an idiom of resistance. Through this practice of commemoration the NBA effectively put the collective memories of the nation's past to use to serve the needs of the present, and they did this by creating and conveying a narrative with a definite moral message.

Crucially, it was a narrative that recognized the freedom struggle and the attainment of Independence through that struggle as fundamental events and achievements – the presence of freedom fighters, the unfolding and hoisting of the Indian flag, indeed, the very celebration of Independence Day testifies to this. However, at the same time it was a narrative which conveys a theme of a national project profoundly out of kilter. 'The tryst with destiny', in this narrative, had gone awry; the promises of freedom and development had been hijacked by elite interests and thus betrayed – leaving large sections of the population by the wayside as outcasts. This betrayal was efficiently brought out by the contrasts evoked in the celebrations: the putrid condition of state schooling versus the vivacity of the *jeevan shalas*; the destruction wrought by the SSP versus the benefits brought to local communities by the micro-hydel project. On the one hand, this makes for an effective and evocative politics of place, which, as Kala (2001: 14) has put it, pits 'the lived space of adivasi and peasant communities' against 'a space of erasure' which is 'the abstract space of the state and of transnational corporations'. However, this is not an "insular" politics of place that turns its back on freedom and development as such. Rather, the celebrations were deployed so as to make a national claim: this is evidenced in the Andolan's press release argued that the notion of tribal self-rule highlighted on the day was 'a pathway to *true independence*' (my emphasis) and that Independence Day, besides being celebration of 'a country's victory over oppression' gained the additional meaning of 'the people's continued resistance against the injustice and exploitation within a nation', and thus that the vision of Independence was 'reshaped'. The narrative that was enunciated through the celebration of Independence Day was expressive of a politics of place that emphasized connection and articulation with wider fields of force and non-local scales, and which posited the NBA as an agent on a mission to reclaim and reinvent the ideals of freedom and development.

Similar narrative structures can be found in the NBA's written assertions of its politics. *Towards Just and Sustainable Development* starts off by placing the struggle against the SSP in the context of a 'nationwide struggle for a new model of development in India' (NBA 1992: 1). The issues that have been thrown up by the struggle against the SSP are posited as 'interrelated, interwoven' and as existing 'in the larger reality of Indian political culture, increasing socio-economic deprivation and inequality, depleting natural resource base, increasing centralization, capitalistic tendencies and vulgar consumerism' as well as 'increasing international debt' (ibid.).

The document proceeds to highlight three themes that, in my opinion, constitute the major loci of contention in the Andolan's discourse of resistance. Firstly, the problem of participatory democracy: the dominant model of development is criticized for having 'led to extreme centralization within the system with no space for the people and their movements, organizations in decision making . . . This results in erosion of basic human rights of people' (ibid.: 2). Secondly, the problem of environmental sustainability: singling out large dams, the Green revolution, intensive industrialization, and urban expansion as targets of critique, it is argued that 'the imposed development has resulted in depleting of whatever natural resource base we have' (ibid.) – a depletion which affects subaltern social groups most immediately and most directly. Thirdly, the problem of social justice: elite-led development 'has further reinforced the inequality in final redistribution' by emphasizing 'capital intensive technology' and 'western indicators of development' rather than the 'peasant cultivator, the landless labourers, unemployed labour force, conservation of soil and our already depleting forest, primary education, health' (ibid.). Furthermore, the indictment of the destructive and exclusionary effects and biases of the dominant model of development is globalized by emphasizing its links to multilateral development banks in the world economy: megaprojects and the centralized political process through which they are brought forward 'can be sustained only on the basis of the partnership between the powerholders in this land and their multinational moneylenders and other allies' and this form of 'neo-imperialism' has been intensified with the adoption of structural adjustment policies in India (ibid.: 2, 3). The basic rationale of the struggle is then defined as follows: 'The struggle aims at protecting people's right to life and for a more humane, egalitarian, sustainable and participatory model and development . . The issues are raised: Whose Development? At whose cost? Is this development sustainable, socially just and suitable for a nation like India?' (ibid.: 3).

What stands out in this manifesto – besides the embedding of the campaign against the SSP in a wider economic, social and political matrix – is the singling out of what the struggle has set out to achieve and the social forces that will carry this out. The goal of the struggle is two-fold: on the one hand, it is a defensive struggle in that it aims to achieve the protection of a basic right, namely 'people's right to life'; on the other hand, it is an offensive struggle in that it seeks to advance a development that will be 'more humane, egalitarian, sustainable and participatory', that is, it seeks to advance a process of change in social structures so as to realize those ideals which are denied and violated by the extant social organization of human practice. The social force that is designated as the agent that will realize this goal is defined broadly as 'the people' – the alternative model of development will be 'raised by and through the people' – which is a social category that can be juxtaposed to the national and global 'elites' which benefit from the hegemonic model and trajectory of development. I discuss these themes in the Andolan's discourse of resistance in more detail later. Now, however, I turn to an examination of the practical manifestation of the politics of alternative development in the NBA's movement project.

Practices of alternative development

Constructive work in the dam-affected adivasi villages had been practised since the very beginning of the trajectory of mobilization in Madhya Pradesh and Maharashtra, but it was only in 1996, with the Supreme Court's imposition and enforcement of an indefinite stay on the construction of the SSP, that *Nav Nirman*, an integrated programme of constructive activities became a central part of the NBA's repertoire of contention. At the time of its inception the NBA described it as 'a gigantic social experiment . . . [that] can offer crucial insights into exploring alternative systems of governance and development' (cited in Dwivedi 1997: 24). Kemalsingh, an adivasi activist from Nimgavhan (Maharashtra), explained the rationale of *Nav Nirman* as follows:

> The movement's idea is not only to oppose the dam, but to do something constructive so as to prove not only that the dams are destructive, and that they should be opposed, but that it's possible to do something constructive to help people.
>
> (interview, March 2003)

Nav Nirman includes activities such as the building and running of schools – Jeevan Shalas (Schools for Life) – with an alternative curriculum in the adivasi areas, introducing skills and practices of forest protection and regeneration, soil conservation and replenishment through bunding and composting, watershed management, community health care systems that seek to integrate indigenous and modern medicine, the use of alternative energy sources, and savings-and-loans activities (field notes, NBA n.d.; Bavadam 2003).

Nav Nirman emerged through the confluence of practical activist experience and distinctive political currents. Reflecting on the development of the *Jeevan Shalas*, Chittaroopa Palit portrayed the encounter with the adivasi communities of Alirajpur as follows:

> It became very clear through working in an adivasi area that there are no schools – those are only on paper, and the government structures have no

> accountability. There's no development work that people were asking for, you know, water-related or whatever. There isn't even ration-shops or proper food grains and so on.
>
> (interview, May 2003)

In response to this, activists sought to pressure the state government into securing that functioning schools were put in place. These attempts, however, were not very successful, which in turn prompted activists to attempt to provide basic services like schools through their own efforts and activities: 'somehow, after beating one's forehead for years and years, finally a decision was taken that "will we let generations go without even literacy skills?" and things like that, so these *Jeevan Shalas* were created' (interview, Chittaroopa Palit, May 2003).

With this move, a new challenge surfaced, namely that the institutions that were created should not merely be functional – i.e. filling the void created by state negligence – but should also play a role in the overall struggle in which they were embedded. The experience of young people who had graduated from the NBA's *Jeevan Shalas* and proceeded to formal education in state-run schools returning to the villages to question the rationale of the anti-dam struggle prompted a realization of the danger of creating 'an understanding that will be different from the experience of those people, even in opposition to, and the same sort of hegemonical understanding of what is development, and what dams are and so on'. To avoid this, the NBA co-operated with radical pedagogues to change the content of what was being taught in the Jeevan Shalas so as to prevent estrangement and promote participation in and solidarity with the activities of the NBA: '. . . there was an attempt to change the *shalas* from, you know, simple, sort of "let us at least give these skills to the students" to a much more interactive mode in which the values of land, water, and, you know, forest and the local economies were valued much more than . . . lifestyles or the developmental [ideology]' (interview, Chittaroopa Palit, May 2003).

The evolution of *Nav Nirman* was also crucially shaped by the precepts of a distinct political culture in which 'the right to resources within the community' is the pivotal principle:

> They would not be against exchange of resources with other communities, but they would try and attain fulfilment of their basic needs at the smallest unit level . . . These units should be the units of planning . . . of this whole action, from planning to execution would really involve the decentralized planning, a local choice of technology would be involved.
>
> (interview, Medha Patkar, June 2003)

The emphasis on decentralized community development of course echoes central tenets of Gandhi's constructive programme. Pioneered during the anticolonial struggle, Gandhian community development contained as one of its key components the notion of *swadeshi* according to which 'a village, locality or nation would be as self-reliant as possible' (Hardiman 2003: 77).[4]

Now, it is crucial to note that community development is not per definition a subaltern practice of opposition. Within the parameters of Nehruvian nation-building, community development served as an modality of rule that took aim at ameliorating relations of domination, but which generally worked to solidify the hegemony of dominant social groups (Frankel 2005; Sinha 2008). At the current conjuncture, the vestiges of community development are currently being revived by the state in the form of participatory development strategies that partly co-opts the constructive activities pioneered by social movements from below (see e.g. Baviskar n.d.).[5] In the postcolonial era, the oppositional deployment of community development was kept alive in the efforts of committed social workers, and then flourished in the 1970s, with the emergence of new social movements and social action groups. The resurgence of community development work outside the auspices of the dominant party system and party politics took the form of the 'new grassroots movement' of the 1970s. What we see in the case of *Nav Nirman* in the Narmada Valley, then, is a particular case of an oppositional deployment of participatory development. The percolation of this tradition to the dam-affected communities in the Narmada Valley was in turn an outcome of the fact that the urban, educated activists that were instrumental in catalyzing resistance emerged precisely from this grassroots movement as NGO workers and action researchers. Let us now consider the challenge to the postcolonial development project that has been articulated as part of this movement project in more depth.

Reclaiming and reinventing development

It has been fashionable among critics from poststructuralist and postcolonial quarters to posit new social movements in the global South as the authors and actors of a political project that simultaneously represents and points towards 'an authentic site of autonomous insurrection beyond development' (Moore 2000: 171). Arturo Escobar's (1995) claim that social movements in the South are searching for 'alternatives to development' is of course formative in this school of thought. In the Indian context, such arguments can be found, for example, in the work of Parajuli (1991: 182, 185, 186) who argues that the political significance of NSMs 'is that they challenge the notion of the integrationist and developmentalist Indian state' by articulating a 'counterdiscourse' of '[situated] knowledge that is locatable in time and space, embodied in struggle and participatory in process' to the 'unmarked, disembodied, unmediated, transcendent knowledge' of the developmentalist state (see also Parajuli 1996).

These perspectives are typically underpinned by a problematic assumption that social movements from below exist in 'hermetically sealed sites of autonomy' (Moore 1998: 347).[6] An alternative, and eminently more tenable, approach views social movements from above and social movements from below as existing in common 'relational spaces of connection and articulation' (ibid.: 347). In this approach, movements from below do not so much seek to pit 'one discursive construction of social life against a completely different alternative' as to 'delegitimate hegemonic genres within a field while appropriating pieces to inflect it with their own subversive meanings' (Steinberg 1999: 747, 751). On this view, the relationship between social movements from below and the postcolonial development project is characterized by the how '[s]ocial movements, by contesting and appropriating it give new shape and form to the development project, deploying it for new political programs, and for creating new bases for social and political life' (Sinha 2003: 308).

This argument is borne out in the analysis of the NBA's movement project for alternative development: it is an immanent rather than an external challenge to the postcolonial development project. This is so in two ways: first, it is a social movement project that emerges from the internal contradictions of a determinate historical trajectory of postcolonial capitalist development; second, it seeks to challenge these contradictions through a critique which appropriates and inverts the central idioms through which legitimacy was sought to be constructed for the postcolonial development project. In terms of the former, rather than articulating a discourse of resistance as a response to modernist encroachments upon otherness, the NBA has arguably given voice to an emergent structure of radical needs and capacities – that is, a structure of needs and capacities that has emerged but cannot be satisfied within the parameters of the dominant trajectory of development.

The three defining loci of contention in this discourse of alternative development – participatory democracy, environmental sustainability, social justice – can each be interpreted as constituting a crystallization of capacities and needs that have emerged within but are simultaneously thwarted by the structures and processes of the postcolonial development project. Participatory democracy, for example, can be understood as being expressive of the capacity and need for participation in decision-making processes that were spawned by the institutionalization of citizenship and universal suffrage to the Indian people at the coming of Independence, but which have since been frustrated by the centralization of power in the hands of social elites and the dominant political parties. Similarly, social justice can be understood as a means by which to achieve the need for equality which loomed large in Nehru's visions for modern India, but which has been negated by the processes of exploitation and dispossession which have defined the transition to capitalist modernity in India, and the ways in which these processes intertwine with pre-modern hierarchies of social stratification and oppression. Environmental sustainability can be understood as being rooted in the potential for resource use determined according to popular social needs rather than commercial colonial imperatives generated by the achievement of democratic rule and national sovereignty, but undermined by the continuation of commercial exploitation through the machinations of the postcolonial state.

In terms of the latter, rather than rejecting development as such, the NBA posits itself, through its manifestoes and symbolic-communicative practices of resistance, as an agent on a mission to reclaim and reinvent development. The Nehruvian project of nation-building sought justification through an ideology which posited development as a neutral process, necessary for the general well-being of the Indian people, dissociated from any particular class interest, and designed according to apolitical and objective scientific evaluations (Chatterjee 1993: 201–4). When the

NBA stages such an event as its Independence Day celebration, which consistently calls attention to the wide discrepancies between the lofty promises of betterment for all and the reality of the systematic marginalization of large sections of the population – a marginalization which is the result of the privileging of elite interests – and thus seeks to draw attention to the glaring contradictions of the dominant model and trajectory of development, it effectively fractures and destabilizes the 'supra-class, eternal character' that dominant social groups have sought to impart to development as an 'ideological sign' (Volosinov 1986: 23). Conversely, by displaying such alternative approaches to development as the *Jeevan Shalas* and the micro-hydel project, the NBA intimates an alternative meaning of development which reflects the social experiences and aspirations of subaltern social groups and seeks to establish 'social tenure' for these meanings (Barker 2002). And throughout, the challenge to the postcolonial development project articulated in the NBA's manifestoes and symbolic-communicative practices of resistance is ostensibly centred on a conception of *alternative development*, rather alternatives *to* development, which in turn is defined along axes and issues that are neither alien nor anathema to typically 'modern' discourses of liberation and emancipation.

Finally, it is crucial to note the populist character of this social movement project. Throughout, the critique of postcolonial development project as well as the politics of alternative development is pursued on behalf and in the interest of 'the people' – undifferentiated by class, gender, caste, ethnicity or other factors of social stratification, which is a defining feature of populist discourses (Taggart 2002). In the case of the NBA and its movement project for alternative development, the category of 'the people' arguably has two referents: 'the people' of the Narmada Valley and 'the people' of India. Both constituencies are united across potential divisions by a common interest in opposing destructive development projects and a socially and ecologically harmful model and trajectory of development. Furthermore, it is a project which opposes the interests and values of 'the people' with those of 'the elite' – both the postcolonial Indian elite and its global companions – and the ways in which the dominant direction and meaning of development in postcolonial India have been hijacked and moulded by these elites according to their interests. As such, and in sum, the NBA's social movement project for alternative development is perhaps best understood as a project of 'oppositional populism' rooted in the radical needs and capacities of subaltern social groups, and which articulates a challenge to the postcolonial development project through a 'disputed and contentious redeployment' of 'the rhetoric of development' (Gupta 2000: 16).

This, however, is not a complete analysis. To assume that the discourses of resistance that can be read off closely orchestrated protest events and carefully worded manifestoes represent a uniform 'collective consciousness' stretching out into every nook and cranny of the movement, would entail a double fallacy. First, it would amount to a neglect of the fact which I highlighted in the previous chapter, namely that different movement participants or groups of participants are 'capable of reading different, divergent, and potentially contradictory meanings' into discourses of resistance (Steinberg 1999: 741; see also Ortner 1995). Second, and closely related to the first point, it would amount to a conflation of the perceptions of leading movement organizers and intellectuals – perceptions which, as Cox (1999b: 61) has argued, are typically the '*least* characteristic elements' of a movement process – with the generic outlook of movement participants (see also Nash 1992). In order to avoid this fallacy, I now turn to deal with some problematic issues related to the politics of representation in the NBA's social movement project for alternative development.

The politics of representation – 1

The first issue concerning the politics of representation that I want to call attention to relates to the basic fact that the conception of a homogenous 'people' that carries forth a project of alternative development against 'the elite' does not match with the Andolan's social base. I have already touched on this issue in Chapter 7, where I showed how the landowning groups that have been at the frontline of the Maheshwar anti-dam campaign tend to represent the conflict in terms of socially harmonious rural communities which are pitted against a powerful coalition of urban industrialists, politicians and transnational capital, and thus obfuscate conflictual forms of difference and intra-community exploitation. The oppositional populism of the NBA's project of alternative development replicates this obfuscation, not just in terms of oppression and exploitation internal to the caste Hindu farming communities of Nimad, but also in terms of the relationship between the Nimadi communities and the adivasi communities. Currently, adivasi migrant labourers from western MP constitute the most exploited section of the working class in Nimad, and historically, the landowning castes of Nimad have ascended to their current position of relative affluence and power through the alienation of adivasi lands in the plains (see Baviskar 1995).

Similar representational contradictions riddle the *Nav Nirman* experiment. Although represented in the NBA's discourse as an expression of the resolve of 'the people of the Valley' to advance a project of alternative development, it has only been practiced in the adivasi areas; Nimad has been left out of this part of the movement's strategy. On the one hand, this could be considered to follow naturally from the fact that whereas the adivasi areas have been systematically deprived of social infrastructure, Nimad is fairly well-endowed with schools and health facilities, electricity and irrigation have been part of the region's economic fabric for decades, and articulate local politicians have seen to it that development works have been carried out in the area. On the other hand, as Baviskar (1995: 221) points out, the social and economic structure of the Nimad communities constitutes something of a negation of the movement's professed adherence to ideals of social equality and environmental sustainability: 'While the [SSP] has rightly come to symbolize unsustainable and inegalitarian development, agriculture in [Nimad] is not based upon sustainable practices either'. The fact that Nimad is left out of the constructive activities for alternative development can be considered as expressive of what might be called the Andolan's internal *realpolitik*. Dwivedi (1999: 58–9) has put it as follows: 'To expect the Nimadi farmer to think beyond issues of fair compensation is to place the burden of fighting the 'development dystopia' on a people whose interests appear more immediate and who are actually beneficiaries of this development' Demanding of prosperous and powerful social groups that they relinquish their social and economic privileges by, say, handing over land to a community collective as was done in the *bhoodan* and *gramdan*[7] movements in the 1950s, or move away from cash crop agriculture, is unlikely to gain much of support. Indeed, it might well lead to the estrangement of an important part of the movement's mass base and the consequent loss of the resources they bring to the movement.

Indeed, the obfuscation of conflictual difference in the Andolan's mass base is of course perfectly understandable in terms of the strategic concerns of the anti-dam campaign. Working against all odds in the first place, it was a crucial and necessary achievement to bring together diverse communities between and within which there were multiple opposing interests and abundant potential for conflict: in short, inter- and intra-group divisions were sidelined in the struggle against a common threat.[8] Still, the uneasy question of Nimad social and economic structures, as well as the exploitation of adivasis in Nimadi agriculture, does not simply go away. As I argued in Chapter 7, the conflictual differences that criss-cross these communities might resurface as constraints upon the development of a movement project in which social justice is a central ambition. This is so in that claims for social justice cannot simply be directed outward; they are equally valid vis-à-vis relations and practices of caste and class internal to and between the communities united in their opposition to an external enemy. Making social justice a reality by transforming such socioeconomic inequalities and dismantling disenfranchising social hierarchies in turn clearly runs counter to the vested interests of dominant groups in these communities. This can be considered as the point at which the limits of the oppositional populism that characterizes the Andolan's movement project for alternative development emerge. To act on this – to raise internal critiques and further the capacity of subaltern groups within the community to mobilize autonomously around such issues – is difficult in the sense that it is likely to destabilize and disintegrate extant movement formations. Not to act on it, though, constitutes a lapse into a romanticized conception of 'the local' and 'the community' which effectively silences the plight of those most exploited and oppressed. Such a lapse would not only constitute an abdication of the ambition of social justice, but would also arguably undermine the likelihood of successfully constructing a powerful social movement project as it fails to give the social majority something to fight for which is genuinely in their interest.

The politics of representation – 2

The second issue related to the politics of representation that I want to discuss here relates to the argument that there is a discrepancy between the official self-representation of the Andolan as a movement for alternative development and the way in which people in the Valley experience the activities of the Andolan.

This is an argument that has been made by both academics and dissident activists, with the former most prominently present in the work of Amita Baviskar

(1995, 1997a/b/c). While the NBA's struggle against displacement 'is a completely just and worthwhile struggle in itself', Baviskar (1995: 227) notes, it nevertheless 'fits somewhat awkwardly into [the Andolan's] general critique of development'. This is partly because 'the awkward parts of the movement' – e.g. intra-community exploitation and non-sustainable economic activities – have been erased from this general critique, but more importantly because '[t]he formulation of a critique of development is not a concern of the people in the valley'. Indeed, for the adivasis, development is 'a paradigm that most of them do not know or care about' (ibid.: 227–8). This in turn raises issues about 'the difference between the beliefs and practices of adivasis and of those who claim to speak on their behalf' (ibid.: 238) – thus, a simple positing of the NBA and its mass base as resistance to the postcolonial development project neglects the actual subjective understandings that guide collective action in the adivasi communities.

It is not only academics who have formulated critiques along these lines; it can also be found among dissident activists. Rahul Banerjee (2000: 38–9), for instance, has argued that while the Bhils have 'a long history of militancy right from ancient times', the Andolan has foisted 'an alien Gandhian culture of satyagraha on to an essentially militant people'. This, he argues, is linked to the NBA's attempt to construct an image of the adivasi as a 'noble savage' and advance a romanticized concept of alternative development, both of which in turn neglects how people in the dam-affected communities 'have to a lesser of greater extent benefited from modern development' and that they consequently do not oppose 'modern development as such but only . . . the particular manifestation of it that has jeopardized their livelihoods'. For Banerjee, the 'pseudo-romantic view of the few indigenous people who are still with the NBA' is most of all a strategy to garner support from urban intellectual groups (ibid.: 39).

An interesting aspect of my fieldwork in the Narmada Valley was the discovery of how leading activists in the Andolan 'talk back' to researchers that have produced critical work on the movement – the criticized, that is, criticize the critics. Chittaroopa Palit, for instance, commented on Baviskar's claims about the gulf separating actual adivasi consciousness and the official politics of the Andolan when I asked her how the movement had come to formulate its critique of the hegemonic direction and meaning of the postcolonial development project:

> . . . as far as my critique of Amita Baviskar's book, you know, is that she somehow seems to see that whole . . . the critique of development was an . . . imposed project, and that basically what the adivasi was talking about was land, you know, wanting land for land. But I never heard anyone saying you know, [we want land for land] . . . And, you know, it was also a question of lifestyles and whether they'd be able to survive, in every way . . . The dignity of living in only adivasi villages is something quite different, where you have labour-sharing institutions and sort of semi-judicial institutions and all sorts of things . . . you are part of something, a clear system, and you recognize to be that, and so on . . . it was not romantic, it was not that they want to live at some lower level of

> existence or something. But they felt that they were living with some poverty and some riches and anything else would be worse off.
>
> (interview, May 2003)

Palit's critique of the critic revolves around an argument that her understanding of adivasi consciousness is too reductive, that the beliefs and aspirations that motivated their collective action transcended a simple struggle for land, and that what did in fact animate adivasi participation in the Andolan was the wish to defend a way of life that was valuable to them in multiple tangible and intangible ways. It was the 'value' of maintaining the community as much as the 'interest' in maintaining their land that propelled them to resist. It follows that since it was the dominant direction and meaning of development that posed a threat to the valued communities that the politics of alternative development was an 'organic' – as opposed to 'imposed' – project.

Similarly, following the publication of Rahul Banerjee's critique of the politics of the NBA, Sanjay Sangvai, a leading urban, educated activist and one of the NBA's movement intellectuals, penned a scathing response. Against the allegation that the NBA has foisted an alien Gandhian idiom of struggle on the militant adivasis, Sangvai (2000b: 3) argued that the NBA's 'idioms' of struggle 'have been contemporary and not anthropological'. Against the claim that the NBA is wielding a pseudo-romantic view of the adivasi societies as the basis for their politics of alternative development he argued as follows:

> From its initial years, the organization in the Narmada Valley always dealt with the issue of adivasis in contemporary terms. The main issue has always been the rights of adivasis over land, forests and rivers, and also to education, health and other government schemes meant for tribal areas . . . From the days of the Narmada Dharangrasta Samiti in 1986–87 to date, the emphasis has always been on rights and material well-being in contemporary terms.
>
> (ibid.: 3–4)

For Sangvai the articulation of a Gandhian idiom of resistance is not an imposition, but the natural outcome of a process of change and development in the forms of adivasi resistance. The allegation that the NBA has advocated a pseudo-romantic notion of alternative development is rejected with reference to the efforts to champion the rights of adivasis to well-being in contemporary terms – both through resistance and construction. Again, the criticism of imposition is countered with an argument focusing on the 'organic'.

This debate over the politics of representation within the Andolan – where critics of the movement emphasize the 'imposed' character of the politics of alternative development and leading activists point to its 'organic' character – can be understood as a debate which revolves around the question of whether or not the alternative direction and meaning of development that looms large in the Andolan's discourse of resistance is an 'inherent' or a 'derived' ideology (Rudé

1980: 29). Inherent ideas are ideas that are based on the social experience and cultural traditions of subaltern groups, whereas derived ideas are those ideas that are transmitted from and by an external agency to subaltern groups. Hence, when critics focus on the imposed character of the politics of alternative development, they are essentially arguing that it is a derived ideology, an ideology that is innately alien to the subaltern groups which are rallied to the cause, and hence not (necessarily) a legitimate ideology. When leading activists focus on the 'organic' character of the politics of alternative development, they are essentially arguing that it is an inherent ideology, an ideology that is fundamentally innate to the subaltern groups which are rallied to its cause, and therefore also (necessarily) legitimate.

Now, a social movement project per definition entails abstraction from the concrete, the particular and the local towards the abstract, the universal, and the global. And consequently, movement projects that are produced as part of this process are likely to emerge as complex amalgamations of particular idioms, symbols, and political claims that are immediately meaningful and relevant in a concrete, local context and universal idioms, symbols, and political claims that resonate with wider parameters of the social totality. Given the complex processes through which the particular and the universal – or the inherent and derived – are mediated in a movement process the terms of the debate are arguably misguided. Of course, this argument does not put a stop to the discussion over conscientization and politicization of a movement's mass base in general, or the degree of conscientization within the NBA in specific. However, it should stand as a call for temperance to those who either criticize the lack of a one-to-one relationship between the outlook of movement intellectuals and leadership, and those who claim that such a relationship exists.[9] Moreover, it should open up possibilities for a more processual understanding of the degree to and ways in which amalgamations of inherent and derived ideological elements have been appropriated and disseminated in a movement's mass base. My own impression of the degree to and ways in which the Andolan's discourse of alternative development has been appropriated by and disseminated throughout the mass base in the Narmada Valley revolves around what can be called *differential appropriation* and *limited dissemination.* Differential appropriation refers to the fact that the social stratification of the mass base is reflected in the ways in which different social groups have appropriated the discourse of resistance in different ways. Limited dissemination refers to the fact that the extent to which the discourse of resistance had been consistently disseminated in the mass base seemed to be limited.

When I asked adivasi activists what they thought development really was or should be, their answers typically went along the lines of 'development should be for all; what is this development where some people drown and other people prosper' and 'for us development means that our land should be preserved, we should get enough to eat for the whole year – we don't want anything else', or 'we want development that does not destroy' with reference to experiments with micro-hydel projects and non-destructive techniques such as small dams that bring tangible improvements in the quality of life in the communities (interviews and field notes, March 2003). Others again would argue that development meant such concrete benefits as having work, access to health care and education, or general material improvements in the standard of living (field notes, March 2003). I would argue that these statements are expressive of the aspirations of social groups whose most basic needs have been neglected and violated by the postcolonial development project and whose existence has thus been characterized by survival at the margins. In the Nimadi farming communities, the rich farmers typically appropriated the Andolan's discourse of resistance as a form of *kisan* consciousness (see Chapter 7). This appropriation is in turn expressive of the specific interests of this social group qua farmers. The landless labourers did not talk of development as such, but referred to 'the good life' as being able to consume what they wanted to consume – i.e. to be free from want – either by means of higher wages or by owning a plot of land (field notes, April 2003). Progress for the landless labourers, then, quite simply meant having what they were currently deprived of. The fact of differential appropriation testifies to the intrinsic difficulties of creating a collective identity and a discourse of resistance through which this identity is expressed in a movement process which unfolds in a context of social stratification.

Limited dissemination is evident in the way that, albeit present in people's consciousness and oral accounts of their aspirations, the notions of or aspirations for an alternative kind of 'development' were restricted to basic notions of justice – exemplified by the question cited earlier: 'what is this development where some people drown while other people prosper' – and an emphasis on the necessity of fulfilling basic, material needs and generating tangible improvements in living standards through non-destructive technologies. This, of course, stands in contrast to the elaborate discourse of resistance expressed in protest events and movement documents. I should stress that limited dissemination seems to be a more prevalent phenomenon in the adivasi areas than in the Nimadi farming communities. This testifies to the fact that a rich peasantry that was literate and familiar with mainstream politics spearheaded the mobilization in Nimad, while illiteracy was widespread in the adivasi communities and these communities had been relatively isolated from both mainstream and oppositional politics. Hence, it can be argued that limited dissemination testifies to a situation where movement intellectuals and leaders have been successful in establishing 'a coherent system of ideas' in the form of a discourse of resistance but have failed to develop 'these ideas through an organic relationship with those to whom they are directed and in whom they are inculcated' and to translate 'the body of ideas into a compelling popular style and idiom' (Johnson 2002: 7).

Now, if the building of a capacity for hegemony revolves around the ability to give direction to or to lead the skilled activity of subaltern social groups, then overcoming limited dissemination must surely be a goal in the sense that giving direction entails establishing some sort of consensus on just what kind of direction this is and where it is supposed to lead. Indeed, a social movement project cannot be expected to move at all unless the social groups from which it draws support experiences a certain affinity to and familiarity with this project. Moreover, it is this kind of affinity and familiarity that in turn fosters the dedication and solidarity that renders the fabric of a movement project cohesive and resilient. Having said this, an important point for me would be that limited dissemination is not an immutable state of affairs, but rather a challenge to be overcome in an as-yet 'incomplete' movement process. The challenge fundamentally revolves around developing methods of collective and participatory learning that can deepen processes of conscientization.

Building a capacity for hegemony

Alliance-building and the capacity for hegemony

Building a capacity for hegemony entails the development of a capacity to lead the skilled activity of different social groups in pursuit of a challenge to a given social totality, such as the postcolonial development project. The *sine qua non* of such a capacity is of course the construction of alliances between social movements from below around a common oppositional project.

According to Medha Patkar, experiments with alliance-building involving the NBA date as far back as the mid-1980s and the incipient processes of mobilization that took place in Maharashtra. Its origins lie in the perceived necessity of building support networks for social movements engaged in contention with the state (interview, June 2003). Through interactions between Patkar and B. D. Sharma, prominent activist and Commissioner for Scheduled Castes and Scheduled Tribes, it was decided that a more elaborate network of movements should be formed to secure support for groups in Bihar, Andhra Pradesh, and Maharashtra among other states. This initiative in turn gave way to the suggestion that 'it shouldn't be called [a network] anymore, we should call it a movement. And we should name it differently' (interview, June 2003). From this process, the Bharat Jan Andolan (BJA) was formed in the mid-1980s.

The process that Patkar recounted was one where a structure that was erected in order to satisfy the needs of localized struggles for support took on a life of its own, transmuted from being a functional adjunct to these struggles to being an institution that is irreducible to its constituent elements, and came to serve a larger purpose – namely that of articulating a political agenda beyond the single issues that these localized struggles engaged with, and into which localized struggles came to be integrated. However, the process of articulating such an agenda was fraught with difficulties as differences arose as to the mass base of the BJA. A majority within the movement argued that tribal issues should be the mainstay of its focus; this was problematic for the NBA: 'in Narmada we couldn't focus only on adivasis, And as Narmada Andolan's perspective was enlarged, expanded . . . So all aspects of a project or development plan really had to be questioned'. Moreover, Patkar's argument that the BJA should be open to trade unions from the organized sector did not fare well with the majority in the movement: "That they were totally opposed to. They felt they were a part of the establishment and we should not take them along"[10] (interview, June 2003).

The Harsud rally in 1989 was the next step towards the creation of an alliance of social movements around a project of alternative development. The guiding motivations of Harsud seem to have been three-fold: first, to bring local groups together in a wider political network; second, to establish an extensive geographical reach across the nation; and, third, to bring together groups from across the range – and indeed from opposite ends of the spectrum – of oppositional politics in India (interview, Medha Patkar, June 2003). These motivations – starting with that of bringing local struggles together – can all be considered as necessary steps in the process of transcending militant particularist politics and moving in the direction of a movement project. Given the salience of regionalism in Indian politics, the second aspect, the establishment of geographical reach, also constitutes an important strategy of abstraction from and translation between militant particularisms. Lastly, bringing together groups from different oppositional camps was an important move in terms of trying to overcome some of the schisms and create some kind of dialogue between the old and the new left, and different groupings within this latter category. All in all, this amounts to a necessary strategy for overcoming various forms of isolation and fragmentation that constituted obstacles to the building of a capacity for hegemony.

Portrayed as 'a movement against the development paradigm being practised in post-independence India' (NBA, cited in Dwivedi 1997: 13) the Jan Vikas Andolan (JVA) emerged from the rally against destructive development at Harsud. Whereas high hopes were pinned on this formation, the JVA failed to become a significant political force, leaving Patkar, amongst others, disheartened. Why was this so? Patkar cites frustration with the modus operandi that emerged within the JVA as the major source of disappointment:

> . . . what happened in Jan Vikas Andolan, it's better to not give names, but individuals, who were very genuine, very supportive of the movements, very close to movements, but they were not part of the movements, they became the committee members, you know, those who could not mobilize masses. So in that situation the Jan Vikas Andolan decisions from meeting to meeting were the decisions to, for example, analyse a government's decision on something during next two months and then issue a statement and that kind of . . . no mass action was emergent. So many of us felt frustrated . . . it was just not moving ahead. It became like policy analysts and critique-giving organization, although perspective-wise there was no difference . . . .
>
> (interview, June 2003)

Thus, whereas the NBA had disassociated itself from the BJA due to differences in terms of the compass of perspective and the composition of the mass base, the disassociation from the JVA seems to have occurred due to differences over strategy, with leading NBA activists wanting to pursue an action-oriented line, which was at variance with the inclination of those groups who came to occupy dominant positions within the JVA.

What has been established so far concerning activist experience with the politics of alliance-building? First, it can be established that necessity is the mother of invention in movement processes. Forming alliances between specific movements and articulating a discourse of resistance that unites these struggles in a challenge to the social totality is arguably the hallmark of social movement projects. However, such alliances initially arose out of the necessities that activists were confronted with in the very early stages of this process – the need for a support network – and then gradually, as activists realized the potentials of this emergent formation, became something more than a response and functional appendage to the immediate needs of militant particularisms or campaigns – they came to serve as institutions for the articulation of an agenda of oppositional politics at a national level. Second, the building of alliances has focused on overcoming the isolated existence of militant particularisms, and the fragmented or antagonistic relationships between these. Third, the process of building alliances has been fraught with disagreements and conflicts over the political and social scope of the alliances and the strategies through which the alliances are to advance their political agenda. These disagreements and conflicts have generated splinters and initiatives for the formation of new alliances operating with alternative political agendas or through alternative political strategies. Thus, alliance building can itself be regarded as a learning process: activists with a shared ambition – an ambition of developing a social movement project – but different approaches as to how to realize this ambition come up against each other in contestations and negotiations over whose approach is to give direction to the building of the alliance and thus come to understand whom and whose approaches they can and cannot work with; a certain approach is applied – whether it is modified or not through the rounds of contestation and negotiation – and the experience of the potentials and limits of the approach constitute the basis for the modification or rejection of this approach; rejection tends to entail the construction of a new approach, and consequently attempts to establish this as the hegemonic approach within the alliance; if these attempts at installing a new approach fail, activists are likely to break away and form new initiatives.

It is from this process that the NAPM emerged in 1996. Patkar recounted the context of the early 1990s when activists again begun to discuss how to mobilize a nation-wide alliance. As Patkar pointed out, these discussions occurred in the context of 'globalization and the Rath Yatra' (interview, June 2003) – that is, the 'elite revolts' of neoliberal restructuring and Hindu communalism that sought to remake India from above in the 1990s (Corbridge and Harriss 2000; see Chapter 2). Whereas the original designs were crafted in 1992, the NAPM as such came into being in 1996, following a national tour that traversed 14 states. At the conclusion of the tour, a conference was held and a basic organizational structure announced, consisting of a national convenors' committee and state-level convenors' committees. The NAPM decided to centre its energies on the Enron debacle in Maharashtra, and by 1997, more than 100 organizations had become official members of the alliance (Multinational Monitor 1997: 1–2).

As an agglomeration of formations involved in subaltern politics, the NAPM pursues a project of alternative development that resonates clearly with that of the NBA. Indeed, this is reflected in the National People's Agenda that the NAPM announced at the conclusion of its 2003 *Desh Bachao, Desh Banao Abhiyan* (Save the Nation, Build the Nation Campaign). The agenda outlines five foci of struggle which reflect the loci of consciousness formation – participation, sustainability, and social justice – that structure the Andolan's discourse of resistance (mentioned earlier). First of these are 'Right of Local Communities to Natural Resources', a principle which states that natural resources are 'a life-support and sources of livelihood' as opposed to 'marketable commodities', and, furthermore, that local communities 'should be granted the first right to the resources in their hands so as to have the first right to plan use of those and have its basic needs fulfilled before a wider unit claims part' (NAPM 2003: 4). Second comes 'Right to life and livelihood' which revolves around a stance of opposing global capitalism and rejecting liberalization and privatization, whilst fighting for social and economic rights such as the right to work and the right to food (ibid.: 5). The third point is 'New Paradigm of Alternative Development ensuring Sustainability and Justice' which includes an assertion of the need to choose and use appropriate technology, the instantiation of village industries based on co-operative management, democratic and decentralized planning for development, and decentralized management of natural resources (ibid.: 6). The fourth point is 'Struggle for Social Action' which is defined as struggles against inequalities based on caste and gender, as well as a call for secularism in politics, and opposition to militarism at a global level (ibid.: 7). Fifth and last, the National People's Agenda calls for 'Fostering Alternative Politics', a point which revolves around championing the 'Right to Information', challenging 'corruption in public life' and opposing 'the use of money and muscle power in electoral politics', an 'Intervention for Social Justice' in the form of committees that can intervene in cases of serious violations of human rights, the development of alternative media, and opposition to anti-terrorist legislation which are labelled as 'anti-people' (ibid.: 8).

The National People's Agenda was declared after a two month yatra which had started at Plachimada, Kerala, where Coca Cola's ravaging of ground water resources constitutes a grave testimony to the social consequences of neoliberal restructuring, and concluded in Ayodhya, Uttar Pradesh, the infamous site of the demolition of the Babri Masjid in 1992 and consequent outbreaks of heinous communal pogroms. This was nothing short of a symbolic positioning of the NAPM's struggle to 'save' and 'build' the nation squarely at the centre of the transformative conjuncture which has been referred to as 'the reinvention of India' (Corbridge and Harriss 2000) – the current process of 'struggle and negotiation' between social movements from above and social movements from below to gain hegemony over the future course of India's development in the wake of the collapse of 'the modernizing mission of the Nehruvian state' (ibid.: xviii). Alliance-building around a progressive project of alternative development is undoubtedly pivotal to the strengthening of subaltern resistance to 'elite revolts' that threaten to wreak havoc upon popular livelihoods and to sunder the social fabric along communal lines, but the question remains whether or not such alliances can in fact generate the capacity for hegemony that is a precondition for the ability of a social movement project to successfully challenge a given social totality.

The problem of limited downward reach

As with the debate over the Andolan's discourse of resistance and the politics of representation, questions emerge vis-à-vis the formation of alliances such as the NAPM as to their actual meaning, relevance and embeddedness in local communities. For instance, in a discussion of the potentials of the NAPM as an organizing force and potential political party, Dwivedi wryly questions the actual mass base of the alliance:

> The NAPM is a formation whose constituents have very little mass-base. Organiszations with mass-base such as Chhattisgarh Mukti Morcha, Adivasi Mukti Sangathan and even the Khedut Mazdoor Chetna Sangath in M.P. have kept out of the NAPM. An alliance of 'peoples movement' [without] people can not [sic] be a right beginning.
>
> (1997: 34)

Whereas I am in no position to comment on the mass bases of the whole range of movements that participate in the NAPM, I will put forward some reflections on my impression of the perception of the alliance in the NBA mass base. What struck me as evident during my fieldwork was that the various alliances that had been formed – such as the JVA and the NAPM – seemed to be remote from the lived experiences of village activists. Even those who had been most active with the NBA would refer superficially to the rally in Harsud as having been 'a big rally where many movements raised the issue of displacement' or 'in Harsud we took an oath that we wanted only small dams, and that big dams are destructive and will be resisted'. When I asked whether they were familiar with the JVA or the NAPM, they would answer that they did not participate much in those activities; some even claimed that they had not heard of these organizations (interviews and field notes, March and April 2003). This situation is similar to what I referred to earlier in my discussion of limited dissemination: whereas the formation of an alliance such as the NAPM represents an achievement in terms of moving towards the articulation of a challenge to the social totality, this alliance and the challenge it poses is not experienced as immediately significant by those whose interests and values it claims to represent.

Now, alliance-building has clearly been an important part of the Andolan's efforts towards the building of a social movement project in that it is a *necessary condition* for developing a capacity for hegemony: there is strength in numbers and unity, and that strength is needed if progress is to be made in terms of the goal of imposing an alternative direction and meaning on India's development. A formation such as the NAPM with more than 100 member organizations across India has clearly achieved the establishment of *extensive outward reach* for its social movement project. However, establishing an alliance with a common view of what kind of alternative direction and meaning should be given to development is clearly not a *sufficient condition* as long as these alliances and their politics are of limited relevance to the communities who are identified as their protagonists. The lack of a subjective experience of alliance politics as meaningful and relevant at a local level can be thought of as a problem of *limited downward reach*. Hence, whereas the forming of alliances can be seen as constituting a first and necessary step in the development of a capacity for hegemony, such capacity can only be achieved if followed by a second step which is focused on building or augmenting *intensive downward reach*. The building of intensive downward reach would be a process through which a social movement project is rendered meaningful and relevant to the lived experiences of members of local communities, and – seeing as the proof of the pudding tends to be in the eating – ensuring that this social movement project has ramifications for these communities. The last point is especially important. As I showed in my analysis of the KMCS, the ideas and strategic proposals that the urban educated activists introduced in the adivasi communities took root because they proved to be effective in practice. Practical efficiency fostered an awareness of the fecundity of resistance and thus also a commitment to the kind of mobilization and organization that these activists were proposing. There is no reason to assume that things should be different when it comes to building a social movement project with a capacity for hegemony. Achieving this kind of awareness, it seems, remains a challenge for the NAPM.

Concluding remarks

This chapter has been devoted to an analysis of how the NBA has sought to embed its campaign against dam-building in a social movement project for alternative development.

This movement project poses an immanent challenge to the postcolonial development project in two senses. First, it arises from its internal contradictions in that it represents an emergent structure of radical needs and capacities related to potentialities for participatory democracy, social justice and environmental sustainability thrown up by the dissolution of colonial rule, but the realization of which is predicated upon the rupturing of the structure of class power that has subsumed the postcolonial development project to the hegemony of dominant proprietary classes. Second, it articulates its critique of the postcolonial development project, as well as its vision for alternative development, through an appropriation and inversion of its major idioms of legitimacy, thereby destabilizing the uniaccentual ideology of development as an inevitable process through which the greater common good of the nation would be realized, and reclaims and reinvents the direction and meaning of development in accordance with subaltern needs and capacities.

Yet, the project of alternative development is riddled with limits and challenges related to the politics of representation. First, being cast in the mould of oppositional populism, it obfuscates forms of conflictual difference and exploitative structures of power internal to the communities it claims to represent, the consequences of which are inimical to a credible project of alternative development which aims to be relevant for subaltern social majorities. Second, there is clearly a discrepancy between the project of alternative development as it is articulated by movement leaders and intellectuals and the developmental aspirations of different groups in the communities which the project claims to represent. Whereas a debate on the degree to which this project is organic/inherent or imposed/derived is arguably a futile exercise, the fact of discrepancy nevertheless raises issues related to limited dissemination and differential appropriation in conscientization processes, and clearly indicates the need to strengthen processes of collective learning in order to give the project of alternative development the social grounding required for it to become a force to be reckoned with.

The articulation of a challenge to the postcolonial development project has been intertwined with a process of alliance-building at the national scale; the construction of alliances, I argued, is a necessary condition for the realization of the movement project for alternative development. However, I also argued that the construction of alliances is not in itself a sufficient condition for the creation of such a capacity for hegemony in that it faces a problem of limited downward reach: i.e. the limited degree to which alliances and their politics are perceived as relevant and meaningful by those communities whom they claim to represent. Like limited dissemination, this restricts the capacity to give direction to the skilled activity of subaltern social groups in opposition to the hegemonic projects of social movements from above.

These limits and challenges that I have identified in relation to the NBA's social movement project can be generalized into an insight about movement processes. Movement processes can be thought of as a kind of journey where activists 'start from the inside and work their way out' (see Cox and Nilsen 2005). The 'inside' refers to the concrete lifeworld in which people are situated – the fragment as opposed to the totality, the particular as opposed to the universal – and the 'common sense' of this lifeworld. Working one's way out refers to the development of 'good sense' and 'local rationalities', the emergence of militant particularisms which turns the concrete lifeworld into a locale of resistance or an insurgent community, the carving out of common ground between different militant particularisms through the building of campaigns, and finally the emergence of social movement projects which address the totality as opposed to the fragment, the universal as opposed to the particular. Expanding on this metaphor, I would argue that the journey outwards is not necessarily completed with the articulation of such a project. The activists who have made this journey will find that, having started from an opposition to everyday routines and connected these struggles with the structures which generate these routines and the movements from above that have been active in constructing and maintaining this totality, they will have to doubleback to where they started from and convince others to come along. In a less metaphorical language this means that when some activists have developed an understanding of how a range of particular conflicts and struggles are embedded in a totality and have developed a political agenda which takes the totality to task – i.e. when some activists have developed a social movement project – they are faced with the challenge of grounding this project in the particular conflicts and struggles that they started from. In other words, a social movement project has to be grounded in the militant particularisms and the local rationalities that it originates from; the universal has to be particularized if social movement projects are to realize the potential of transcending and transforming the totality in which they have emerged and against which they level systemic and counter-hegemonic challenges.

9 Whither the rage?

Learning from the Narmada Valley movement process

In this study, I have presented an analysis of dispossession and resistance in the Narmada Valley which has sought to elucidate the underlying political economy of the distributional biases of the Narmada dam projects, to decipher the dynamics of the expansive movement process that has unfolded in opposition to dispossession, and to extract strategic insights from both the achievements and the failures of the Narmada Bachao Andolan (NBA). It is time now to summarize my argument and to discuss what social movements from below can learn from the Narmada Valley movement process.

Summary of the argument

The Narmada dam projects are at the heart of a process of accumulation by dispossession which is shaped by a wider political economy in which state development strategies have served as modalities for the reproduction, extension, and entrenchment of capitalist relations of production in postcolonial India.

In the case of the Sardar Sarovar Project (SSP), I showed how regional agroindustrial elites in central and southern Gujarat have exercised their political power to promote a dam project which will secure them access to irrigation and electricity, at the cost of adivasi and caste Hindu peasant communities engaged in subsistence and petty commodity production in western Madhya Pradesh, that become subject to pressures towards proletarianization as a consequence of displacement. In the case of the Maheshwar Hydroelectric Project (MHP), I showed how the privatization of the dam has provided a profitable investment opportunity for national and transnational industrial and finance capital, whilst displacement again leads to pressures towards proletarianization in peasant communities engaged in petty-commodity production in western Madhya Pradesh. These cases of accumulation by dispossession, I argued, are not singular, but rather symptomatic of a distributional bias that has been an intrinsic feature of India's multi-purpose river valley development schemes, and this is in turn expressive of how the workings of state development strategies have been instrumental in effecting 'the historical process of divorcing the producer from the means of production' (Marx 1990: 875) in a passive revolution shaped by a social movement from above, rooted in the country's dominant proprietary classes, which has been capable of setting limits to and exerting pressures on postcolonial development planning. I also showed how this dynamic continues through neoliberalism as a social movement from above that seeks to transcend certain barriers to accumulation that were inherent to Indian developmentalism.

Following this, I turned my attention to the development of resistance to the Narmada dam projects, taking as my point of departure the emergence of militant particularist struggles for resettlement and rehabilitation (R&R) in Madhya Pradesh, Maharashtra and Gujarat, and the transformations of local rationalities that energized these struggles.

In tracing the emergence of the Khedut Mazdoor Chetna Sangath (KMCS), I showed how adivasi communities in western Madhya Pradesh were subjected to a range of coercive and extortive practices that I referred to as everyday tyranny at the hands of local state officials. Rooted partly in national forest legislation and partly in caste ideology, everyday tyranny was in effect a local state-society relationship defined by the de facto absence of the rights of citizenship and reproduced through a local rationality of fear, deference and submission that foreclosed open resistance in and by the adivasi communities. It was through the catalytic work of urban, educated activists that came to engage with these communities and spearhead a challenge to the practices of local officials that everyday tyranny was finally ruptured: local rationalities were transformed through a series of catalytic events in which the activists were eventually successful in forcing high ranking state officials to concede the culpability of forest rangers, police officers and revenue officials – thus reversing debilitating collective memories of defeat and betrayal and demonstrating that resistance could be fertile rather than futile. Through this process, people developed the cognitive resources, emotional dispositions and practical skills necessary for assertive engagement in rightful resistance centred on an innovative defence of customary use rights and the claiming of rights of citizenship that was articulated by the KMCS.

I then traced the process through which militant particularist struggles emerged in the dam-affected adivasi communities in Maharashtra and Gujarat, as well as in the caste-Hindu farming communities of Nimad in western Madhya Pradesh. Discussing the Narmada Dharangrasta Samiti and the ARCH Vahini, I argued that, similar to the KMCS in Madhya Pradesh, they came into being through catalytic work which centred on subverting local rationalities of fear, submission and deference and enabled the communities to make rightful claims on the state. I also showed how multiscalar infrastructures of contention were built within and beyond the Narmada Valley so as to channel such claims towards regional, national and transnational opponents. In Nimad, the already extant Narmada Ghati Navnirman Samiti was resuscitated and its mode of operation transformed through the intervention of activists from the NDS; rather than being predicated upon the subversion of everyday tyranny, this militant particularism emerged as a result of overcoming collective memories of defeat and co-optation and through constituting the organization outside the domain of regional party politics. The end result of this phase of the movement process was the politicization of a development project which the state had tried to keep beyond the realm of political contestation, and its subjection to rights-based claims for information and resettlement and rehabilitations from dam-affected communities at multiple scales.

I then moved on to show how these claims came to be radicalized and abstracted from their state-specific contexts in a process that led to the formation of the NBA as a pan-state anti-dam campaign, and, furthermore, analyzed the cycles of struggle through which this campaign unfolded from 1990 to 2000.

The radicalization that led to the emergence of the anti-dam campaign can be traced to two intertwined processes of knowledge production: first, conflictual learning – that is, the knowledge that activists garnered about their opponents lack of will, ability and commitment to implement adequate R&R for the dam-affected groups through a series of abortive interactions with the responsible state authorities; second, counter-expertise – that is, the production of a body of critical knowledge about the dam which contradicted official claims about its impacts in terms of displacement, the viability of R&R, its benefit-cost ratio and so on and so forth. The counter-expertise produced by the NBA in turn served as a multi-faceted discourse of resistance that not only challenged the SSP on its own terms, but also destabilized the ideological representation of Indian development planning as 'a field external to "the squabbles and conflicts of politics"' (Chatterjee 1993: 202), and constituted the dam-campaign in terms that abstracted from the particular circumstances of the riparian states, and linked the struggle to wider questions of elite dominance at national and transnational scales. I also discussed how the emergence of the anti-dam campaign was criss-crossed by processes of divergence and convergence by showing how the ARCH Vahini's decision to work in tandem with the Government of Gujarat (GoG) was informed by the particular trajectory of their demand for R&R, and how the formation of the NBA was embedded in the crystallization of a national coalition of opposition to large dam projects.

The next part of my analysis delineated and deciphered the cycles of struggle through which the anti-dam campaign unfolded from 1990 to 2000. The first cycle of struggle revolved around jury politics: on the basis of the counter-expertise the NBA had amassed, the demand was made that the state should implement a review of the social and environmental impacts, benefit-cost ratio and technical feasibility of the SSP. However, due to staunch opposition from the GoG and the class forces that underpinned it, this demand was never met. This prompted a strategic reorientation that was manifest in a new cycle of struggle centred on symbolic-communicative practices of resistance in the adivasi villages in Maharashtra and Madhya Pradesh. Laden with references to the collective memory of the freedom struggle, this cycle can be seen as an expression of a movement's capacity for innovative strategic reinvention, but critical activist voices have also maintained that it reflected an erosion of mobilizational capacity on the ground in the Narmada Valley. I dealt more briefly with the third cycle of struggle, which was centred on transnational advocacy to force the withdrawal of World Bank funding from the SSP. I traced the successful trajectory of the International Narmada Campaign to a reorientation of intensely co-ordinated lobbying efforts from the World Bank's Operations Staff to its Executive Directors, as well as towards the parliamentary representatives of crucial nation states such as the USA and Japan. However, I also argued that, despite its testimony to the potential efficacy of transnational advocacy networks, the impacts of this particular victory eventually turned out to be less significant than initially expected. This became evident through the examination of the fourth and final phase of the struggle, in which the NBA revived its demand for a state-led review of the SSP. Whilst concessions were gained in the form of the constitution of the Five Member Group and the Supreme Court's imposition of a four-year stay on the construction of the dam, the anti-dam campaign was eventually vanquished in 2000, when the Supreme Court ordered the completion of the SSP. This, I argued, was expressive of how the anti-dam campaign implicitly challenged basic structures of class power and thereby came up against the constraints that these structures of class power impose upon the workings of the Indian state.

The following step in the analysis turned to a discussion of the factors that enabled the rapid mobilization of a campaign against the MHP, and the factors that might constrain the campaign from evolving into a more radical social movement project.

I identified extant skills and experience as the main factor of enablement in the making of the campaign against the MHP. These skills and experiences were both exogenous and endogenous to the communities affected by the MHP. Exogenous skills and experience was brought to the process by NBA activists that had been involved in the struggle against the SSP. Rich in confidence due to the imposition of a stay on the construction of the SSP by the Supreme Court, these activists extracted a generic knowledge of how to handle different aspects of a mobilization process and reapplied it to the specific context of mobilization in east Nimad. Endogenous skills and experience were brought to the process by the class of economically prosperous and politically powerful farmers at the apex of the Nimadi social pyramid. Experienced in local and regional politics, these farmers commanded respect and wielded clout both within the dam-affected communities, and in relation to state-level politicians; the former enabled them to form a bridgehead to the Nimadi communities for the NBA activists, and the latter entailed a certain rapport with important figures within the Government of Madhya Pradesh (GoMP). I then discussed the role of women in the Maheshwar campaign. Whilst women have been central activists in the campaign, I argued that it was doubtful whether this could be attributed to a distinctly female relationship to nature and place, pointing instead to gendered vulnerabilities to displacement as a plausible motivating factor for participation. More importantly, I argued that the reversals of patriarchal power upon which women's participation was predicated – partial and temporary though it was – illustrated how movement processes can also trigger emancipatory dynamics internally in insurgent communities. Closely related to this point, my discussion then turned to factors of constraint in the campaign against the MHP. I pointed to how the NBA had been unsuccessful in mobilizing around issues of caste-based oppression and class-based exploitation in the Nimadi communities, and how this in turn had engendered a core-periphery structure at community-level, where rich farmers had appropriated the NBA's counter-expertise and deployed it in a discourse of resistance which effectively occluded intra-community divisions and conflicts. This, I argued, would quite possibly constitute a barrier to the development of a more radical counter-hegemonic politics in the Nimadi communities.

Finally, I turned to an analysis of how the NBA has embedded its anti-dam campaign in a social movement project that posits India's postcolonial development project as a target of critique and transformation, and then engaged with the NBA's involvement in the construction of alliances of new social movements around a politics of alternative development at a national scale.

Framed as an oppositional populism which pits the people of the Narmada Valley and the people of the Indian nation against national and transnational elites, the NBA has crafted discourses and practices of resistance which seek to reclaim and reinvent, and thereby also give an alternative direction and meaning to, India's future development. I argued that these discourses and practices are rooted in an emergent structure of radical needs and capacities centred on social justice, environmental sustainability, and participatory democracy that has been spawned within and as a part of the postcolonial development project, but that has also been constrained by the ways in which dominant proprietary classes have moulded the machinations of this project so as to reproduce and extend their hegemony. I then moved on to discuss some problematic issues related to the politics of representation. First, I pointed out how the discourse of oppositional populism obfuscates inequalities and oppressive power relations internal to the agent that is represented as a unitary 'people' and that this – much like the dominance of rich farmers in the campaign against the MHP – might stymie the articulation of a movement project with the capacity to advance a radical politics of social justice. Second, I engaged with academic and activist debates over the extent to which the NBA's project of alternative development can be considered to be an inherent or a derived ideology. I argued that this debate is in essence misguided, as it disregards how social movements from below always exhibit a multiplicity of interpretations of the meanings and goals of struggle. A more fecund approach would address this issue as a question of differential appropriation and limited dissemination, and view this question, in turn, as a challenge in terms of the development of genuinely participatory learning processes in a movement.

I then turned to the construction of alliances around the politics of alternative development at a national scale. Tracing the trajectory of the NBA's involvement in the Bharat Jan Andolan, the Jan Vikas Andolan and finally the National Alliance of People's Movements, I argued that alliance-building has originated in instrumental needs for the building of support networks and then taken on a life of its own as alliances have come to constitute a political space for the articulation of counter-hegemonic political projects. The emergence and dissolution of alliances, in turn, has been animated by activist debates over the social scope and political modes of operation. Finally, I argued that whereas a formation such as the NAPM constituted a significant achievement in terms of the establishment of extensive outward reach around the movement project of alternative development, it still seems to suffer from limited downward reach in the sense of being experienced as relevant by the communities which it claims to represent. This is potentially a serious constraint on the ability of social movements from below to build a capacity for hegemony which will enable them to challenge social movements from above, and brings to the fore the necessity of grounding social movement projects in the subaltern needs and capacities from which they have originated.

Whither the rage?

The writing of this book and most of the research on which it is based have been carried out at a time when the NBA was entering into a phase of abeyance. Now, it is of course possible to let the defeat of one of India's most significant movements since the 1970s curtail the optimism of the will and fuel the pessimism of the intellect to the extent of an abandonment of hope in the transformative capacities of social movements from below, but to do so would be a grave error. At the current conjuncture, India is witnessing the amplification and multiplication of processes of accumulation by dispossession as the social movement from above that has driven neoliberalism forward since the early 1990s grows more unified and virulent. Dismissing the capacity of subaltern social groups to act as the agents of their own empowerment and emancipation would, I believe, amount to putting an implicit stamp of approval on the poverty, inequality, marginalization and violence that are the outcomes of these processes. Rather, the task at hand is that of approaching the variegated experiences of particular movement processes in politically enabling ways, with a view to distilling generic strategic insights for the struggles that lie ahead and the movements from below that are in the making. To that end, I shall conclude with some reflections on the role of the state and state power in the strategies of social movements from below, and the challenges involved in the construction of social movement projects.

A recurring question in my discussion of the trajectory and politics of the NBA has been this: to what extent can social movements from below advance their oppositional projects via the practices, institutions and discourses of the Indian state? I have addressed this question in relation to differing experiences of engaging with the state during different phases of the movement process in the Narmada Valley, and in terms of conflicting perspectives on the capacity of the Indian state to function as a site of subaltern empowerment.

I first touched upon this discussion in relation to the KMCS's politics of rightful resistance, which successfully empowered adivasi communities against oppressive local state officials by appealing to the higher echelons of the state and creating an awareness of constitutional rights and entitlements in these communities. Drawing on the work of Corbridge and Harriss (2000) I argued that this particular case could be viewed as being symptomatic of a wider tendency in which subaltern politics in contemporary India can and do make good use of the state and its discourses of democracy and citizenship, and in so doing also criticized Sangeeta Kamat's (2002) blanket condemnation of political strategies centred on the demystification of the state – first, this critique is insensitive to the particular context in which such strategies are developed and deployed, and second, it ignores the processual nature of subaltern collective action: rightful resistance based on the democratic discourses of the state may be a first and necessary step in what might be a trajectory of radicalization for social movements from below.

I returned to this question in my discussion of the trajectory of the NBA's anti-dam campaign, which, contrary to the KMCS's relative success in curbing the excesses of everyday tyranny, eventually ended in failure. The jury politics of the campaign, I argued, was constructed around a very similar rationality to that which underpinned the rightful resistance of the initial militant particularist struggles in the Narmada Valley: based on the assumption that a review of the SSP would reveal the multiple ways in which the project would violate norms and stipulations that attach to large-scale development projects, the NBA in effect sought to hold the state accountable both to its legal underpinnings and to its role as a democratic and neutral arbiter between conflicting interests in society. I attributed the failure of this strategy to the fact that the NBA's opposition to the SSP constituted an implicit challenge to the basic modalities through which the state has reproduced and extended capitalist relations in postcolonial India, and argued that this brings into view the limits to projects of subaltern empowerment centred on the democratic accountability of the state. Thus, the challenge at hand is that of striking a strategic balance between what Jessop (1982: 253) has referred to as the 'conjunctural opportunities' and the 'structural constraints' that movements from below might encounter in their encounters with state power.

What does this entail for social movements from below? It entails, I would argue, that it is necessary to steer a strategic course between anti-statism on the one hand and state-centrism on the other hand. The basic argument against anti-statism would be this: an awareness of the structural limits to the changes that can be achieved via the state-system and the state-idea does not translate into a principled rejection of any engagement with the state. Social movements from below develop historically in relation to the hegemonic projects of social movements from above, and in contexts where the state-system and the state-idea have figured so centrally in those hegemonic projects as is the case in postcolonial India, then the trajectory of those movements will naturally tend to involve some kind of recourse to state-centred practices, institutions and discourses. Given the conjunctural nature of state power, this might also bear fruits. However, this does not entail a position in which interaction and negotiation with the state is seen as the beginning and the end of the strategic scope of oppositional collective action. Rather, it is a position in which social movements from below are encouraged to think carefully about which bets to place on the normal political process within an institutionalized social order and which bets to place elsewhere. In other words, it is a position that advocates an instrumental rather than a committed engagement[1] with the state-system and the state-idea – that is, an approach to interaction with the state based on limited expectations of what can be gained and, simultaneously, a clear perception of what cannot be gained and what is risked in pursuing this avenue. And this position also entails the awareness that a challenge to the relations of power on which the state rests is a bet best placed on the construction of a social movement project which seeks to develop the collective skilled activity of subaltern groups to the point where it can successfully challenge extant power structures and the workings of their institutional manifestations (see Nilsen 2007b, 2008).

In extension of this, I would also argue that this position entails taking social movement projects in the form of anti-systemic, counter-hegemonic challenges to a historical totality seriously as a possible and indeed necessary aspect of the praxis that animates movement processes, rather than writing them off as part and parcel of 'a Jacobin conception of politics which depends upon an idea of perfectibility or an "ideal outside"' (Corbridge *et al.* 2005: 186).

Insisting that it is possible and necessary for social movements from below to pursue counterhegemonic projects does not entail a conception of these movements as either originating in 'authentic sites of autonomous insurrection' (Moore 2003: 171) or as moving towards a future perfect cast 'in some fantastic utopian mold' (Harvey 2000: 191). Rather, it entails a view of social movements from below as immanent forces that emerge on the basis of needs and capacities that are simultaneously spawned within and frustrated by a given historical totality – sometimes through submerged everyday struggles, sometimes through making claims on the state within the parameters of an institutionalized social formation, and at other times again through challenging the basal relations of power upon which a social formation is based (see Cox 1999a: 22; Geoghegan and Cox 2001: 8). An important dimension of the latter form of subaltern praxis is of course that for all their immanence, there resides in movements from below the contingent potentiality that they may become forces with the potential to transcend and transform the social formation in which they have emerged as their praxis develops – not through the impositions of a vanguard elite, but when ordinary people go far beyond what they previously believed to be possible in terms of challenging the status quo through 'tangible transformations of the raw materials given to [them] in [their] present state' (Harvey 2000: 191). And whereas Corbridge *et al.* (2005: 199–201) are right to raise the normative question of the 'opportunity costs' involved in the social upheavals that would be required to carry out such transformations – a question which is typically at the heart of the strategic debates which animate actual movement processes – an equally legitimate concern attaches to the consequences of ruling out anti-systemic politics at a conjuncture where the systemic processes that violate and constrain subaltern needs and capacities are gaining ever more momentum (see Harriss-White 2005).

In a recent article that interrogates the dispossessory ramifications of the neoliberal project in India, Chandra and Basu point out how a material basis is crystallizing for the formation of alliances across and between struggles: 'Understanding all these diverse processes [of dispossession] in the framework of primitive accumulation has several strategic implications. Perhaps most urgently, this can provide a framework to locate the numerous struggles going on in the country . . .' (2007: 5). If this is the basis upon which activists must engage in the complex labour of joining the dots between their struggles in order to build a capacity for hegemony that can challenge the totality in which these struggles are embedded, what lessons can be drawn from the Narmada movement process to guide this effort? I shall restrict myself here to two brief reflections.

First, it is imperative to address and overcome the limits of oppositional populism. The basic problem with oppositional populism is the way in which it conceals oppressive and exploitative relations within the collective agent which is posited as a unitary 'people' – both at a practical and discursive level – and this is a two-pronged problem. At a moral level, the failure to address forms of oppression and exploitation within the communities that are mobilized in struggle constitutes a circumscription of the ambit of the project of social justice to the extent that if fails to encompass the situated lifeworlds of the subaltern majorities that ultimately carry a movement project forward. At the practical level of mobilization, oppositional populism lays the foundation for a dynamic in which a movement from below – if it is successful in its challenge to a given sociohistorical totality – may be transformed into a social movement from above, characterized by 'a progressive sidelining of those exploited groups . . . whose allegiance was necessary to take power' (Cox 1999a: 181). This, of course, is the basic dynamic which gave rise to the passive revolution of capital in the Indian context, and its reoccurrence can only be prevented if social movements from below engage with the multi-scalar nature of the relations of power that prevent the satisfaction of subaltern needs and the development of subaltern capacities. Second, and related to this point, is the necessity of grounding social movement projects in the communities which they claim to represent. The successful pursuit of a challenge to a sociohistorical totality is ultimately predicated upon the capacity to give direction to the development of the collective skilled activity of subaltern social groups, but such a capacity is unlikely to emerge unless these groups perceive a movement project as relevant to their determinate experiences of domination and their hopes and ambitions for a different future. The articulation of movement projects, then, needs to be a participatory process, rather than a domain of movement elites.

These are lessons for the long term – for a 'war of position' (Gramsci 1998) in which movements from below will have to strive to identify 'how struggles in different socio-spatial arenas and across spatial scales might link with one another' (Hart 2002: 820). To paraphrase Karl Marx, the trajectory of such a war of position is certain to be one of constant self-criticism, of self-interruption, and of returning to the apparently accomplished in order to begin it afresh. Undoubtedly, it will be a trajectory in which movements from below throw down their adversaries only to have them draw new strength from the earth and rise again – more gigantic than ever. And yes, the trajectory will be one of recoiling from the indefinite prodigiousness of the aims of insurgency. But such is the nature of the praxis which is capable of engendering those situations in which all turning back is impossible – in which the conditions themselves cry out: 'Hic Rhodus, hic salta! Here is the rose, here dance!'

Notes

1 The river and the rage

1 The evidence on failed resettlement and rehabilitation in the case of the SSP is discussed extensively in Chapter 2.
2 The term adivasi is used here to refer to communities that are classified as belonging to the category of Scheduled Tribes as per the Fifth and Sixth Schedules of the Indian constitution. See Béteille (1986), Singh (1985), Prasad (2003, 2004), Guha (1999), Ratnagar (2003), Kela (2006a), Ghosh (2006) and Shah (2007) for a selection of perspectives in the Indian debate about indigeneity.
3 See Patnaik (1986, 1999).
4 See D'Souza (2005) for an impressive study of the Upper Krishna Project.
5 Indeed, this shift in the orientation of the colonial state is representative of a general shift in the orientations of the colonial powers in the first part of the twentieth century, when a colonial development project emerged so as to address the increasingly evident problem of economic stagnation and the emergence of surplus populations in the colonies (see Cowen and Shenton 1996; Cooper and Packard 1998).
6 See Khagram (2004) and Dwivedi (2006) for detailed accounts of the early investigations into dam-building on the Narmada.
7 1 crore = 10 million.
8 The information in this section is drawn from the websites of the SSNNL (www.sardarsarovardam.org) and the NVDA (www.mp.nic.in/nvda/sardarsarovar), accessed July 2004.
9 See Sangvai (2000), Khagram (2004) and Dwivedi (2006) for detailed accounts of the conflict between Gujarat and Madhya Pradesh and the following deliberations of the Narmada Water Disputes Tribunal.
10 The report was that of Bissell, Singh and Warth (1999); see Venkatesan (2000) for a comment on the report.
11 A more detailed account of the involvement of financial institutions in funding the MHP is presented in Chapter 2.
12 The Sarvodaya Samaj was formed in 1948 by the Gandhian Vinoba Bhave, who was inspired by Gandhi's suggestion that the Congress should be dissolved in favour of an organization promoting constructive work in village communities. Championing decentralized governance and development, and rejecting parliamentary politics, the movement advocated *bhoodan* and *gramdan* – initiatives to promote landlords to donate land to the landless and bring village land under community control respectively. JP joined Bhave in his work, but was later estranged from him, and he also set up the Chhatra Yuva Sangharsh Vahini to organize youth to work among poor and low caste groups so as to further his programme of "total revolution" (see Hardiman 2003).
13 I want to note from the outset that I use the term new social movements strictly in a temporal sense to refer to movements that emerged from the late 1960s onwards. Attempts

to draw fine lines between old and new in social movement research is arguably a futile endeavour as in most cases the supposedly 'old' is present in the 'new' and the supposedly 'new' is present in the 'old' – whether it pertains to groups, issues, strategies, or ideologies. Shah's (1988) overview of grassroots mobilizations in India brings out the deep historical lineage of most of the movements that authors typically designate as 'new'. See Shah (1990) and Rao (2000) for instructive overviews of Indian social movements.

14 The Narmada Bachao Andolan was a central actor in the planning and execution of the Harsud rally; this is discussed in more detail in Chapter 8.

15 Constraints of space do not allow for a full discussion of Marx's philosophical anthropology here. It will have to suffice to note that this particular conception of human species being remained constant in Marx's thought from his discussion of 'objectification' in the *Economic and Philosophical Manuscripts of 1844*, via the outline of the fundamental principles of the materialist conception of history in *The German Ideology*, to the designation of 'the labour process' as the kernel of the mediation of needs and capacities in human life-activity in *Capital* (Marx 1981; Marx and Engels 1999; Marx 1990; see also Geras 1983; Fracchia 1991, 2005; Nilsen 2007).

16 This definition draws heavily on Cox (1999a: 99).

17 These concepts are of course ideal-types, and movement processes are uneven as opposed to homogenous trajectories. As Nash (1992) has pointed out, a social movement is in itself a field containing a plethora of experiences and articulations of such experiences (see also Cox 1999a/b). The analysis that is presented in this study stresses the multiplicity of experiences in the movement processes that unfolded in the Narmada Valley, as well as its fractural aspects and negotiated character.

18 A social movement project that successfully develops a capacity for hegemony is likely to be associated with periods of what Gramsci (1998) refers to as 'organic crisis', the development of dual power institutions, and the onset of a revolutionary situation animated by 'a dialectic between reactionary and progressive forces in search of a solution, a new order' (Gill 2003: 33).

2 Losing ground

1 The construction of Bargi dam led to the flooding of more than 160 villages – far in excess of the 100 or so villages that the state government of Madhya Pradesh had projected as dam-affected – whilst resettlement and rehabilitation remained a chimera for most of close to 40,000 oustees (indeed, 26 of the proposed resettlement sites for the Bargi oustees were submerged when the floodgates closed in 1990 (see Dharmidhikary n.d.; Schücking 1999; D'Souza 2002).

2 See also De Angelis (2001, 2007) and Bonefeld (2001) as well as Mandel (1975).

3 See www.sardarsarovardam.org/benefits.html, accessed July 2004.

4 The NWDT put the water flow at 27 MAF. Critics, drawing on more recent estimates by the Government of Madhya Pradesh, put the water flow at 22 MAF.

5 An aspect of this 'distributional critique' concerns claims made by the Government of Gujarat that the drought-prone regions of Kutch and Saurashtra will benefit from the harnessing of the Narmada's waters by the SSP. Metha (1997: 7) points out that only two per cent of Kutch stand to benefit from the Kutch Branch Canal, and irrigation delivery is rendered difficult by a series of logistical factors: setbacks in the completion of the main Narmada canal, reduced levels of irrigation delivery due to high evaporation levels, and, finally, the bias of canal construction in Kutch towards the industrial areas in the region, rather than drought-prone agricultural areas. A closely related official claim about the benefits of the SSP to Kutch and Saurashtra is that the region will receive drinking water from the Narmada. The Morse Commission cast doubt on this claim when their 1992 inquiry found that there were no actual plans in existence for the delivery of drinking water to these regions (Roy 2002: 131–2). Some ten years later, things were not much

improved: when in 2004 the Government of Gujarat announced that Narmada waters had reached Kutch, it was eventually revealed that this water actually came from the Mahi dam in Saurashtra, and not the SSP (Bavadam 2007). See also Ram (1993) for a critique of official claims concerning drinking water from the SSP.

6 However, it should be noted that South Gujarat exhibits a profoundly *uneven* pattern of capitalist development. The eastern part of Surat is predominantly tribal, characterized by subsistence agriculture, extensive cultivation due to poor soil fertility and irregular rainfall; the western coastal stretch along the Arabian sea is typified by a populace of low caste fishermen and peasants. In short, it is the central plain of Surat which constitutes the locus of capitalist transition (see Breman 1996).

7 However, forms of semi-bondage still exist in capital-labour relations in South Gujarat (see Breman 1996).

8 See, for instance, Modi's speech to non-resident Indians under the auspices of the Federation of Indian Chambers of Commerce and Industry (www.ficci.com/media-room/speeches-presentations/2003/Jan/pbd-narendramodi.html) and his speech at the Vibrant Gujarat Global Investors' Summit (www.gujaratindia.com/media/speeches/Ahmedabad.pdf), accessed July 2004.

9 The region of Nimad is ostensibly somewhat ill-defined. The current administrative districts of West and East Nimad (also referred to as Khargone and Khandwa [see GoMP 2002]) are located in the southwestern corner of M.P. In conventional usage, however, and in terms of agro-ecological and socio-cultural features, Nimad also refers to parts of the districts of Badwani and Dhar (see e.g. Dwivedi 1999 and Shankar 2005). My fieldwork was focused on West Nimad (Khargone), Dhar and Badwani.

10 In terms of policy failures in Madhya Pradesh, they criticized the restrictive definition of PAPs in the state's policy regime: a person has to have cultivated lands for three years prior to notification of land acquisition in order to qualify as PAP, rather than one year as is stipulated by the NWDT Award; major sons are not granted land-for-land compensation; encroachers have to prove that their land was encroached prior to April 1987 in order to be entitled to land-for-land compensation, but it is unlikely that papers proving the time of encroachment exist; finally, 'in Madhya Pradesh, as elsewhere . . . records of ownership tend to be out of date and provide an inadequate picture of current land ownership' (Morse and Berger 1992: 177). The reports on the conduct of R&R in Maharashtra are strikingly similar: see TISS (1993) and Indian People's Tribunal IPT (2000). Moreover, a 2001 Task Force that investigated the extent of submergence in Maharashtra as the height of the SSP was raised from 90 to 95 metres found that 2176 families living in villages slated for submergence in Maharashtra were not registered as project-affected families (see IPT 2004).

11 A survey of dam-affected villages in Alirajpur carried out by the NBA in 2004, in a context where the NCA was discussing whether to give clearance for raising the dam height from 100 to 110 metres, found an almost identical scenario to that identified by the Housing and Land Rights Network (NBA 2004). These findings were confirmed later the same year by the Indian People's Tribunal which found a similar pattern of non-recognition of land rights and more generally a failure to implement R&R in a satisfactory manner (IPT 2004).

12 This, in turn, is part of a larger regional scenario in which, throughout the adivasi border region of Western India, which comprises areas of Madhya Pradesh, Rajasthan and Gujarat, in any year as much as 'half of the adult population will be absent for half of the year, most often working intermittently as casual seasonal labourers in urban construction sites, leaving only the old or the injured; in some villages there will be almost nobody' (Mosse 2007: 16; see also Mosse *et al.* 2005). Mosse *et al.* (2005: 16) notes that 'the experience and outcome of migration is highly differentiated . . . Successful migrants invest surplus in agriculture or repay debts . . . but for many migration does not offer an exit from poverty and debt'.

13 Madhya Bharat was formed in 1948 as a union of 25 former princely states in west central India. It later merged with Vindhya Pradesh to form the state of Madhya Pradesh.

14 See also Mander (2002) on tribal land alienation as a problem throughout Madhya Pradesh.
15 In addition to farming, economic life in Nimad is also characterized by sand-quarrying, riverbed farming, and fishing, all of which share the basic features of petty commodity production. Due to space constraints I restrict my treatment of the Nimadi economy to agriculture, but see Nilsen (2006) for details on this.
16 Indeed, if there has been a group that has been able to dominate politics in the state it has been the upper castes that previously held power in the princely states (see Gupta 2005). As Jaffrelot (2003) points out, there has more recently been a challenge to the position of these groups from the Other Backward Castes (OBCs). However, this can in no way be compared to the convulsions associated with the rise to power of OBCs in Uttar Pradesh and Bihar (Gupta 2005: 5096).
17 See Abhyankar (2005) for a critical analysis of power sector reform in MP.
18 As critics of the project noted at the time, the rating was in flagrant violation of the regulations of the Securities and Exchange Board of India, as the chairman of CARE was also the chairman of the SMHPCL (*Central Chronicle*, 28 February 2007).
19 See Klingensmith (2007) for an excellent analysis of the cultural politics of dam-building and the crucial role that large dams played in the attempts to establish the legitimacy of the developmental state in postcolonial India.
20 Indeed, it is a global pattern that, because of the confluence of 'structural inequities, cultural dissonance, pervasive and institutional racism and discrimination, and political marginalization', indigenous people 'have suffered disproportionately from the negative impact of large dams, while often being among those who have been excluded from sharing the benefits' (Colchester 2000: 8; see also McCully 1998).
21 The BJP-led NDA government in 2004 introduced a draft version of a National Rehabilitation Policy and a new draft version was publicized by the Congress-led UPA government in 2006. In February 2009, an amended Land Acquisition Bill and what had by then become the Resettlement and Rehabilitation Bill were passed by the Indian parliament. At the time of writing, the Bills have not yet become law, and activists are campaigning vigorously in relation to the new legislation. For critiques of the new resettlement policy, see Palit (2004) and Iyer (2007).
22 IFL was a breakaway faction from the AITUC, founded in 1941. The Communist Party of India came to control AITUC after 1942 as a consequence of the widespread imprisonment of Congress leaders after the advent of the Quit India movement (Chibber 2003: 117).
23 A crucial structural factor adding to the weakness of labour in the Indian context was of course that the majority of the working class remained unorganized – a fact which remains to this day (see e.g. Breman 1996). This, however, does not make the trajectory of the labour movement irrelevant in terms of the dynamics of mobilization and equations of power that shaped India's postcolonial political economy. As Chibber (2005a: 33) argues, the structural conditions that weaken labour relative to capital – conditions such as 'a massive reserve army of the unemployed or underemployed, the small size of the organized factory sector, the migratory character of much industrial labour' – may 'be mitigated by the institutional framework which governs the labour-capital relation'. The point here is that such an institutional framework failed to be put in place in India, as a consequence of the curbing of labour's mobilizational capacities. See Heller's (1999) study of labour in Kerala for an example of what can be achieved when labour mobilization is encouraged rather than curbed.
24 Moore adds an important qualifier: 'The allies this bourgeois impetus has found, the enemies it has encountered, vary sharply from case to case' (ibid.: xii). See Hill (1980), Teschke (2003), Halperin (2004), and Davidson (2005a/b) for instructive discussions of the complex problematics that attach to bourgeois revolutions.
25 Such ambitions did exist within the Indian capitalist class during the independence struggle. As Mukherjee (2002: 45) points out, in the 1940s the dominant section of

Indian capital argued for 'comprehensive reforms in agriculture . . . geared precisely towards the undermining of the existing feudal and semi-feudal tendencies in Indian agriculture'.

26 The classical account of the conflicts that have bedevilled this coalition of dominant proprietary classes is that of Bardhan (1998). See Kaviraj (1997) and Vanaik (1990) for instructive discussions of the relationship between the three constitutive elements of the alliance.

27 However, the significant outlier case of Kerala should be noted; as Heller (2005) shows, the state witnessed significant mobilization in the early years of independence, culminating with the 'electoral watershed' of CPI in 1957, and resulting in 'the most socialized economy and developed welfare state in the region' (ibid.: 85).

28 As Atul Kohli (2006a) has noted, whilst the character of state intervention took a decisive pro-business turn under "the two Gandhis" in the 1980s, this was far from a shift towards the market as such. The pro-business turn was in many ways foreshadowed by the Emergency of 1975–77, which had a clear class bias in that it provided short-term benefits for the propertied rural and urban classes: 'both the profits and assets of big business went up' and this was achieved 'more from the repression of labour than from any real improvements in productivity' (Corbridge and Harriss 2000: 87; see also Kohli 2006a).

29 The CII emerged as a consequence of a breakaway from FICCI. Tensions arose, Pedersen (2000: 269) argues, as small- and medium-scale industrialists concentrated in western and southern India found that the Marwari-dominated FICCI failed to accommodate and represent their interests.

30 See e.g. *Times of India* (04 July 2009) and *Indian Express* (05 July 2009)

3 Everyday tyranny and rightful resistance

1 *Gherao* literally means encirclement and is a form of protest in which a person or group of persons is prevented from leaving a place or a building until a set of demands have been heard or met.

2 See Hardiman (1987, 1997) on the relationship between adivasi communities and moneylenders.

3 Atrocities against adivasis are a widespread phenomenon in the state of Madhya Pradesh (see Baviskar 1995: Chapter 8; 2001: 10–11). Among other examples this is evidenced in the shooting of four adivasis protesting accusations of illegal tree felling by police in Mehendikheda village in Dewas district in April 2001 (see Swaminathan 2001) and, more recently, police firing against adivasis who protested forced eviction in Ghatega village in Rewa district in April 2007 (http://web.amnesty.org./library/print/ENGASA200102007), accessed July 2007.

4 Corbridge *et al.* (2005) propose the notion of 'seeing the state' as an alternative to Scott's (1998) notion of 'seeing like a state'. They argue that states 'are best thought of as bundles of everyday institutions and forms of rule' and their workings best studied in terms of 'the ways in which different groups of the rural poor might be said to see or encounter the developmental state' (Corbridge *et al.* 2005: 5, 19).

5 As regards sexual brutality, a former KMCS activist also pointed out that officials in Alirajpur would often claim "first right" to adivasi brides (interview, Chittaroopa Palit, May 2003). Baviskar (2001: 16) also cites the example of the gang rape of the wife of an adivasi man who was in conflict with – and was later killed by – the police as an example of the gendered nature of everyday tyranny. As Baviskar (2001) notes, caste Hindu state officials often attribute promiscuity to adivasi women with reference to adivasi marriage customs, and use this to justify sexual violence.

6 A *panchayat* is a political institution which caters to governance at village, block and district levels.

7 See e.g. Kaviraj (1991), Inden (1995), Brass (1997) and Jalal (1995).
8 See also Yadav (2000) and Jaffrelot (2000, 2003). This is indeed a rupture as Indian parliamentary politics in the postcolonial era was characterized by the Congress party's accommodation of the upper castes and classes (see Chapter 2 for a discussion).
9 Most recently, such politics is evident in the rise to state power of the dalit-based Bahujan Samaj Party in Uttar Pradesh.
10 See Fuller and Harriss (2001), Chatterjee (2004) and Corbridge *et al.* (2005) for related arguments.

4 Discovering the dam

1 Interviewees never mentioned the NBNBS; in fact, some interviewees asserted that such an organization had never existed. Whereas this is doubtful, its absence from people's memories of mobilization suggests that it was an insignificant initiative.

5 Towards opposition

1 Cited in NBA (1988).
2 This was an organization set up by the NDS to mobilize the oustees of Kevadia Colony – the site built for the SSP engineers – in Gujarat, following the ARCH Vahini's decision not to join the anti-dam campaign. The ARCH Vahini's divergence from the other organizations in the Narmada Valley will be discussed later.
3 My translation from the original Norwegian.
4 See also Dwivedi (1999: 52–3; 2006: Chapter 6).
5 See http://www.narmada.org/AMTE/vanaprastha1.html (accessed July 2004) for an account of Baba Amte's life and work. This section is otherwise based on Sen (n.d.).
6 Patel's critique of the turn to dam opposition cited earlier comes very close to making such claims.
7 Manibeli is an adivasi village in the submergence zone of Maharashtra, which was central in the NBA's monsoon satyagraha, an annual protest event that was inaugurated in 1991.

6 Cycles of struggle

1 My treatment of the international campaign will be relatively brief as this is arguably the aspect of the NBA's anti-dam campaign that has received the most attention in scholarly literature and I have little to add to these analyses; see for example Udall (1995), Wade (1997), Sen (n.d.) and Khagram (2004).
2 The World Bank was at this point in time considering the implementation of an independent review of the SSP.
3 According to Hardiman (2003: 59) similar tactical equations motivated Gandhi's use of non-violence in the struggle against colonial rule.
4 See also Chabot and Duyvendak (2002) on the proliferation of Gandhian protest methods.
5 However, this promise was quickly retracted when he was made aware that such actions would jeopardize the Janata Dal's electoral success in Gujarat (Jayal 2000: 168). Janata Dal was eventually successful in the state assembly elections in Gujarat, and Chimanbhai Patel, a staunch supporter of the SSP (see Chapter 2), was ushered back to the apex of power in the state.
6 From 1991 to 1994, the satyagraha was concentrated around the village of Manibeli in Maharashtra. From 1995 onwards, following the submergence of Manibeli and further intrusion of the SSP reservoir and backwaters into Madhya Pradesh, it came to focus on Jalsindhi (MP) and Domkhedi (Maharashtra).

7 See Green (2000), Davies and Flett (2000), Uehling (2000), and Gongaware (2003) for more elaborate perspectives on how collective memories are used in social movements.
8 See Dwivedi (2006: 247–9).
9 The cautionary note was well-founded as the NBA had experienced fierce repression at the hands of state governments, police, and dam supporters from 1991, when the first satyagraha was staged in Manibeli, to 1992 (see Jayal 2000).
10 Following the electoral victory of Digvijay Singh of the Congress, the GoMP reverted on this decision and made a submission to the FMG in the last phase of the review, arguing for a reduction in the height of the dam (Dwivedi 2006: 258).
11 Construction work continued, however, in violation of this order, and it was only after the NBA took out a protest march on Delhi towars the end of the year that construction was actually stalled. The Supreme Court's stay order was then observed until 1999 (discussed later).
12 As Rajagopal (2004: 30–1) notes, a meeting between the chief ministers of the three riparian states during the summer of 1996 supposedly established consensus between the three states, but it was later revealed that MP had not accepted the terms of the agreement and that the consensus reached 'was basically a decision of the Prime Minister' (ibid.: 31).

7 Enablements and constraints

1 The Maheshwar struggle started while the stay on the SSP imposed by the Supreme Court was still in place (see Chapter 6).
2 A sarpanch is a democratically elected head of the village panchayat.
3 See e.g. Agarwal (1989, 1992, 1994) and Nanda (2004).
4 This was chiefly an outcome of the fact that in most cases when I approached central female activists in the villages my requests for interviews were more or less consistently turned down.
5 A *mohalla* is a neighborhood or locality in cities and towns.
6 '*Kisan*' is the Hindi word for 'farmer'.
7 *Jagirdari* refers to the feudal landholding system in colonial India; see Chapter 2.

8 Development, not destruction

1 The satyagraha never rose to such dramatic heights in 2000 as the monsoon failed to set in. The failure of the monsoon brought its own hardships in the form of a severe drought.
2 The term 'tryst with destiny' is drawn from Nehru's speech delivered at midnight, 15 August 1947: 'Long years ago, we made a tryst with destiny, and now the time comes when we shall redeem out pledge, not wholly or in full measure, but very substantially. At the stroke of the midnight hour, when the world sleeps, India will wake to life and freedom' (cited in Metcalf and Metcalf 2002: 216).
3 On the dismal state of education in the adivasi areas and the development of the jeevan shalas, see Sangvai (2000a).
4 This is not to suggest that Gandhi was the originator of community development in India. As Sinha (2008) has shown, community development has complex and composite rules in transnational flows of development practice that emerged during the British Raj.
5 See Cooke and Kothari (2001) on the 'anti-politics' of participatory development; see Williams (2004) and Hickey and Mohan (2005) for instructive engagements with the possibilities for the radicalization of participatory development.
6 Hall (1983) has produced a particularly apt critique of such assumptions in the study of popular culture. Sarkar (1998), O'Hanlon (2003) and Sivaramakrishnan (2003) have put forward persuasive critiques of the ramifications of this assumption within the Indian Subaltern Studies school, and Moore (1996, 1998, 2003) has produced a seminal critique

of its operation in post-development theory. See also Corbridge (1998), Rangan (1993, 1996, 2000), Pieterse (1998, 2000), Kiely (1999), and Cooper and Packard (1997) for a selection of critical commentaries on post-development theory. See Nilsen (2007b) for a detailed critique of the representation of Indian NSMs in post-development theory.

7 See note 12, Chapter 1.

8 However, the commonality of the threat is of course also subject to discussion: as Dwivedi (1999, 2006) has pointed out, different groups within the mass base are differently equipped in terms of their capacity to deal with the impact of displacement, with landless labourers, adivasis and women being by far the most vulnerable groups.

9 More recently, Baviskar (2005: 174) seems to adopt a stance more along these lines.

10 The fact that the dominant tendency in the BJA wanted to exclude trade unions is expressive of a general tendency in the politics of India's NSMs where class politics is increasingly left behind and new oppositions and contradictions are highlighted – in particular oppositions and contradictions between the city and the countryside (see Omvedt 1993; Brass 1991, 1995a/b/c, 2000; Brass, T. 1997).

9 Whither the rage?

1 I owe this distinction to Laurence Cox.

Bibliography

Abhyankar, N. (2005) 'Power Sector Restructuring in Madhya Pradesh', *Economic and Political Weekly*, Vol. 48, No. 40: 5038–47.

Abrams, P. (1988) 'Notes on the Difficulty of Studying the State', *Journal of Historical Sociology*, Vol. 1, No. 1: 58–89.

Agarwal, B. (1989) 'Rural Women, Poverty and Natural Resources: Sustenance, Sustainability and Struggle for Change', *Economic and Political Weekly*, Vol. 24, No. 43: 46–65.

—— (1992) 'The Gender and Environment Debate: Lessons from India', *Feminist Studies*, Vol. 18, No. 1: 118–58.

—— (1994) *A Field of One's Own: Gender and Land Rights in South Asia*, Cambridge: Cambridge University Press.

Aggarwal, A. (2006) 'Special Economic Zones: Revisiting the Policy Debate', *Economic and Political Weekly*, Vol. 41, No. 43: 533–6.

Bannerjee, R. (1994) 'Case Study of an Independent Trade Union in Jhabua District of Madhya Pradesh', *Indian Journal of Labour Economics*, Vol. 37, No. 4: 811–17.

—— (2000) 'There's No Such Thing as Instant Revolution', *Humanscape*, January: 36–40.

—— (2003) 'Sahukars Rule the Roost: Status of Informal Rural Financial Markets in Adivasi Dominated Regions of Western Madhya Pradesh', report available at http://www.panchayats.org/downloads/Sahukars%20Rule%20the%20Roost.PDF (accessed December 2004).

Banerjee, S. (1984) *India's Simmering Revolution: The Naxalite Uprising*, London: Totowa.

—— (2007) 'Moral Betrayal of a Leftist Dream', *Economic and Political Weekly*, Vol. 42, No. 14: 1240–2.

Bardhan, P. (1998) *The Political Economy of Development in India: Expanded Edition*, New Delhi: Oxford University Press.

Barker, C. (2002) 'A Modern Moral Economy? Edward Thompson and Valentin Volosinov Meet in North Manchester', paper presented at the conference Making Social Movements: The British Marxist Historians and the Study of Social Movements, Edge Hill College of Higher Education, England, June.

Barker, C. and Cox, L. (2002) 'What Have the Romans Ever Done for Us? Academic and Activist Forms of Movement Theorizing', paper available at the Tools for Change website, http://www.iol.ie/~mazzoldi/toolsforchange/afpp/afpp8.html (accessed February 2005).

Basu, A. (1987) 'Grassroots Movements and the State: Reflections on Radical Change in India', *Theory and Society*, Vol. 16, No. 5: 647–74.

Bavadam, L. (2001) 'A New Phase of Resistance', *Frontline*, Vol. 18, No. 14.

—— (2003) 'The Bhilgaon Model', *Frontline*, Vol. 20, No. 21.

—— (2004a) 'Water and Votes', *Frontline*, Vol. 21, No. 10.

—— (2004b) 'Guarantee for Maheshwar', *Frontline*, Vol. 21, No. 4.

—— (2006) 'Drowned in Politics', *Frontline*, Vol. 23, No. 8.

—— (2007) 'Submerged Hopes', *Frontline*, Vol. 24, No. 2.

—— (2009) 'Farmers' Victory', *Frontline*, Vol. 26, No. 13.

Baviskar, A. (1991) 'Narmada "Sangharsh Yatra": State's Response and its Consequences', *Economic and Political Weekly*, Vol. 26, No. 9–10: 477–8.

—— (1995) *In the Belly of the River: Tribal Conflicts over Water in the Narmada Valley*, New Delhi: Oxford University Press.

—— (1997a) 'Reverence is Not Enough: Ecological Marxism and Indian Adivasis', in Dupuis, E. M. and Vandergeest, P. (eds): *Creating the Countryside: The Politics of Rural and Environmental Discourse*, Philadelphia: Temple University Press.

—— (1997b) 'Tribal Politics and Discourses of Environmentalism', *Contributions to Indian Sociology*, Vol. 31, No. 2: 196–223.

—— (1997c) 'Displacement and the Bhilala Tribals of the Narmada Valley', in Drèze, J., Samson, M. and Singh, S. (eds): *The Dam and the Nation: Displacement and Resettlement in the Narmada Valley*, New Delhi: Oxford University Press.

—— (2001) 'Written on the Body, Written on the Land: Violence and Environmental Struggles in Central India', Berkeley Workshop on Environmental Politics, Working Paper 02–10.

—— (2005) 'Red in Tooth and Claw? Looking for Class in Struggles over Nature', in Ray, R. and Katzenstein, M. (eds) *Social Movements in India: Poverty, Power and Politics*, New York, Rowman and Littlefield.

—— (n.d.) 'The Dream Machine: The Model Development Project and the Remaking of the State', manuscript obtained from the author.

Baviskar, A. and Sundar, N. (2008) 'Democracy versus Economic Transformation?', *Economic and Political Weekly*, Vol. 43, No. 46: 87–9.

Bernstein, H. (1994) 'Agrarian Classes in Capitalist Development', in Sklair, L. (ed.) *Capitalism and Development*, London: Routledge.

Bevington, D. and Dixon, C. (2005) 'Movement-Relevant Theory: Rethinking Social Movement Scholarship and Activism', *Social Movement Studies*, Vol. 4, No. 3: 185–208.

Bissell, R. E., Singh, S. and Warth, H. (2000) *Maheshwar Hydroelectric Project: Resettlement and Rehabilitation – An Independent Review Conducted for the Ministry of Economic Cooperation and Development (BMZ) Government of Germany*, report summary published by the Narmada Bachao Andolan.

Bonefeld, W. (2001) 'The Permanence of Primitive Accumulation: Commodity Fetishism and Social Constitution', *The Commoner*, No. 2, available at www.thecommoner.org.uk (accessed February 2002).

Bose, S. (1997) 'Instruments and Idioms of Colonial and National Development: India's Experience in Comparative Perspective', in Cooper, F. and Packard, R. (eds) *International Development and the Social Sciences: Essays on the History and Politics of Knowledge*, Berkeley: University of California Press.

Bosshard, P. (2002) *Power Finance: Financial Institutions in India's Hydropower Sector*, Berkeley: International Rivers Network.

Brass, P. (1997) *Theft of an Idol: Text and Context in the Representation of Collective Violence*, Princeton: Princeton University Press.

Brass, T. (1991): 'Moral Economists, Subalterns, New Social Movements, and the

(Re-)Emergence of a (Post-)Modernised (Middle) Peasant', *Journal of Peasant Studies*, Vol. 18, No. 2: 173–205.

—— (1995a): 'Introduction: The New Farmers' Movements in India', *Journal of Peasant Studies*, Vol. 21, No. 3–4: 3–26.

—— (1995b): 'The Politics of Gender, Nature and Nation in the Discourse of the New Farmers' Movements', *Journal of Peasant Studies*, Vol. 21, No. 3–4: 27–71.

—— (1995c): 'Post-Script: Populism, Peasants and Intellectuals, or What's Left of the Future?', *Journal of Peasant Studies*, Vol. 21, No. 3–4: 247–86.

—— (1997) 'The Agrarian Myth, The "New" Populism and the "New' Right"', *Journal of Peasant Studies*, Vol. 24, No. 4: 201–45.

—— (2000) *Peasants, Populism and Postmodernism*, London: Frank Cass Publishers.

Breman, J. (1978/9a/b) 'Seasonal Migration and Co-operative Capitalism: The Crushing of Cane and of Labour by the Sugar Factories of Bardoli, South Gujarat – Parts 1&2', *Journal of Peasant Studies*, Vol. 6, Nos. 1 and 2: 41–70 and 168–205.

—— (1985) *Of Peasants, Migrants and Paupers: Rural Labour Circulation and Capitalist Production in West India*, New Delhi: Oxford University Press.

—— (1996) *Footloose Labour: Working in India's Informal Sector*, Cambridge: Cambridge University Press.

Byres, T. J. (1981) 'The New Technology, Class Formation and Class Action in the Indian Countryside', *Journal of Peasant Studies*, Vol. 8, No. 4: 405–54.

Central Chronicle (2007) 'Complaint Against CARE Rating of Maheshwar Project', February 27.

Cernea, M. (1999) 'Development's Painful Social Costs', in Parasuraman, S. (ed) *The Development Dilemma: Displacement in India*, London: Macmillan Press.

Chabot, S. and Duyvendak, J. W. (2002) 'Globalization and Transnational Diffusion Between Social Movements: Reconceptualizing the Dissemination of the Gandhian Repertoire and the "Coming Out" Routine', *Theory and Society*, Vol. 31, No. 6: 697–740.

Chandra, P. and Basu, D. (2007) 'Neoliberalism and Primitive Accumulation in India', article available at the *Z magazine* website, http://www.zmag.org/znet/viewArticle/2082 (accessed July 2007).

Chandrasekhar, C. P. (2004) 'To the Markets This March', *Frontline*, Vol. 21, No. 6.

—— (2006) 'Primitive Accumulation', *Frontline*, Vol. 23, No. 20.

Chandrasekhar, C. P. and Ghosh, J. (1999) 'Disinvestment: At What Price', article available at http://www.macroscan.org/pol/dec99/print/prnt281299Disinvestment.htm (accessed August 2003).

—— (2002) *The Market that Failed: A Decade of Neoliberal Reforms in India*, New Delhi: Leftword.

Chatterjee, P. (1986) *Nationalist Thought and the Colonial World*, New Delhi: Oxford University Press.

—— (1993) *The Nation and Its Fragments*, Princeton: Princeton University Press.

—— (2004) *Politics of the Governed: Reflections on Popular Politics in Most of the World*, New York: Columbia University Press.

Chibber, V. (2003) *Locked in Place: State-Building and Late Industrialization in India*, Princeton: Princeton University Press.

—— (2005a) 'From Class Compromise to Class Accommodation: Labor's Incorporation into the Indian Political Economy', in Ray, R. and Katzenstein, M. (eds) *Social Movements in India: Poverty, Power and Politics*, New York: Rowman and Littlefield.

—— (2005b) 'Reviving the Developmental State: The Myth of the National Bourgeoisie', in Panitch, L. and Leys, C. (eds) *Socialist Register 2005*: 226–45.

Colchester, M. (2000) *Sharing Power: Dams, Indigenous People and Ethnic Minorities*, report available at the World Commission on Dams website, http://www.dams.org/docs/kbase/thematic/tr12main.pdf (accessed November 2002).

Cooke, B. and Kothari, U. (eds) (2002) *Participation: The New Tyranny*, London: Zed Books.

Cooper, F. (1997) 'Modernizing Bureaucrats, Backward Africans, and the Development Concept', in Cooper, F. and Packard, R. (eds) *International Development and the Social Sciences: Essays on the History and Politics of Knowledge*, Berkeley: University of California Press.

Cooper, F. and Packard, R. (1997) 'Introduction', in Cooper, F. and Packard, R. (eds) *International Development and the Social Sciences: Essays on the History and Politics of Knowledge*, Berkeley: University of California Press.

Corbridge, S. (1998) '"Beneath the Pavement Only Soil": The Poverty of Post-Development', *Journal of Development Studies*, Vol. 34, No. 6: 138–48.

Corbridge, S, and Harriss, J. (2000) *Reinventing India: Liberalization, Hindu Nationalism and Popular Democracy*, Cambridge: Polity Press.

Corbridge, S., Williams, G., Srivastava, M., and Véron, R. (2005) *Seeing the State: Governance and Governmentality in India*, Cambridge: Cambridge University Press.

Cowen, M. and Shenton, R. W. (1996) *Doctrines of Development*, London: Routledge.

Cox, L. (1998) 'Gramsci, Movements and Method: The Politics of Activist Research', paper presented to the fourth annual Alternative Futures and Popular Protest conference, Manchester Metropolitan University, April.

—— (1999a) *Building Counter Culture: The Radical Praxis of Social Movement Milieux*, unpublished PhD dissertation, Trinity College, Dublin.

—— (1999b) 'Power, Politics and Everyday Life: The Local Rationalities of Social Movement Milieux', in Bagguley, P. and Hearn, J. (eds) *Transforming Politics: Power and Resistance*, Basingstoke: Macmillan.

Cox, L. and Nilsen, A. G. (2005) '"At the Heart of Society Burns the Fire of Social Movements": What Would a Marxist Theory of Social Movements Look Like?', in Barker, C. and Tyldesley,M. (eds) *Tenth International Conference on Alternative Futures and Popular Protest – Conference Papers, Volume 2*, Faculty of Humanities and Social Science, Manchester: Manchester Metropolitan University.

D'Souza, D. (2002) *The Narmada Dammed: An Inquiry into the Politics of Development*, New Delhi: Penguin.

D'Souza, Radha (2005) *Insterstate Diputes Over Krishna Waters: Law, Science and Imperialism*, Hyderabad: Orient Longman.

D'Souza, Rohan (2003) 'Damming the Mahanadi River: The Emergence of Multi-Purpose River Valley Development in India (1943–46)', *The Indian Economic and Social History Review*, Vol. 40, No. 1: 81–105.

—— (2006) *Drowned and Dammed: Colonial Capitalism and Flood Control in Eastern India*, New Delhi: Oxford University Press.

Davidson, N. (2005a) 'How Revolutionary Were the Bourgeois Revolutions?', *Historical Materialism*, Vol. 13, No. 3: 3–34.

—— (2005b) 'How Revolutionary Were the Bourgeois Revolutions? – Continued', *Historical Materialism*, Vol. 13, No. 4: 3–54.

Davies, M. and Flett, K. (2000) 'Forgetting and Remembering: Memory and Political Action', paper presented to the Alternative Futures and Popular Protest conference, Manchester Metropolitan University, April.

De Angelis, M. (2001) 'Marx and Primitive Accumulation: The Continuous Character of

Capital's "Enclosures"', *The Commoner*, No. 2, article available at www.thecommoner.org.uk (accessed November 2001).

—— (2007) *The Beginning of History: Value Struggles and Global Capital*, London: Pluto Press.

Dhamgawar, V. (1997) 'The NGO Movements in the Narmada Valley: Some Reflections' in Drèze, J., Samson, M. and Singh, S. (eds) *The Dam and the Nation: Displacement and Resettlement in the Narmada Valley*, New Delhi: Oxford University Press.

Dhamgawar, V., Thukral, E. G., and Singh, M. (1995) 'The Sardar Sarovar Project: A Study in Sustainable Development?', in Fisher, W. F. (ed.) *Towards Sustainable Development? Struggling Over India's Narmada River*, London: M.E. Sharpe.

Dharmidhikary, S. (n.d.) 'Large Dams – Destruction not Development: The Experience of the Dams in the Narmada Valley in India (with the exception of Sardar Sarovar)', report available at the World Commission on Dams website, www.dams.org/kbase/submissions/showsub.php?rec = soc025 (accessed November 2002).

Drèze, J., Samson, M. and Singh, S. (eds) (1997) *The Dam and the Nation: Displacement and Resettlement in the Narmada Valley*, New Delhi: Oxford University Press.

Dubash, N. K. and Rajan, S. C. (2001) *The Politics of Power Sector Reform in India*, report available at the website www.pdf.wri.org (accessed July 2004).

Dwivedi, R. (1997) 'People's Movements in Environmental Politics: A Critical Analysis of the Narmada Bachao Andolan in India', Working Paper Series No. 242, Institute of Social Studies.

—— (1999) 'Displacement, Risks and Resistance: Local Perceptions and Actions in the Sardar Sarovar', *Development and Change*, Vol. 30, No. 1: 43–78.

—— (2006) *Conflict and Collective Action: The Sardar Sarovar Project in India*, London: Routledge.

Escobar, A. (1995) *Encountering Development: The Making and Unmaking of the Third World*, Princeton: Princeton University Press.

Eyerman, R. and Jamison, A. (1991) *Social Movements: A Cognitive Approach*, Cambridge: Polity Press.

Featherstone, D. (2005) 'Towards the Relational Construction of Militant Particularisms: Or Why the Geographies of Past Struggles Matter for Resistance to Neoliberal Globalisation', *Antipode*, Vol. 37, No. 2: 251–71.

Fisher, W. F. (1995): 'Development and Resistance in the Narmada Valley', in Fisher, W. F. (ed.) *Towards Sustainable Development? Struggling Over India's Narmada River*, London: M.E. Sharpe.

Foucault, M. (1977) *Discipline and Punish: Birth of the Prison*, London: Penguin Books.

Fracchia, J. (1991) 'Marx's Aufhebung of History and the Foundations of Historical-Materialistic Science', *History and Theory*, Vol. 30, No. 2: 153–79.

—— (2005) 'Beyond the Human-Nature Debate: Human Corporeal Constitution as the "First Fact" of Historical Materialism', *Historical Materialism*, Vol. 13, No. 1: 33–62.

Frankel, F. (1971): *India's Green Revolution*, Princeton, Princeton University Press.

—— (2005) *India's Political Economy: The Gradual Revolution 1947–2004*, New Delhi: Oxford University Press.

Fuller, C. J. and Harriss, J. (2001) 'For an Anthropology of the Modern Indian State', in Fuller, C. J. and Béneï, V. (eds) *The Everyday State and Society in Modern India*, London: Hurst and Company.

Gadgil, M. and Guha, R. (1993) *This Fissured Land: An Ecological History of India*, New Delhi: Oxford University Press.

Geoghegan, M. and Cox, L. (2001) 'Outside the Whale: (Re)thinking Social Movements and the Voluntary Sector', paper available at the Tools for Change website, http://www.iol.ie/~mazzoldi/toolsforchange/afpp/afpp7.html (accessed December 2005).

Geras, N. (1983) *Marx and Human Nature: Refutation of a Legend*, London: New Left Books.

Ghose, S. (n.d.) 'The Maheshwar Dam Project: Factsheet', factsheet available at the Friends of the Narmada website, http://www.narmada.org/maheshwar/maheshwar.factsheet.html (accessed July 2000).

Ghosh, J. (2003) 'Sleaze-Ridden Capitalism', *Frontline*, Vol. 20, No. 9.

—— (2006a) 'The Sardar Sarovar Dam: The Legacy of an Indifferent State', article available at the Macroscan website, http://www.macroscan.org/cur/jun06/cur140606Indifferent_State.htm (accessed October 2007).

—— (2006b) 'Repeated Sins of Commission', article available at the Macroscan website, http://www.macroscan.org/cur/jun06/cur300606Commission.htm (accessed October 2007).

Gill, S. (2003) 'Grand Strategy and World Order: A Neo-Gramscian Perspective', mimeo/lecture delivered at Yale University in ISS's Grand Strategy Series, 20 April 2000.

GoMP (2002) *The Madhya Pradesh Human Development Report 2002: Using the Power of Democracy for Development*, Bhopal: Government of Madhya Pradesh.

Gongaware, T. B. (2003) 'Collective Memories and Collective Identities: Maintaining Unity in Native American Educational Social Movements', *Journal of Contemporary Ethnography*, Vol. 32, No. 5: 484–520.

Gosh, K. (2000) 'Between Global Flows and Local Dams: Indigenousness, Locality, and the Transnational Sphere in Jharkhand, India', *Cultural Anthropology*, Vol. 21, No. 4: 501–34.

Gramsci, A. (1998) *Selections from the Prison Notebooks*, London: Lawrence and Wishart.

Green, J. R. (2000) *Taking History to Heart: The Power of the Past in Building Social Movements*, Amherst: University of Massachusetts Press.

Guha, R. (1989) *The Unquiet Woods: Ecological Change and Peasant Resistance in the Himalaya*, New Delhi: Oxford University Press.

—— (2002) *Elementary Aspects of Peasant Insurgency in India*, New Delhi: Oxford University Press.

Guha, S. (1999) *Environment and Ethnicity in India, 1200–1991*, Cambridge: Cambridge University Press.

Gupta, A. (2000) *Postcolonial Developments: Agriculture in the Making of Modern India*, Durham: Duke University Press.

Gupta, S. (2005) 'Socio-Economic Base of Political Dynamics in Madhya Pradesh', *Economic and Political Weekly*, Vol. 40, No. 48: 5093–100.

Hall, S. (1983) 'Notes on Deconstructing "the Popular"', in Samuel, R. (ed.) *People's History and Socialist Theory*, London: Routledge and Kegan Paul.

Halperin, S. (2004) *War and Social Change in Modern Europe:* The Great Transformation *Revisited*, Cambridge: Cambridge University Press.

Hardiman, D. (1987) 'The Bhils and Shahukars of Eastern Gujarat', in Guha, R. (ed.) *Subaltern Studies V: Writings on South Asian History and Society*, New Delhi: Oxford University Press.

—— (1997) *Feeding the Baniya: Peasants and Usurers in Western India*, New Delhi: Oxford University Press.

—— (2002) *Gandhi – In His Time and Ours*, New Delhi: Permanent Black.

Harriss-White, B. (2005) 'Poverty and Capitalism', QEH Working Paper, available at the

Queen Elizabeth House website, http://www3.qeh.ox.ac.uk/pdf/qehwp/qehwps134.pdf (accessed February 2008).

Hardiman, D. (2003): *Gandhi – In His Time and Ours*, New Delhi: Permanent Black.

Hart, G. (2002) 'Development/s Beyond Neoliberalism? Power, Culture, Political Economy', *Progress in Human Geography*, Vol. 26, No 6: 812–22.

Harvey, D. (1996) *Justice, Nature and the Geography of Difference*, Oxford: Blackwell.

—— (1999) *The Limits to Capital*, London: Verso.

—— (2000) *Spaces of Hope*, Edinburgh: Edinburgh University Press.

—— (2003) *The New Imperialism*, Oxford: Oxford University Press.

—— (2005) *A Brief History of Neoliberalism*, Oxford: Oxford University Press.

Hay, D., Linebaugh, P., Rule, J. G. Thompson, E. P., and Winslow, C. (1975) *Albion's Fatal Tree: Crime and Society in Eighteenth Century England*, London: Allen Lane.

Heller, A. (1976) *The Theory of Need in Marx*, London: Allison and Busby.

Heller, P. (1999): *The Labour of Development: Workers and The Transformation of Capitalism In Kerala, India*, Ithaca: Cornell University Press.

Hickey, S. and Mohan, G. (2005) 'Relocating Participation Within a Radical Politics of Development', *Development and Change*, Vol. 36, No. 2: 237–62.

Hill, C. (1980) 'A Bourgeois Revolution?', in Pocock, J. (ed.) *Three British Revolutions*, Princeton: Princeton University Press.

Housing and Land Rights Network (2002) *The Impact of the 2002 Submergence on Housing and Land Rights in the Narmada Valley: Report of a Fact-Finding Mission to Sardar Sarovar and Maan Dam Projects*, Delhi: Habitat International Coalition.

Inden, R. (1995) 'Embodying God: From Imperial Progress to National Progress in India', *Economy and Society*, Vol. 24, No. 2: 245–78.

Independent People's Commission (2004) *Without Land or Livelihood – The Indira Sagar Project: State Accountability and Rehabilitation Issues*, report available at the Friends of the Narmada website, http://www.narmada.org/nvdp.dams/indira-sagar/ISP_Report.pdf (accessed March 2005).

Indian Express (2009) 'Left Out, UPA to Fast-Track Disinvestment', 5 June.

Indian People's Tribunal IPT (2000) *Dammed Future: Report of the Independent Inquiry into the Status of Rehabilitation of Project Affected Families (PAFs) of the Sardar Sarovar Project (SSP) in Maharashtra*, report available at the Indian People's Tribunal website, http://iptindia.org/pdf/Dammed%20Future.pdf (accessed March 2005).

—— (2004) *Narmada: Inquiry Into Displacement, Resettlement and Rehabilitation of People Affected by the Sardar Sarovar Project*, report available at the Friends of the Narmada website, http://www.narmada.org/IPT_Report.pdf (accessed March 2005).

Iyer, R. R. (2007) 'Towards a Just Displacement and Rehabilitation Policy', *Economic and Political Weekly*, Vol. 42, No. 30: 3103–7.

JACSES/Urgewald (2004) *The Omkareshwar Dam in India: Closing Doors on People's Futures*, report available at the Japan Centre for a Sustainable Environment and Society, http://www.jacses.org/sdap/omkare/Omkareshwar-Briefing.pdf (accessed March 2005).

Jaffrelot, C. (2000) 'The Rise of the Other Backward Classes in the Hindi Belt', *Journal of Asian Studies*, Vol. 59, No. 1: 86–108.

—— (2003) *India's Silent Revolution: The Rise of the Lower Castes in North India*, London: Hurst and Company.

Jalal, A. (1995) *Democracy and Authoritarianism in South Asia: A Comparative and Historical Perspective*, Cambridge: Cambridge University Press.

Jayal, N. G. (2000) *Democracy and the State: Welfare, Secularism and Development in Contemporary India*, New Delhi: Oxford University Press.

Jessop, B. (1982) *The Capitalist State: Marxist Theories and Methods*, Oxford: Martin Robertson.

Johnson, A. (2002) 'Leadership and Historical Materialism: Reading Christopher Hill', paper presented to the Making Social Movements: The British Marxist Historians and the Study of Social Movements conference, Edge Hill College of Higher Education, June.

Jones, D. E. and Jones, R. W. (1976) 'Urban Upheaval in India: The 1974 Nav Nirman Riots in Gujarat', *Asian Survey*, Vol. 16, No. 11: 1012–33.

Kala, P. (2001) 'In the Spaces of Erasure: Globalisation, Resistance and Narmada River', *Economic and Political Weekly*, Vol. 38, No. 27: 3025–38.

Kamat, S. (2002) *Development Hegemony: NGOs and the State in India*, New Delhi: Oxford University Press.

Katzenstein, M. and Ray, R. (2005) 'Introduction: In the Beginning There Was the Nehruvian State', in Ray, R. and Katzenstein, M. (eds) *Social Movements in India: Poverty, Power, and Politics*, New York: Rowman and Littlefeld.

Kaviraj, S. (1991) 'On State, Society and Discourse in India', in Manor, J. (ed.) *Rethinking Third World Politics*, London: Longman.

—— (1997) 'A Critique of the Passive Revolution', in Chatterjee, P. (ed.) *State and Politics in India*, Delhi: Oxford University Press.

Keck, M. E. and Sikkink, K. (1998) *Activists Beyond Borders: Advocacy Networks in International Politics*, Ithaca: Cornell University Press.

Kela, S. (2003) 'Towards Elections: Disaffection and Co-Option', *Economic and Political Weekly*, Vol. 38, No. 27: 1991–2002.

—— (2006a) 'Adivasi and Peasant: Reflections on Indian Social History', *Journal of Peasant Studies*, Vol. 33, No. 3: 502–25.

—— (2006b) 'Forms of Resistance: Adivasi Movements in India', paper presented at the annual conference of the Norwegian Forum for Devélopment Research, September 2006.

Khagram, S. (2004) *Dams and Development: Transnational Struggles for Water and Power*, Itaca: Cornell University Press.

Kiely, R. (1999) 'The Last Refuge of the Noble Savage: A Critical Assessment of Post-Development Theory', *The European Journal of Development Research*, Vol. 11, No. 1: 30–55.

Kilgore, D. W. (1999) 'Understanding Learning in Social Movements: A Theory of Collective Learning', *International Journal of Lifelong Education*, Vol. 18, No. 3: 191–202.

Klingensmith, D. (2003) 'Building India's 'Modern Temples': Indians and Americans in the Damodar Valley Corporation, 1945–60', in Sivaramakrishnan, K. and Agrawal, A. (eds) *Regional Modernities: The Cultural Politics of Development in India*, Stanford: Stanford University Press.

—— (2007) *'One Valley and a Thousand': Dams, Nationalism and Development*, New Delhi: Oxford University Press.

Kohli, A. (2006a) 'Politics of Economic Growth in India, 1980–2005: Part 1: The 1980s', *Economic and Political Weekly*, Vol. 41, No. 13: 1251–9.

—— (2006b) 'Politics of Economic Growth in India, 1980–2005: Part 2: The 1990s and Beyond', *Economic and Political Weekly*, Vol. 41, No. 14: 1363–71.

Kothari, R. (1984), 'The Non-Party Political Process', *Economic and Political Weekly*, 4 February, Vol. 19, No. 5: 216–24.

Land Reforms Unit (2002) 'A Report on Land Reforms in Madhya Pradesh', in Jha, P. K. (ed.) *Land Reforms in India, Volume 7: Issues of Equity in Rural Madhya Pradesh*, New Delhi: Sage Publications.

Linebaugh, P. (2003) *The London Hanged: Crime and Civil Society in the Eighteenth Century*, London: Verso.

Mahapatra, L. K. (1993) 'Customary Rights in Law and Forest and the State', Miri, M. (ed.) *Continuity and Change in Tribal Society*, Shimla: Indian Institute of Advanced Study.

Mahalingam, S. (2000): 'A Dam and Some Questions', *Frontline*, Vol. 17, No. 2.

Mandel, E. (1975) *Late Capitalism*, London: Verso.

Mander, H. (2002) 'Tribal Land Alienation in Madhya Pradesh: The Problem and Legislative Remedies', in Jha, P. K. (ed.) *Land Reforms in India, Volume 7: Issues of Equity in Rural Madhya Pradesh*, New Delhi: Sage Publications.

Marx, K. (1981) *Contribution to the Critique of Political Economy*, London: Lawrence and Wishart.

—— (1990) *Capital: A Critique of Political Economy – Volume 1*, Hammondsworth: Penguin.

Marx, K. and Engels, F. (1999) *The German Ideology*, London: Lawrence and Wishart.

McCully, P. (1998) *Silenced Rivers: The Ecology and Politics of Large Dams*, London: Zed Books.

Metcalf, B. D. and Metcalf, T. R. (2002) *A Concise History of India*, Cambridge: Cambridge University Press.

Metha, L. (1997) 'Water, Difference and Power: Kutch and the Sardar Sarovar (Narmada) Project', IDS Working Paper 54.

—— (2002) 'The Double Bind: A Gender Analysis of Forced Displacement and Resettlement', paper available at the website of the Institute of Development Studies, University of Sussex, www.ids.ac.uk (accessed March 2005).

Middleton, D. and Edwards, D. (1990) 'Introduction', in Middleton, D. and Edwards, D. (eds) *Collective Remembering*, London: Sage Publications.

Moore, B. (1991) *Social Origins of Dictatorship and Democracy: Lord and Peasant in the Making of the Modern World*, London: Penguin.

Moore, D. S. (1996) 'Marxism, Culture, and Political Ecology', in Peet, R. and Watts, M. (eds) *Liberation Ecologies: Environment, Development, Social Movements*, London: Routledge.

—— (1998) 'Subaltern Struggles and the Politics of Place: Remapping Resistance in Zimbabwe's Eastern Highlands', *Cultural Anthropology*, Vol. 13, No. 3: 1–38.

—— (2000) 'The Crucible of Cultural Politics: Reworking "Development" in Zimbabwe's Eastern Highlands', *American Ethnologist*, Vol. 26, No. 3: 654–89.

—— (2003) 'Beyond Blackmail: Multivalent Modernities and the Cultural Politics of Development in India', in Sivaramakrishnan, K. and Agrawal, A. (eds) *Regional Modernities: The Cultural Politics of Development in India*, Stanford: Stanford University Press.

Morse B. and Berger, T. (1992) *Sardar Sarovar: The Report of the Independent Review*, Ottawa: Resource Futures International.

—— (1995) 'Findings and Recommendations of the Independent Review', in Fisher, W. F. (ed.) *Towards Sustainable Development? Struggling Over India's Narmada River*, London: M.E. Sharpe.

Mosse, D. (2007) 'Power and the Durability of Poverty: A Critical Exploration of the Links between Culture, Marginality and Power', CPRC Working Paper 107, available at the Chronic Poverty Research Centre website, http://www.chronicpoverty.org/pdfs/107 Mosse.pdf (accessed February 2008).

Mosse, D., Gupta, S. and Shah, V. (2005) 'On the Margins in the City: Adivasi Seasonal

Labour Migration in Western India', *Economic and Political Weekly*, Vol. 40, No. 28: 3025–38.

Mukherjee, A. (2002) *Imperialism, Nationalism and the Making of the Indian Capitalist Class 1920–1947*, New Delhi: Sage Publications.

Multinational Monitor (1997) 'Against Globalization and for Power to the People – An interview with Medha Patkar', interview available at www.multinationalmonitor.org (accessed April 2005).

Nanda, M. (2004) *Prophets Facing Backward: Postmodern Critiques of Science and Hindu Nationalism in India*, New Brunswick: Rutgers University Press.

NAPM (2003) *Ayodhya Declaration – National People's Agenda*, document obtained from NAPM leadership.

Nash, J. (1992) 'Interpreting Social Movements: Bolivian Resistance to Economic Conditions Imposed by the International Monetary Fund', *American Ethnologist*, Vol. 19, No. 2: 275–93.

NBA (1988) 'The Statement Issued by Organisation in Narmada Valley to Oppose Sardar Sarovar Project, on 18th August, 1988', in Sangvai, S. (ed.) (2000) *The River and Life: People's Struggle in the Narmada Valley*, Mumbai: Earthcare Books.

—— (1992) 'Towards Just and Sustainable Development: The People's Struggle in the Narmada Valley', document obtained from the NBA offices in Baroda, Gujarat.

—— (1999) 'Big Dams in the Narmada Valley: The Need for Alternatives', report published by the Narmada Bachao Andolan.

—— (2000a) *People vs. Verdict*, Vadodara: NBA.

—— (2000b) 'September 17, Conclusion of Narmada Satyagraha, Jalsindhi and Domkhedi', press note available at the Friends of the Narmada website, www.naramada.org (accessed October 2000).

—— (2004) *Displacement Without Rehabilitation: Adivasis of Alirajpur Tehsil, Jhabua District, Madhya Pradesh*, report available at the Friends of the Naramda website, www.narmada.org/nvdp.dams/ssp/alirajpur.doc (accessed March 2005).

—— (2007) 'Urgent Appeal: Two Lakh People, Adivasis and Farmers, From the Narmada Valley Cry Halt to Destruction', press note available at the Friends of the Narmada website, www.narmada.org (accessed January 2008).

—— (n.d.) *Narmada: The Struggle for Life, Against Destruction*, Baroda: Chittaroopa Palit.

Nilsen, A. G. (2006) 'The Valley and the Nation – The River and the Rage: A Study of Dispossession and Resistance in the Narmada Valley, India,' unpublished PhD thesis, Faculty of Social Sciences, University of Bergen.

—— (2007a) 'History Does Nothing: Notes Towards a Marxist Theory of Social Movements', *Sosiologisk Årbok* 1–2: 1–30.

—— (2007b) 'On New Social Movements and "the Reinvention of India"', *Forum for Development Studies*, No. 2: 271–93.

—— (2008) 'Political Economy, Social Movements and State Power: A Marxian Perspective on Two Decades of Resistance to the Narmada Dam Projects', *Journal of Historical Sociology*, Vol. 21, No. 2–3: 303–30.

—— (2009) 'The Authors and the Actors of Their Own Drama: Notes towards a Marxist Theory of Social Movements', forthcoming in *Capital and Class*.

Nilsen, A. G. and Cox, L. (2006) '"The Bourgeoisie, Historically, Has Played a Most Revolutionary Part": Understanding Social Movements From Above', in Barker, C. and Tyldesley, M. (eds) *Tenth International Conference on Alternative Futures and Popular Protest – Conference Papers, Volume 3*, Faculty of Humanities and Social Science, Manchester: Manchester Metropolitan University.

O'Brien, K. and Li, L. (2006) *Rightful Resistance in Rural China*, Cambridge: Cambridge University Press.

O'Hanlon, R. (2003) 'Recovering the Subject: Subaltern Studies and Histories of Resistance in Colonial South Asia', in Ludden, D. (ed.) *Reading Subaltern Studies: Critical History, Contested Meaning and the Globalisation of South Asia*, 135–86.

Omvedt, G. (1993) *Reinventing Revolution: New Social Movements and the Socialist Tradition in India*, New York: East Gate.

—— (1995) '"We Want the Return for Our Sweat": The New Peasant Movement in India and the Formation of a National Agricultural Policy', *Journal of Peasant Studies*, Vol. 21, No. 3–4: 107–64.

Ortner, S. (1995) 'Resistance and the Problem of Ethnographic Refusal', *Comparative Studies in Society and History*, Vol. 37, No. 1: 173–93.

Palit, C. (2003) 'Monsoon Risings: Mega-Dam Resistance in the Narmada Valley', *New Left Review*, Vol. 21: 81–100.

—— (2004) 'Short-Changing the Displaced: National Rehabilitation Policy', *Economic and Political Weekly*, Vol. 39, No. 27: 2961–3.

Parajuli, P. (1991) 'Power and Knowledge in Development Discourse: New Social Movements and the State in India', *International Social Science Journal*, No. 127: 173–90.

—— (1996) 'Ecological Ethnicity in the Making: Developmentalist Hegemonies and Emergent Identities in India', *Identities*, Vol. 3, No. 1–2: 15–59.

Parasuraman, S. (1997) 'The Anti-Dam Movement and Rehabilitation Policy', in Drèze, J., Samson, M. and Singh, S. (eds) *The Dam and the Nation: Displacement and Resettlement in the Narmada Valley*, New Delhi: Oxford University Press.

—— (1999) *The Development Dilemma: Displacement in India*, London: Macmillan Press.

Patel, A. (1995) 'What Do the Narmada Valley Tribals Want?', in Fisher, W. F. (ed.) *Towards Sustainable Development? Struggling Over India's Narmada River*, London: M.E. Sharpe.

—— (1997) 'Resettlement Politics and Tribal Interest', in Drèze, J., Samson, M. and Singh, S. (eds) *The Dam and the Nation: Displacement and Resettlement in the Narmada Valley*, New Delhi: Oxford University Press.

Patkar, M. (1995) 'The Struggle for Participation and Justice: A Historical Narrative', in Fisher, W. F. (ed.) *Towards Sustainable Development? Struggling Over India's Narmada River*, London: M.E. Sharpe.

Patnaik, P. (2003) *The Retreat to Unfreedom: Essays on the Emerging World Order*, Delhi: Tulika Books.

Patnaik, U. (1986) *The Agrarian Question and the Development of Capitalism in India*, New Delhi: Oxford University Press.

—— (1999) *The Long Transition: Essays on Political Economy*, Delhi: Tulika Books.

Pedersen, J. D. (2000) 'Explaining Economic Liberalization in India: State and Society Perspectives', *World Development*, Vol. 28, No. 2: 265–82.

Perelman, M. (2000) *The Invention of Capitalism: Classical Political Economy and the Secret History of Primitive Accumulation*, Durham: Duke University Press.

Pieterse, J. N. (1998) 'My Paradigm or Yours? Alternative Development, Post-Development, Reflexive Development', *Development and Change*, Vol. 29, No. 2: 343–73.

—— (2000) 'After Post-Development', *Third World Quarterly*, Vol. 21, No. 2: 171–95.

Piven, F. F. and Cloward, R. A. (1977) *Poor People's Movements: Why They Succeed, How They Fail*, New York: Vintage Books.

Polanyi, K. (2001) *The Great Transformation: The Political and Economic Origins of Our Time*, Boston: Beacon Press.

Prasad, A. (2003) *Against Ecological Romanticism: Verrier Elwin and the Making of an Anti-Modern Tribal Identity*, Delhi: Three Essays Collective.

—— (2004) *Environmentalism and the Left: Contemporary Debates and Future Agendas in Tribal Areas*, New Delhi: Leftword.

Rajagopal, B. (2004) 'Limits of the Law in Counterhegemonic Globalization: The Indian Supreme Court and the Narmada Valley Struggle', working paper available at the Jawarharlal Nehru University website, http://www.jnu.ac.in/cslg/workingpaper/cslg%20wp%2004–04%20balakrishnan%20rajgopal.pdf (accessed October 2007).

Ram, R. N. (1993) 'Muddy Waters: A Critical Assessment of the Benefits of the Sardar Sarovar Project', report available at the Friends of the Narmada website, http://www.narmada.org/MW/contents.html (accessed July 2009).

Ramakrishnan, V. (2006) 'Conflict Zones', *Frontline*, Vol. 23, No. 20.

Randeira, S. (2003a) 'Glocalization of Law: Environmental Justice, World Bank, NGOs and the Cunning State in India', *Current Sociology*, Vol. 51, No. 3–4: 305–28.

—— (2003b) 'Between Cunning States and Unaccountable International Institutions: Social Movements and Rights of Local Communities to Common Property Resources', Discussion Paper Nr. SP IV 2003–2502, Wissenschaftszentrum Berlin/Universität Zürich.

Rangachari, R., Sengupta, N., Iyer, R. R., Banerji, P. and Singh, S. (2000) *Large Dams: India's Experience*, report available at the website of World Commission on Dams, http://www.dams.org/docs/kbase/studies/csinmain.pdf (accessed July 2004).

Rangan, H. (1993) 'Romancing the Environment: Popular Environmental Action in the Garwhal Himalayas', in Friedmann, J. and Rangan, H. (eds) *In Defense of Livelihood: Comparative Studies on Environmental Action*, West Hartford: Kumarian Press.

—— (1996) 'From Chipko to Uttaranchal: Development, Environment, and Social Protest in the Garwhal Himalayas, India', in Peet, R. and Watts, M. (eds) *Liberation Ecologies: Environment, Development, Social Movements*, London: Routledge.

—— (2000) *Of Myths and Movements: Rewriting Chipko into Himalayan History*, New Delhi: Oxford University Press.

Rao, M. M. (2005) 'Taming the Krishna', *The Hindu*, 18 December.

Rao, M. S. A. (ed.) (2000) *Social Movements in India*, Delhi: Manohar.

Ratnagar, S. (2003) 'Our Tribal Past', *Social Scientist*, Vol. 31, No. 1–2: 17–36.

Routledge, P. (2003) 'Voices of the Dammed: Discursive Resistance Amidst Erasure in the Narmada Valley, India', *Political Geography*, Vol. 22, No. 3: 243–70.

Roy, A. (2002) *The Algebra of Infinite Justice*, New Delhi: Penguin.

—— (2004) 'The Road to Harsud: The Death of a Town', article available at the website of *Z magazine*, http://www.zmag.org/znet/viewArticle/8179 (accessed October 2008).

Rudé, G. (1980) *Ideology and Popular Protest*, London: Lawrence and Wishart.

Rutten, M. (1995) *Farms and Factories: Social Profile of Large Farmers and Rural Industrialists in West India*, New Delhi: Oxford University Press.

Sampat, P. (2008) 'Special Economic Zones in India: Reconfiguring Displacement in a Neoliberal Order', *Economic and Political Weekly*, Vol. 43, No. 28: 25–9.

Sangvai, S. (2000a) *The River and Life: People's Struggle in the Narmada Valley*, Mumbai: Earthcare Books.

—— (2000b) 'Rejoinder: How to Strengthen the Struggle in the Valley', *Humanscape*, April 2000 (internet edition).

Sarkar, S. (1997) *Writing Social History*, New Delhi: Oxford University Press.

Schücking, H. (1999) *The Maheshwar Dam in India*, report available at the Friends of the Narmada website, http://www.narmada.org/urg990421.html (accessed July 2000).

Scott, J. C. (1985) *Weapons of the Weak: Everyday Forms of Peasant Resistance*, New Haven: Yale University Press.

—— (1990) *Domination and the Arts of Resistance: Hidden Transcripts*, New Haven: Yale University Press.

—— (1998): *Seeing Like A State: How Certain Schemes To Improve The Human Condition Have Failed*, New Haven: Yale University Press.

Sen, J. (2000a) 'The Sardar Sarovar Case: A Universal Concern', article available at the Friends of the Narmada website, http://www.narmada.org/articles/JAI_SEN/sardarsarovarcase.html (accessed July 2005).

—— (2000b) 'The Reclaiming of Eminent Domain: The Sovereignty of the People, the Legitimacy of the State, the Relevance of the Narmada Hearings', article available at the Friends of the Narmada website, http://www.narmada.org/articles/JAI_SEN/reclaim.html (accessed July 2005).

—— (n.d.) 'A World to Win – But Whose World is it Anyway?', manuscript obtained from the author.

Sewell, W. H. (1992) 'A Theory of Structure: Duality, Agency, and Transformation', *American Journal of Sociology*, Vol. 98, No. 1: 1–29.

—— (1996) 'Historical Events as Transformation of Structures: Inventing Revolution at the Bastille', *Theory and Society*, Vol. 25, No. 6: 841–81.

Shah, A. (2007) 'The Dark Side of Indigeneity: Indigenous People, Rights and Development in India', *History Compass* Vol. 5–6: 1806–32.

Shah, G. (1977) *Protest Movements in Two Indian States: A Study of the Gujarat and Bihar Movements*, New Delhi: Ajanta Publications.

—— (1988) 'Grass-Roots Mobilization in Indian Politics', in Atul Kohli (ed.) *India's Democracy*, Princeton: Princeton University Press.

—— (1990) 'Caste Sentiments, Class Formation and Dominance in Gujarat', in Frankel, F. and Rao, M. S. A. (eds) *Dominance and State Power in Modern India – Volume 2*, New Delhi: Oxford University Press.

—— (1990) *Social Movements in India: A Review of the Literature*, New Delhi: Sage Publications.

Shankar, P. S. V. (2005) 'Four Decades of Agricultural Development in MP: An Agro-Ecological Sub-Region Approach', *Economic and Political Weekly*, Vol. 40, No. 48: 5014–24.

Shridar, V. (2007) 'Subversive Enclaves', *Frontline*, Vol. 23, No. 20.

Silver, B. (2003) *Forces of Labour: Workers' Movements and Globalization Since 1870*, Cambridge: Cambridge University Press.

Singh, K. S. (1985) *Tribal Society in India: An Anthropo-Historical Perspective*, Delhi: Manohar.

Singh, S. (1997) *Taming the Waters: The Political Economy of Large Dams in India*, New Delhi: Oxford University Press.

Sinha, S. (2003) 'Development Counter-Narratives: Taking Social Movements Seriously', in Sivaramakrishnan, K. and Agrawal, A. (eds) *Regional Modernities: The Cultural Politics of Development in India*, Stanford: Stanford University Press.

—— (2008) 'Lineages of the Developmentalist State: Transnationality and Village India, 1900–1965', *Comparative Studies in Society and History*, Vol. 50, No. 1: 57–90.

Sinha, S., Gururani, S. and Greenberg, B. (1997) 'The "New Traditionalist" Discourse of Indian Environmentalism', *Journal of Peasant Studies*, Vol. 24, No. 3: 65–99.

Sivaramakrishnan, K.(2003) 'Situating the Subaltern: History and Anthropology in the Subaltern Studies Project', in Ludden, D. (ed.) *Reading Subaltern Studies: Critical History, Contested Meaning and the Globalisation of South Asia*, 212–55.

Skirbekk, G. (1984) *Ord: Essay i Utval*, Oslo: Samlaget.

Steinberg, M. W. (1999) 'The Talk and Back Talk of Collective Action: A Dialogic Analysis of Repertoires of Discourse Among Nineteenth-Century English Cotton Spinners', *American Journal of Sociology*, Vol. 105, No. 3: 736–80.

Sundar, N. (1997) *Subalterns and Sovereigns: An Anthropological History of Bastar*, New Delhi: Oxford University Press.

Swaninathan, S. (2001) 'A Tale of Continued Oppression: Government Atrocities on Tribals in Dewas', *Economic and Political Weekly*, May 5–11: 1510–12.

Taggart, P. (2002) *Populism*, Buckingham: Open University Press.

Tarrow, S. (1998) *Power in Movement: Social Movements and Contentious Politics*, Cambridge: Cambridge University Press.

Teschke, B. (2003) *The Myth of 1648*, London: Verso.

Thompson, E. P. (1975) *Whigs and Hunters: The Origin of the Black Act*, New York: Pantheon Books.

Tilly, C. (1977) 'Getting it Together in Burgundy – 1675–1975', *Theory and Society*, Vol. 4, No. 4: 479–504.

Times of India (2009) 'Govt Plans Big-Bang Disinvestment', 4 June.

TISS (1993) *The Sardar Sarovar Project: Experiences with Rehabilitation and Resettlement 1987–93*, Bombay: Tata Institute of Social Sciences.

Udall, L. (1995) 'The International Narmada Campaign: A Case of Sustained Advocacy', in Fisher, W. F. (ed.) *Towards Sustainable Development? Struggling Over India's Narmada River*, London: M.E. Sharpe.

Uehling, G. (2000) 'Social Memory as Collective Action: The Crimean Tatar National Movement', in Guidry, J. A., Kennedy, M. and Zald, M. N. (eds) *Globalizations and Social Movements: Culture, Power, and the Transnational Public Sphere*, Ann Arbor: University of Michigan Press.

UNHCR (2006) 'Human Rights Experts Express Concern about Impact of Raising Height of Dam in Narmada River, India', United Nations press release, available at the UNOG website, http://www.unog.ch/80256EDD006B9C2E/(httpNewsByYear_en)/E10911FAE046D011C125714F005ABB7C?OpenDocument.

Upadhyaya, A. (1980) 'Class Struggle in Rural Maharashtra: Towards a New Perspective', *Journal of Peasant Studies*, Vol. 7, No. 7: 212–34.

Vanaik, A. (1990) *The Painful Transition: Bourgeois Democracy in India*, London: Verso.

—— (2001) 'The New Indian Right', *New Left Review*, Vol. 9: 43–67.

Varshney, A. (1995) *Democracy, Development, and the Countryside: Urban-Rural Struggles in India*, Cambridge: Cambridge University Press.

Venkatesan, V. (2000) 'A Moral Victory for the NBA', *Frontline*, Vol. 17, No. 15.

Vester, M. (1978) *Proletariatets Opståen som Læreproces: Fremkomsten af Antikapitalistisk Teori og Praksis i England 1792–1848*, Kongerslev: GMT.

Volosinov, V. N. (1986) *Marxism and the Philosophy of Language*, London: Seminar Press.

Wade, R. (1997) 'Greening the Bank: The Struggle over the Environment, 1970–95', in Kapur, D., Lewis, J. P., and Webb, R. (eds) *The World Bank – Its First Half Century – Volume Two: Perspectives*, Washington, D.C.: Brookings Institution Press.

Wainwright, H. (1994) *Arguments for a New Left: Answering the Free-Market Right*, Oxford: Blackwell.

Walton, J. and Udayagiri, M. (2002) 'Global Strategies and Local Counter Movements – Comparative Studies of Asia and Latin America', paper presented to the Next Great Transformation? Karl Polanyi and the Critique of Globalization conference, University of California, Davis.

Watts, M. (2001) '1968 and all that . . .', *Progress in Human Geography*, Vol. 25, No. 2: 157–88.

Whitehead, J. (2003) 'Space, Place and Primitive Accumulation in Narmada Valley and Beyond', *Economic and Political Weekly*, Vol. 38, No. 40: 4224–30.

Williams, G. (2004) 'Evaluating Participatory Development: Tyranny, Power and (Re)politicization', *Third World Quarterly*, Vol. 25, No. 3: 557–78.

Williams, R. (1989) *Resources of Hope: Culture, Democracy, Socialism*, London: Verso.

World Commission on Dams (2000) *Dams and Development: A New Framework for Decisionmaking*, London: Earthscan Publications.

Wood, J. R. (1975) 'Extra-Parliamentary Opposition in India: An Analysis of Populist Agitations in Gujarat and Bihar', *Pacific Affairs*, Vol. 48, No. 3: 313–34.

Yadav, Y. (2000) 'Understanding the Second Democratic Upsurge: Trends of Bahujan Participation in Electoral Politics in the 1990s', in Frankel, F., Hasan, Z., Bhargava, R. and Arora, B. (eds) *Transforming India: Social and Political Dynamics of Democracy*, Oxford: Oxford University Press.

Index

This book deals with the controversies on developmental aspects of large dams, with a particular focus on the Narmada Valley projects in India. Based on extensive ethnographic fieldwork and research, the author draws on Marxist theory to craft a detailed analysis of how local demands for resettlement and rehabilitation were transformed into a radical anti-dam campaign linked to national and transnational movement networks.

The book explains the Narmada conflict and addresses how the building of the anti-dam campaign was animated by processes of collective learning, how activists extended the spatial scope of their struggle by building networks of solidarity with transnational advocacy groups, and how it is embedded in and shaped by a wider field of force of capitalist development at national and transnational scales. The analysis emphasizes how the Narmada dam project is related to national and global processes of capitalist development, and relates the Narmada Valley movement to contemporary popular struggles against dispossession in India and beyond.

Conclusions drawn from the resistance to the Narmada dams can be applied to social movements in other parts of the global south, where people are struggling against dispossession in a context of neoliberal restructuring. As such, this book will have relevance for people with an interest in South Asian studies, Indian politics and development studies.

Alf Gunvald Nilsen is a postdoctoral fellow in the Department of Sociology, University of Bergen, Norway. His research interests cover social movement theory and research, critical development research, and Marxist approaches to the political economy of capitalist development, all with special reference to India and South Asia.